Logistics and
Supply Chain Integration

Logistics and Supply Chain Integration

Ian Sadler

SAGE Publications
Los Angeles • London • New Delhi • Singapore

First published 2007

SAGE Publications Ltd
1 Oliver's Yard
55 City Road

London EC1Y 1SP
SAGE Publications Inc.
2455 Teller Road
Thousand Oaks, California 91320

SAGE Publications India Pvt Ltd
B 1/I 1 Mohan Cooperative Industrial Area
Mathura Road
New Delhi 110 044

SAGE Publications Asia-Pacific Pte Ltd
33 Pekin Street #02-01
Far East Square
Singapore 048763

Library of Congress Control Number: 2006939433

British Library Cataloguing in Publication data

A catalogue record for this book is available from the British Library

ISBN 978-1-4129-2978-3
ISBN 978-1-4129-2979-0 (pbk)

Typeset by C&M Digitals (P) Ltd., Chennai, India
Printed in Great Britain by Athenaeum Press, Gateshead, Tyne & Wear
Printed on paper from sustainable resources

Contents

4 International Logistics (with David Taylor) — 99

5 Information Communication — 124

Foreword

We are pleased to introduce a new text *Logistics and Supply Chain Integration* which combines relevant concepts with practical applications and cases. Supply chains are now seen as a new, additional vantage point from which to manage the value streams that deliver products and services to consumers.

In our work at the Lean Enterprise Research Centre of Cardiff University, we use these concepts in supply chain management every day with both practitioners and students. Our clients range from health services to vegetable processing; from automotive assembly to sheep dis-assembly. The wide strategies of supply chain integration aim to involve all company employees in achieving customers' exact needs. Doing this without wasteful processes has proved a powerful paradigm for achieving business excellence, for those prepared to stay the course.

We have been involved in this book since its inception. It makes a worthwhile contribution to supply chain education for postgraduates, undergraduates and logistics managers. This novel contribution includes balanced coverage of information communication, inter-company relationships, service chains, international chains and supply chain improvements. The cases at the end of each chapter are a valuable aid to the aspects of knowledge covered. We commend Ian for producing this book.

Peter Hines
Director of the Lean Enterprise
Research Centre,
Cardiff University

David Taylor
Senior Research Associate
Lean Enterprise Research
Centre, Cardiff University

Contents Summary

Preface

APPROACH

The special perspective on business provided by supply chain management has been growing in importance over the last twenty years. This started with an emphasis on physical distribution management, then comprised the entire logistics of a company from receiving materials to despatch of finished goods. Recently, the emphasis has widened to include all the business partners required to source, make and deliver goods to end customers. With the universal availability of information and with supply chains that extend around the world, it is now clear that companies compete according to the strength of their entire chains, not according to the stature of one link in the chain. Hence companies should aim to have a supply chain for each product group which is healthy, satisfies customers and competes with other chains at a long-term profit. This set of chains needs to reflect current conditions and needs to be flexible when markets and resource costs change. The chains are an integral part of the formation and implementation of business strategy. This book addresses these company aims.

The text provides several innovative features over existing texts. The big picture is examined through a generic 'Double-Bell' model which deals with multiple levels of suppliers in the first bell and multiple levels of distributors in the second bell. The manufacturing (or service) processes are sited between the two bells in a *focal* company. The logistics of service businesses is considered at length. Information communication is treated broadly by setting out both a framework and the specific systems which managers use to plan and execute logistics decisions accurately. A combination of personal contact and electronic information is involved in this process. Using the Internet and enterprise resource planning systems, correct information can replace inventory and enable accurate fulfilment of customer orders around the globe.

There is a lack of suitable texts to support a postgraduate course in Supply Chain *Management* which are both conceptually sound and useful in practice. Many texts take a marketing approach, which is light on operational practice. Others have a strong analytical emphasis, which tends to provide an average answer with limited use to the individual situation. This work acknowledges that each supply chain is unique, although each will have commonalities with others in its industry.

The author takes a management approach. This approach recognises that supply chains depend upon communications between people, shared understanding and decisions made from commercial knowledge rather than from mathematical calculations. The managerial challenge is to integrate numerous processes in different places and different firms so that both the short-term objectives of customer satisfaction and the strategic objectives of business development and efficiency are attained. The broad approach examines key concepts and practical considerations for designing, running and changing supply chains.

As the book's title suggests, the key issue missing from many companies' thinking is *integration*, the synergy of contributions within the design and execution of product-delivery systems. Integration requires a *systems* approach by analysts and management decision-makers. Supply chain management must be given its correct place in the chain of companies at each of the decision levels from strategic to operational in order for greater value to be obtained for customers and stakeholders. Therefore the book devotes two chapters to important advice for integrating partner companies into a seamless supply chain. A further chapter addresses the means to attain operational and strategic improvement.

The text reflects the belief that supply chain success requires:

- insight into managers' behaviour,
- a realistic management approach to individual chain links, and
- visionary leadership to integrate the whole chain.

It is primarily intended for use as a university textbook for teaching supply chain management at advanced undergraduate or Master's level. It is also intended for current and prospective logistics managers who wish to develop their thinking through its research and insights.

ORGANISATION AND CONTENT

Given this managerial approach to chains, the book is organised into a wide foundation of supply chain knowledge in the first three chapters; key additional topics in the next two chapters; and the theory and practice of integration in the final three chapters.

Figure 0.1 below shows the relationships between the various chapters. Chapter 1 defines supply chains and provides an overview of information communication, management and integration for chains. Chapters 2 and 3 focus on the organisation and functions of the focal companies in supply chains, covering manufacturing companies and logistics in service organisations, customer service and transport respectively. The next two chapters add important parameters to the whole chain: international logistics which becomes ever more important as globalisation of business progresses, and information communication which is critical to drive product delivery.

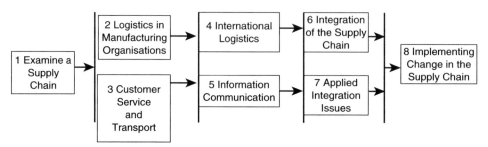

Figure 0.1   **Layout of the book**

After the first five chapters provide a wide foundation of chain theory and practice, the next two chapters examine supply chain integration. Chapter 6 considers the way in which the key links in chains can be integrated, focusing on primary processes, the creation of flows of products and services and the choice of relationships between link-companies. Chapter 7 studies the more complex areas of chain integration such as chain restructuring and leadership issues. Chapter 8 considers supply chain performance, immediate improvements and a process of strategic planning to achieve revolutionary change for the benefit of end customers and chain companies.

EDUCATIONAL METHODS

This book provides numerous educational aids. The reader's *learning objectives* are given at the start of each chapter. The end of the text of each chapter has a *summary* and a set of *review questions,* so that participants can check that they have understood the material and attained the learning objectives. Brief *answers* to odd-numbered questions are on the book's website. *Boxes* are used for mini-cases or analysis, to separate them from the main flow of the text.

Each chapter concludes with a *case,* related to its material, which is valuable for participants to use in groups. The cases are based on practical situations, modified to protect confidentiality and to improve the knowledge that they exemplify. The last section in each chapter is a *list of references* for further reading. A *glossary* is provided at the end of the book as an easy reference to meanings of terms and because the newness of supply chain management means that many terms have different meanings in the literature and commerce. Terms in the text in *italics* denoted by an asterisk* are defined in the glossary. The length of the book is determined by the amount of content which can be studied in a one-semester subject.

The book's website also contains;

- a set of PowerPoint slides for instructors to explain each chapter,
- teaching notes for each chapter,
- sample answers to cases,
- several assignments for student assessment, and
- exam questions.

Logistics and Supply Chain Integration provides a state-of-the-art explanation of concepts and implementation issues for students and experienced managers. It is intended to cater for postgraduate and third-year undergraduate students. Directors and managers (where 'managers' is shorthand for all the people in companies who make things happen for customers) in logistics and related areas can use the concepts and well-developed cases to inform supply chain decisions, from strategic to operational. The melding of concepts, axioms and practical applications is a resource for academic researchers to use as a reference in any work which relates to supply chains.

Acknowledgements

This book would not have been accomplished without the help of colleagues and the executives at Sage Publications. I offer sincere thanks to my colleagues, in Australia and Britain, who inspired and supported me in this work.

I exprcss my sincere gratitude to all who assisted me with specific areas:

- David Taylor of the Lean Enterprise Research Centre (LERC) at Cardiff University, who helped me write Chapter 4 and provided the material for the case 'Shoes go global'.
- G. Peter Dapiran, Senior Fellow in the Faculty of Engineering, The University of Melbourne, who gave generously of his teaching materials for the Benetton case, distribution centre strategy, logistics security, and outsourcing logistics.
- Martin Christopher, Professor of Marketing and Logistics at Cranfield University, whose writings have enthused me for twenty years and who kindly provided the original case on which 'Designing a European supply chain' is based.
- Peter Gilmour, late Professor of Logistics at Macquarie University, New South Wales, for his specific work on logistics customer service levels and his inspiration over the whole field.
- Professor Nigel Slack, of Warwick University Business School, whose writings and personal contact informed my work on the operations aspects of the book.
- Professor Robert Johnson, of Warwick University Business School, whose writings stimulated the chapter on service supply chains.
- Terry Hill, Emeritus Professor at Templeton College, Oxford, who developed the concepts of order-winning criteria and strategic operations planning.
- Ken Platts, Reader in Engineering Management at Cambridge University, whose 'Manufacturing audit approach' inspired the strategic planning process described in Chapter 8.

I thank Professor Michael Muetzelfeldt, previous Head of the School of Management at Victoria University, who stimulated me to write the book, and Professor Peter Hines, the Director of LERC, for his advice that the book was worth publishing in a growing field.

In writing this book I made use of the knowledge available and 'picked the brains' of my colleagues. I express my thanks to all who helped me, especially Professor Don Bowersox of Michigan State University; Dr Mark Francis and David Simons of LERC at Cardiff University; Richard Gough, Associate Professor Bernadine van Gramberg and Dale Harvey of the School of Management at Victoria University, Melbourne; Alan Harrison and Remko van Hoek of Cranfield University; Dan Jones of the Lean Enterprise Institute in Ross-on-Wye, Wales; and Thomas Vollmann of the International Institute for Management Development.

I am also very grateful to many friends, consultants and company contacts for practical help. Special thanks go to Ulf Åslund of Malmo in Sweden; David Doherty of the SCLAA Association in Melbourne; Jesper Hovrell of SingTel Optus in Sydney; the late Richard Normann and Rafael Ramirez, authors of the book *Designing Interactive Strategy*, Kenichi Ohmae of Ohmae and Associates in Tokyo; authors of the Supply Chain Operations Reference model, Graham Stevens of Peat Marwick McLintock in London , John Stuart of JV Support Services, Melbourne and Ken Yendell of Publishing Solutions.

Although all the cases are my own work, many of them are based on prior work, which I adapted to suit this particular text. In addition to those mentioned above, I gratefully acknowledge the following sources:

- 'Serving motorists' is based on work by my Master's students J Kale and H Keskar.
- 'Betta Struts develops an e-supply chain' was developed from a presentation by Mark Ottery.
- 'Preparing for a seamless supply chain' is a revision of a case published by Dan Dimancescu, Peter Hines and Nich Rich.
- Lucent Technologies Company' was developed from work by my Master's students C Duan and T Kanjanakajit.

I wish to thank Jennifer Pegg, of Thomson Learning, who first considered publishing my book. I especially thank Delia Alphonso and Anne Summers for reviewing my book and giving much sound advice during its publication. Katherine Haw was a tremendous help during production. They 'held the hand' of a first author on the other side of the world. I thank all the staff at Sage Publishing who have assiduously helped to achieve this outcome.

I express my heart-felt thanks to my Australian editor, Margery Joan, who has unstintingly advised, edited, formatted and proofed all my work.

PUBLISHER'S ACKNOWLEDGEMENTS

I am grateful to the following for permission to reproduce copyright material:

Figures 1.7 and 4.1 after *Logistics Management and Strategy*, by Harrison A and van Hoek R, reprinted by permission of Pearson Education Limited, copyright 2002, 2005.

Figures 2.4 and 5.7 from *Manufacturing Planning and Control Systems for Supply Chain Management*, 2005, by Vollmann TE, Berry WL, Whybark DC and Jacobs FR, reprinted with permission of The McGraw-Hill Companies.

Figure 3.6 after *Service Operations Management*, by Johnston R and Clark G, reprinted by permission of Pearson Education Limited, copyright 2001, 2005.

Figure 3.9 reprinted from *Journal of Purchasing and Supply Management*, Volume 9, Harland C, Brenchley R and Walker H, 'Risks in Supply Networks', page 55, copyright 2003, with permission from Elsevier.

Figure 4.4 after *Supply Chain Management*, by Chopra S and Meindl P, reprinted by permission of Pearson Education, USA (2004).

Table 4.2 after *Supply Chain Logistics Management*, 2006, by Bowersox DJ, Closs DJ and Cooper MB, reproduced with permission of The McGraw-Hill Companies.

Box 5.3 after *Operations Management*, by Slack N, Chambers S and Johnston R, reprinted by permission of Pearson Education Limited, copyright 2001.

Table C6.2 page 183 adapted and reprinted by permission of AMACOM Inc (Dimancesceau D, Hines P and Rich N, 1997).

Figure 7.2 reprinted from *Relationship Marketing* by Peck H, Payne A, Christopher M and Clark M, copyright 1999, with permission from Elsevier.

Figures 2.11 and 8.5 from *Manufacturing Strategy*, ed. Voss CA (Jouffrey and Tarondeau, 1992).

Every effort has been made to trace all the copyright holders. However, if any have been unwittingly overlooked, I will be pleased to make the necessary arrangements.

List of Figures

List of Tables

Examine a Supply Chain

1

The art of seeing the forest and the trees.[1]

Objectives

- To be able to identify the major stages in the location, transformation and movement of materials and goods in a supply chain of a manufacturing or service company
- To describe the increasing importance of supply chain management to all businesses in achieving a competitive advantage and controlling costs so that operations are profitable
- To apply the supply chain management concept to information and physical movement within logistics chains
- To understand how a supply network can be partitioned into a supply chain for each product family to achieve the desired flow of products and services to consumers
- To understand how the relationships between supply chain partners can be developed so that high value is generated for customers and partners

INTRODUCTION

This chapter introduces supply chains as groups of companies which work together to source, produce and deliver goods and services to end customers. To survive, and to be competitive, it is not sufficient for firms to restrict their vision to their own processes. Instead they must consider the whole flow of materials and goods and the information which communicates the specific needs of consumers to the various levels of suppliers. Firms should also consider the management of those flows and the part which they play within the coordination of the entire supply network. The challenge is for companies in *partnership** to collaborate in design and delivery of products and services so that a more effective service is given to consumers and each company prospers.

A basic supply chain comprises:

- a focal company, which forms goods or services for a set of consumers,
- a range of suppliers of raw materials and components,
- distributors, which deliver the goods to consumers, and
- modes of transport which move products between each location in the chain.

The overt chain is the physical movement of materials and products between each partner firm along the chain until they reach the consumer in the required form when needed. Other factors necessary to integrate the supply chain are information communication, management coordination and chain leadership. Information exchange between partners enables them to work closely in line with end consumer needs, even though the firm may be several stages removed from product or service delivery. The term 'management' refers to the organisation and control of all the internal logistics functions within one link, or partner firm, in the chain, while the coordination of the whole chain, to ensure that it functions as an effective system to provide goods and services, is called chain leadership.

Consider one link firm in the supply chain which handles the materials or goods on their way to consumers. The link's task is to provide a product by purchasing components, converting them into products and despatching those products to the next level in the chain. On receiving specific orders, the link firm holds an inventory of components, and schedules conversion so that the movement satisfies its customers' requirements. This entails cooperation between many departments and processes and the use of external services such as transport and maintenance. Information communication within the firm derives from the actual or forecast mix of product needed in a period, leading to all the data required to process that order, which are typically stored in a comprehensive enterprise resource planning system. The operations manager then has the task of planning all the required activities, organising their execution, measuring performance, and controlling outcomes so that customers receive their goods without expending an unreasonable amount of resources. This operations task would, optimally, be coordinated along the whole supply chain.

The impetus for working on complete supply chains arises because the activities across all the firms are never perfect in creating value for customers and retaining value for operating firms. Investigation by operators drawn from each link in the chain can allow elimination of costs while improving customer service. The first step is to design a chain, starting with its strategic purpose in delivering to a set of customers. The second step is to integrate the physical and information processes across each link, achieving an effective flow of goods and provision of services. This requires consideration of issues such as the decoupling point (at which materials or products are committed to a customer order), order-winning criteria and the type of product or service being provided.

A more frequent situation than designing a supply chain from scratch arises when we set out to change an existing chain to make it more effective for customers and owners. Then we need to:

- bring the owners together,
- obtain an overall view of the supply chain, its boundaries, scope and strategy,
- adopt a method to investigate activities carried out along the chain, and
- decide on simplifications which will deliver the precise needs of end consumers without wastage of effort by chain owners and operators.

Box 1.1 provides an example of the supply chain required to manufacture sweaters and distribute them to retailers throughout the world.

Box 1.1   The Benetton Supply Chain: successful vertical integration

Benetton[2] is a highly successful manufacturer and deliverer of sweaters and other woollen clothing. It makes these sweaters in Italy and sells them in its own licensed shops throughout the world. Benetton's supply chain starts with the purchase of wool yarn in northern Italy. The wool is woven into garments by dozens of small knitting firms. The garments are stored in a central warehouse. When orders are received, the sweaters and scarves are dyed into a huge range of colours, producing the exact combination of colours, sizes and styles which customers want in 6,000 shops in 83 countries on every continent.

Benetton's 6,000 outlets sell 60 million garments each year. Their one range of clothes is sold in small boutique-style shops, strictly merchandised and heavily advertised. Benetton's target market is young and multiracial. They operate in a highly competitive, mature industry with a fickle consumer base demanding a large variety of products. They change their product line ten times a year. Benetton's Italian owners match the demands of fashion by flexibility and speed. They rapidly adapt to consumer tastes while gaining efficiencies of scale. To do this their supply chain must operate very competently to support the incessant pace.

The lynch-pin of Benetton's supply chain is information communications. Benetton's agents in each country use electronic data interchange (EDI) to transmit orders daily to the head office near Venice. Eliminating the filters between customer and production, Benetton manufactures only those garment styles, colours and sizes required.

The traditional manufacturer of clothing dyes the yarn, then knits the garment. But knitting is slow and would lead to high levels of finished garments. Benetton's solution is to manufacture clothes from bleached yarn and delay the dyeing until colour information comes from customers via EDI. The process is:

- Garments are designed in-house using CAD technology
- Design data are transferred directly to computer-controlled garment cutters and knitting machines
- Garment assembly is done by sub-contractors, small family operations
- Garment dyeing is done by Benetton, retaining control of the high-technology elements
- Garments are sent to an automated distribution centre in Italy, packed in standard boxes
- On receipt of an order from their agent in one country, Benetton picks the required boxes to make up the order and air freights them direct to the destination country.

Benetton has replaced a raft of carriers, freight forwarders and customs brokers with its own integrated distribution function to manage internal freight forwarding

(Continued)

(Continued)

and customs clearance. Again EDI is used to transmit documents ahead of consignment arrival to allow speedy clearance and on-forwarding to retail shops in the destination country.

Benetton uses a blend of in-house expertise and outsourced resources throughout the value chain. For example, manufacturing is carried out by sub-contractors who receive support for production planning, quality control and advice on technology. In return, Benetton demands exclusivity. The partnership arrangement is a version of the Italian extended family. This gives Benetton a high level of flexibility. Risks and rewards are shared without the use of legal contracts. At each stage of the supply chain Benetton consciously decides whether to process in-house or sub-contract, considering the effect on cost, flexibility, speed and service.

- Why is Benetton so successful?
- What is the key innovation which enables this success?
- How does Benetton handle information about orders and shipping?
- What are the key parts of this supply chain?

This chapter provides the answers to these questions.

1.1 THE SUPPLY CHAIN CONCEPT

The biggest challenge facing companies today is not the Internet, by itself, or globalisation or stakeholder needs. Rather, the greatest challenge is the integration of *supply chains** from vendors through manufacturers and distributors to satisfy end *customers** and obtain value for those companies. Supply chain management is the planning and *flow** of materials and products between a number of companies to deliver goods and services to end consumers. The insight examined in this book is that business supply chains are more likely to survive, grow and profit if they integrate the development of new products with a balanced supply chain in which each *link** combines to provide the goods that consumers want.

We suggest that *managers** in all the links in the supply chain need to plan and achieve a seamless stream of products in order to fully satisfy chosen customers while making a good return for each link. However there are some potential problems. Directors of different companies do not trust each other sufficiently. Managers of some chain links have more power than others and therefore push their own needs rather than working with their partner links to optimise the entire chain. A *link* is a company which performs some function within a supply chain, joining other parts into a complete chain. We accept that *entrepreneurs** will promote strategies which manipulate the chain for their own ends.

---

*Definitions of asterisked words in italics can be found in the glossary. Elsewhere italics are used for emphasis.

This book explains how the present view of supply chains has come about and suggests how managers in companies can work with *upstream** and *downstream** counterparts to harness the power of the concept to position and tune businesses for success. This concept can help them work with other *partners** in the supply chain to meet customer needs precisely without unnecessary actions.

Supply chain integration provides a key opportunity for you, as future *leaders** and managers of companies along the chain, to work together through shared information and joint provision and delivery of goods and services for customers. Picture a simple supply chain of one vendor transporting materials to a manufacturer who converts them into finished products and despatches them to a wholesaler's warehouse for delivery, at the right time, to a retailer for customers to purchase when they wish. Assume that the supply chain processes and information systems are already well designed for their purpose of supplying those goods at a profit over the costs of operating the various firms in the chain. As managers of the links in the supply chain you then have three tasks:

- to plan the flow of materials and goods along the chain by information exchange,
- to make the necessary physical movements and conversions in the required quantities and at the required times for end consumers, and
- to manage changes and developments to the benefit of all companies without disadvantaging customers.

The opportunity requires the chain managers to plan the way in which all the tasks required will be carried out before receiving customer orders. Frequently, the tasks are complicated due to the number of components in the finished product and the need to respond very quickly to customer orders from any location in the world. However, the power to share information in digital form and transfer it instantly from one firm to another gives them an enormous opportunity to optimise supply chain preparation.

Unfortunately, the firms along the supply chain are independent companies with separate owners, managers and stakeholders. Such *sovereign companies** are not used to working closely together for the good of the whole chain. Their managers keep product volume and cost information to themselves; if pressed they will provide inflated volumes, 'to be on the safe side' and ambit claim costs, to allow for negotiation and squeezing by, for example, powerful retailers. They work predominantly with their immediate suppliers and customers. They aim just to finish today's work, within a plethora of questions by employees and government regulations. So the challenge is to overcome the inertia of past practices (mainly manual records, batch computer systems and islands of data) and to implement transparent planning, scheduling and operating for every *transaction** (rather than batch or mass production) for every product in the chain. In short, to integrate the supply chain.

A useful analogy, to help visualise a supply chain, is a *stream** along which materials and products flow to the consumer. Imagine the stream, or *channel**, contains water flowing downhill, or left to right in Figure 1.1. Raw materials enter on the left, they are converted to components and products, and they flow to the right where customers buy them because they see value in having them. This stream analogy suggests that barriers (between companies responsible for part of the chain) should be minimised. Any

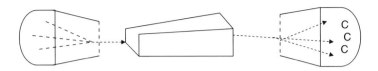

Figure 1.1   **Chain representation: from tributaries through product manufacture to distribution**

(C = Customers)

bends, constrictions or delays will slow the rate of flow so the customer has to wait longer for her product and hence sees less value. The flow of the stream, or turnover of the business supply chain, will be reduced. To improve the flow, waste must be reduced throughout the supply chain, so that the customer receives more value and the companies get more return for their efforts. This concept of waste removal is developed below. In the channel, tributaries on the left represent multiple suppliers delivering different materials and components. A delta with multiple mouths to the sea represents the many product groups and delivery routes to different customers. The central box stands for a manufacturer or distributor. The information that makes the stream flow is not shown.

A basic chain

The major components of a supply chain are physical movements, *information flow**, management coordination and leadership of the chain. The first task is to create a flow of information between chain partners so that physical flow takes place exactly as required. The second task is a series of physical movements: procuring parts, manufacture of the finished product and its *delivery** to the customer. The third task is the management of chains, and the fourth task is chain leadership.

Assume that you want to buy a new car because your present model is worn out. You need a four-cylinder sedan with automatic gearbox, four doors and air conditioning. This car requires 8,000 parts from 300 suppliers in all parts of the globe. Consider the simplified supply chain for a car model named 'Camry' which comprises an ignition module made by a firm called Bosch from metal components supplied by Kawasaki Steel and assembled into the finished car by Toyota Australia, which keeps an inventory of finished cars. You intend to purchase the finished car from a dealership in Melbourne, Australia. The simplified supply chain is shown in Figure 1.2.

The physical task of operating an integrated supply chain commences when a customer places an order with a distributor or manufacturer. Figure 1.2 shows the flow of materials and components for conversion by the manufacturer into a finished product. Inventory of finished cars is shown, indicative of inventory held at many places in the chain. The flow of finished product by distribution from the manufacturer to the end customer is also shown.

Of equal, or greater, importance is to plan the flow of materials and goods along the chain in response to your order. This will require information and communication to confirm your order, to plan production, to purchase materials and components and all the other preparatory tasks necessary before the physical operations shown in Figure 1.2 can be carried out. These planning tasks are shown in Figure 1.3. Such information typically flows in the opposite direction to the physical flow, from right to left in

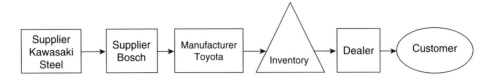

Figure 1.2   **Basic supply chain – physical movements**

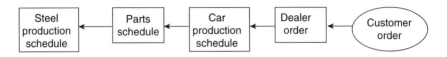

Figure 1.3   **Basic supply chain – information drives flow up the chain**

Figure 1.3 from the customer order until steel production is scheduled. All these informational tasks are needed before the physical tasks can be carried out.

The other task is the management of each link in the chain and the coordination of all the links. It involves all the decisions that directors, managers and operators at Benetton or Toyota, and their suppliers and contractors, make as they design, organise, inform, schedule and control the supply chains for clothing and cars. This task is described in the next section.

Chain and network definitions and major factors in each chain process

The term 'supply chain' is used because of its current popularity. The definitions underpin the development of concepts in this book:

- A supply chain is the *information-directed* flow of one *product family** from sources to end customers, managed by a number of partner firms, with reference to one *focal company**.
- *An integrated supply chain** requires movement of material, parts and product, and the provision of service, in the value chain. These moves are planned and managed as part of a system which is known as a supply chain for one group of products and as a network for all the range of products (and services) provided through a focal company.
- Supply chains use *electronic communication** and person-to-person communication, throughout the processes in the firms, to provide value for customers and firms.
- Better *design** and *execution** of *provision** and flow, by all partner firms in concert, will improve the efficiency of the operation. The system-wide perspective allows the firms to make appropriate *trade-offs** between variable costs such as purchasing, production, transport, inventory and distribution and between the resource costs of equipment, information systems and people.
- Close coordination between these operations and the strategic environment produces high levels of service and performance for customers while reducing the total costs incurred, so that value is sustainably generated for all chain partners.

- The objective of the supply chain is to maximise the overall value generated, where value is the difference between what the final product is worth to the consumer and the effort the chain expends in filling the customer's request.
- A *supply network** is the sum of supply chains across all products and services provided to end customers through a focal company.

*Value stream**, an equivalent term to supply chain, emphasises the flow of products along a stream and the value that partners must provide for themselves and customers. The concept of a value stream originated with Michael Porter,[3] who said that it should be disaggregated into strategic activities from *inbound logistics** to product distribution. The firms in the value stream generate competitive advantage by performing these important activities better or more cheaply than their competitors. Porter splits value stream activities into primary activities (inbound logistics, operations, outbound logistics, marketing and sales and service) and support activities (infrastructure, human resource management, technology development and procurement). Support activities are integrating functions that span the primary activities of the firms in the value stream.

Competitive advantage is derived from the way in which firms organise and perform these activities within the supply chain. To gain competitive advantage over its rivals, a firm must deliver value to its customers by carrying out these activities more efficiently or in a different way.[4] The word 'integrated' is added to supply chain to emphasise that we advocate a system view across the entire chain. It is not useful to improve only one partner in the supply chain. Rather chain leaders should strive to make each part work highly effectively in the performance of the entire chain. 'Integrated' also distinguishes this term from the careless use of 'supply chain' to refer to the logistics of one company.

This book focuses, firstly, on manufacturing operations and the service components of the resultant products. Secondly, service businesses, where the main or sole objective is to supply a service, such as credit from a bank or 'wellness' from a hospital, are included (see Chapter 3). Many of the principles of manufacturing supply chain integration apply to service chain management. Many manufactured products include a service component, such as the two-year warranty which a new car has. Such concomitant services, and the use of services in manufacturing and in the supply chain, are covered. All supply chains include transport, maintenance and professional services (such as process design and information systems). These are also included.

The *objective* of supply chain integration is to synchronise the requirements of the customer with the flow of material from suppliers in order to achieve a balance between the goals of high customer service, low inventory investment and low unit cost. These goals are often seen as conflicting but this is not necessarily so. We examine methods of designing and implementing supply chains so that the aims of all the interested parties are achieved. The design and operation of an effective supply chain are of fundamental importance to every business.

Each process in the integrated supply chain can be considered as comprising four factors: information communication, physical product flow, management coordination and chain leadership (see Figure 1.4). Information and product flow have already been defined. The third factor in the supply chain process involves management. Management[5] is the detailed planning, organisation, coordination and application necessary to move goods. It includes the *performance measurement** towards the supply chain's goals to ensure resources match destination aims. Activities in the

Figure 1.4   **Major constituents of a process**

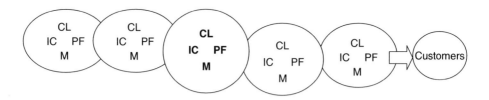

Figure 1.5   **Supply chain as a series of company links (processes) providing goods and services to customers**

(CL = chain leadership; LC = information communication; PF = product flow; and M = management)

links of the chain are carried out by employees who are steered and guided by managers. Managers are the people who use knowledge to encourage and allow employees to behave democratically and with enterprise to achieve broad company goals through free application of resources to provide products and services for customers.

Chain leadership signifies the application to the local process of the vision for where the overall supply chain is going. Leadership includes the means of getting to that required goal by instructions, regulations and coaching. Leadership also signifies strategic organisation and control of the value chain by the focal company and its partners, as exemplified by Benetton (Box 1.1).

Building on the major parts of a supply chain process just discussed, Figure 1.5 brings together those logistics processes in five firms to span the supply chain for a set of end customers. The four factors in each link of the chain need to be properly designed so that the overall chain capability is achieved. The supply chain, as a total *system**, will only work effectively and efficiently if proper consideration is given to these factors.

Developing the basic chain into an integrated supply network

The information and material flows and management described can now be assembled together with some extra detail of the partners involved into an integrated supply network. For the purpose of this discussion we adopt the assumptions in Box 1.2 to simplify the explanation. Building on the basic chain in Figure 1.1 and the major factors of each process along the chain, we now develop the *Double-Bell model** of the integrated supply network, as depicted in Figure 1.6. Each process in the chain from sources to end customers contains the four key components just discussed.

Box 1.2   **Simplifying assumptions**

- *Make-to-stock** manufacturing business.
- Orders are placed on a distribution centre, which replenishes its stock from the manufacturer.
- Supply chain comprises about 100 vendors supplying materials and components into a single factory where manufacture and assembly are carried out.
- Manufacturer distributes to 5–10 wholesale distributors. They deliver to retailers who sell to end consumers.
- Transport is a commodity in the chain which does not have a strategic effect on chain operation. It can be bought competitively from transport companies as and when it is required.

The 'Double-Bell model' is a generic representation of a complete supply network from sources of materials to end consumers. The left-hand bell indicates large numbers of suppliers of materials and components proceeding through several *tiers** and journeys to the focal manufacturer. The central ellipse is the conversion process in which materials are transformed into finished products and services. The right-hand bell represents the distribution of those goods to numerous end consumers through *intermediaries** and delivery transport. The Double-Bell model represents the main links and relative components in a generalised supply network. Typically, the network comprises 5–10 supply chains catering for each major group of products or services. The model can also be used to represent service supply chains. In this case the central ellipse

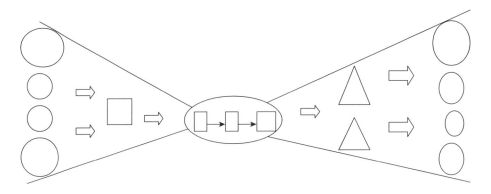

Figure 1.6   **The Double-Bell model of the supply network for business**

The left-hand bell shows many suppliers (circles) sending materials and components into the factory (central ellipse) by transport (arrows). The factory contains several processes (rectangles) producing or mixing finished goods,which are placed in a despatch bay. The right-hand bell represents the movement of products through distribution stores (triangles) to many end customers (ovals) by transport. In one sense, this model only represents the physical movement of materials and products along the supply chain. If each symbol, or process, is regarded as comprising goods, information drivers, management and leadership, the model starts to represent an integrated supply network.

becomes the chain partner which delivers the service. The model aims to help students to think about a particular supply chain. What is its extent? What range of customers is supplied? Which partners are most important? What are the flow paths for products and for information? How will the chain be managed and coordinated?

At the start of the physical chain, there are, say, a hundred suppliers arranged in two tiers. Tier-one suppliers deliver materials and components direct to the manufacturing factory according to the purchasing schedule. Tier-two suppliers deliver such resources to the tier-one suppliers. Vehicles are used to move the materials between the suppliers and the *factory**. Stocks of materials are also involved to enable on-time supply of long lead-time items.

The factory receives materials and converts them into finished products by means of a number of production processes. Handling of materials between the processes is also required. Finished goods are packed for their journey to the customer and built up into multiple units on pallets and in containers. Frequently, such products are placed in a despatch warehouse until suitable *freight transport** is arranged.

The finished products now proceed through a distribution system to large numbers of end customers. Typically, goods are transported in bulk to a distribution centre and stored in it. *Distribution centre** is a name for a warehouse which is a staging post on the way to customers. At the distribution centre the exact mix of goods required by the customer order is assembled, packed and delivered to the customer by a form of transport.

A fuller description of the information, which drives the 'double-bell' integrated supply chain, is given in section 1.3.

Another model, which has been suggested for the underlying structure of supply networks, is that shown in Figure 1.7 by Harrison and van Hoek.[6] In this model the chain is structured around three factors: flow of materials and products, flow of information and the time taken to respond to demand from the source of supply. The *network** is a system of interdependent processes and it extends from the focal firm at the centre across suppliers and customers. The end customers, on the right, initiate demand for products and services. After that, the system takes over. This model treats upstream suppliers and downstream customers in the same way as the Double-Bell model. Harrison and van Hoek's supply network is run by *supply chain management** which comprises *planning** and controlling all the processes from raw material production to purchase by the end user and recycling of used products. This chain management views the supply chain as a single entity which:

- requires strategic decision-making,
- views balancing inventories as a last resort, and
- demands system integration.

Harrison and van Hoek's model considers the aim that:

> Supply chain processes (supply, source, make, distribute and sell) are integrated together to meet end-customer demand. Demand signals are shared across the chain rather than being massaged by the 'sell' process next to the market. Demand fulfilment is also envisaged as an integrated process, as materials are moved from one process to another in a seamless flow. Information is the 'glue' that binds the supply chain processes together.[6] (p. 15)

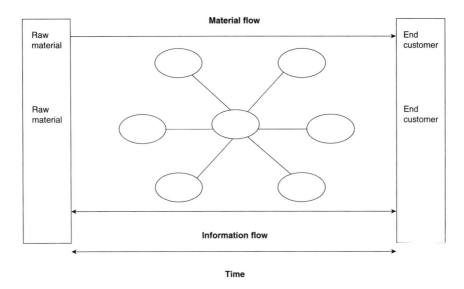

Figure 1.7   **Supply network structure**[6]

Source: Logistics Management and Strategy, by Harrison A and van Hoek R, reprinted by permission of Pearson Education Limited, copyright 2002, 2005.

How does a service supply chain compare with the product chain described above? Service chains are typically simpler than product chains because they place more emphasis on intangible assistance by people. If we consider a retailer or a restaurant to be typical service businesses, then the inbound supply chain has all the levels of supply companies but is usually simpler on distribution: customers come to these businesses themselves. In a professional service, such as an accountant or a consultant, the supply chain concept has very little relevance. The emphasis is on employing a number of people who render specialised advice to clients. There are few materials or products involved. In a mass transport service, such as a railway or an airline, the supply chain comprises building the *infrastructure** to enable the transport of people or goods and then providing the service to customers as they require.

Why work on supply chains?

One of the biggest challenges for businesses is to integrate supply chains for the benefit of customers and to make a profit. One key reason that this is necessary is because most current businesses are not very efficient. Numerous studies[7] show that almost all businesses contain enormous amounts of *waste**: misdirected efforts, poor or missing information, ineffectual management, lack of leadership, authority or trust, power plays, delays and excessive inventory. Hence the need to reduce waste throughout the supply chain must be considered, so that the customer receives more value and the companies get more return for their efforts. The people who first realised this ubiquitous waste were Japanese manufacturers, especially Toyota. Waste is any human activity which absorbs resources but creates no value.

For example, Womack and Jones[7] have a rule of thumb that states the gains expected
when waste is removed from a production system:

> Converting a classic batch-and-queue production system to continuous flow with effec-
> tive pull by the customer will double labour productivity all the way through the system
> (for direct, managerial and technical workers, from raw materials to delivered product)
> while cutting production throughput times by 90 per cent and reducing inventories in the
> system by 90 per cent as well. (p. 27)

If we accept that amount of waste within a business system run by one management,
then there is likely to be even more waste when three firms in a supply chain provide a
product. Since each company is autonomous, it is busy running its own business. Such
inward focus is unlikely to be efficient in terms of the whole supply chain. It will contain lots of waste.

So far we have examined a supply chain which is in place, carrying out the short-
term planning and activities necessary to provide a range of products to end consumers. Later we want to talk about the strategic planning and development of a chain
for some products, either because they are new products or because the chain is operating in the wrong ball park, that is it is fundamentally wrong in some way. We define
the integration which creates value for customers and operators in section 1.5. The
overall issue of creating supply chains is discussed in Chapters 6 to 8.

If company managers are running an existing *value stream*, they are interested in creating *value* for the customer and for their company. ('Value stream' is an alternative
phrase for a supply chain which emphasises the intention of creating value for customers and companies.) Managers overseeing the manufacture of Toyota cars want
customers to recognise sufficient value in their cars so that they recommend them to
their friends. They also want Toyota to pay their salaries and make a profit for reinvest-
ment. But there is a second important meaning to the *value* in value stream. Value
streams will only work if people put values, good company and partnership behaviours
ahead of numbers. Soft values of contributing and sharing outweigh the short-term
gains of outsmarting and putting down. Jack Welsh, the highly successful CEO of
GE, says:

> Early in my career ... there was way too much focus on the numbers ... and a lot less
> focus on the softer values of building a team, sharing ideas, exciting others.[8] (p. 22)

Every supply chain is unique. It differs in some way from other chains. Exceptions can
be found for all the statements in this chapter. This makes the study of chains and their
practical *implementation** an interesting and frequently challenging task. Different
industries and varied products create different situations. This book covers a wide range
of industries to give specific points of reference. There is a great contrast between clothing manufacture, car manufacture, meat processing and selling petrol. Generally, supply chains only comprise part of the range of activities carried out by the firms which
constitute links in the chain. Supply chains are frequently not linear, they are really
networks. Chains do not last forever: they form, work for a while and then change their
configuration.

Having considered the basic elements of a supply chain, we recommend you study
the case at the end of this chapter, 'Designing a European supply chain'. This case

Table 1.1   **Comparison between supply chains**

Product/Industry	Number of levels	Number of suppliers	Number of products	Lead-time	Number of customers
Newspapers	3	2	1	6 hours	300,000
Milk	4	200	3	24 hours	150,000
Fast-food meal	3	30	6	5 mins	500
Sausages	6	4	12	4–12 days	15,000
Beer	3	6	3	10 days	2.5 million
Furniture	4	5	200	3–5 weeks	800
Pharmaceuticals	3	150	50	6 weeks	5 million
Hire car	2	5	15	1–2 days	1000
Car manufacture	5	1,100	8	3 weeks	200,000
Car parts	3	800	80,000	3–24 hours	400,000
Steel reinforcing	2	2	20	1 week	300

examines the practical organisation of supply chains when faced with the need to streamline operations.

1.2 VARIED CHAINS SATISFY CUSTOMER NEEDS THROUGH DESIGN

Supply chains occur in infinite variety to serve the product and service that the customer requires. Is the product a commodity, like milk, or customised, like picture framing? Is the product small and immediate, like a newspaper, or expensive and long delivery, such as a luxury car? Is the product a pure good, such as a pair of socks, or a mixture of goods and services, such as fast food? Is the product made for immediate sale, like a bottle of beer, or for stock until a need arises, such as spare parts for cars? Does the product have a distinct use-by date, such as milk or sausages? Is product sale regulated, as occurs with pharmaceutical drugs and cigarettes? Table 1.1 compares some characteristics of chains used to achieve these contrasting products. The 'lead-time' column refers to the length of time taken to supply the product.

The response in terms of supply chains varies between these products. The newspaper supply chain has few levels. It is very fast to produce a single product which has a very short lifetime, measured in hours. Fresh milk has a longer supply chain but the product has a life of a week. Milk is collected in tankers from the dairy farm, processed and packed in a factory, delivered via a cold store to a supermarket and selected by the customer off the shelf. Sausages have many players in their value chain, from farm to abattoir, meat packer, sausage maker, cold store and retailer.

An extended product and service is provided when someone buys a fast-food meal. All the partners in the meat chain, as with sausages, are present. Similar types of supplier deliver bread and vegetables. Then these food ingredients have to be converted into a hot, cheap meal in a minute or two after you have placed an order at the counter.

A further set of supply chains is required to provide industrial products. Where a company rather than an individual buys the product, the parameters are frequently quite different. Delivery at the agreed time, quality and correctness are the most important criteria. There is less emphasis on the product packaging and more emphasis on repeat purchases in a permanent relationship.

The overall aim of a supply chain is to satisfy the needs of the end consumer, who uses the goods produced. This aim is achieved by each partner in the chain treating the downstream link that it supplies as a customer. Focusing on one partner with a number of production processes, again each process should treat its downstream process as a customer. This relationship, which was first brought into prominence in *total quality management**, is an important means of obtaining maximum value from the chain with the use of minimum resources.

How then should one design a supply chain? We examine the situation where there is an existing supply chain, comprising a number of constituent partner firms, which requires extensive modification to match current and future conditions. Saw and McCullen[9] say, there are four design tasks which must be addressed in parallel:

- process design,
- information system design,
- organisation design, and
- physical network design.

There is very little published information on groups of companies designing supply chains in their entirety. In fact, logistics design has barely progressed beyond distribution audits in the literature. It is likely that a number of companies have held meaningful *strategic planning** meetings with their whole supply chain partners, but if they have, they are not telling anyone about it! Our own experience leads us to think that true supply chain planning, open-ended, trusting and sharing, is extremely rare. Hence we use theory which we consider helpful, if not yet adopted by many companies. These authors go on to propose four design rules:

- control systems principles,
- time compression,
- information transparency principles, and
- link elimination.

Design can also be seen as containing three elements:

1. Content – the area of 'order winners'[4] and policies, covering processes, information and physical operations, which are tools to obtain a customer-satisfying strategy.
2. Process – the method by which a supply chain strategy will be constructed by a group of managers and approval obtained for the resultant action plans.
3. Implementation – the way in which the action plans will be operationalised sequentially through all the necessary firms and employees. This involves multi-organisation change processes, project management and perseverance.

An example of such elements was the derivation and implementation of a strategy for fresh sausages by a meat-processing company. A planning process was facilitated during seven meetings over a three-month period to give the required content in the form of an action plan for the next two years. The planning team proceeded to implement the sausage strategy with enormous success over a 12-month period, a 10-fold increase in turnover to Aus$4 (£1.5) million per year. One problem with this example was that the strategy did not address information communication to any extent. The need for information communication is examined in the next section.

An important part of supply chain design is the trade-offs between the functions of links and processes in the chain. Considering a supply chain as a system, one is concerned about the output of the whole chain. Individual processes do not need to have optimum design. Trade-offs exist between processes that assist total system performance. The aim is to get the required performance at an economic cost, rather than to optimise travel times or inventory levels. If the trade-offs are correctly chosen, the integrated supply chain may produce superior results compared to a series of individually optimised components.

1.3 INFORMATION COMMUNICATION SUPPORTS MANAGEMENT

Building on the Double-Bell model described above, we now delve further into the information required by the supply chain. How can information be moved to the right places in the right forms so that managers can organise, measure performance and control the chain and its *stages*?

We saw how communication of information is necessary before the supply chain can perform its physical task. The basic information comprises:

- an order,
- a production schedule,
- a purchase order,
- an inventory record, and
- a despatch advice.

An order is a list of products and quantities required by the customer. A production schedule is an instruction to manufacture products in a particular order. A *purchase order** is a list of materials or components required from a supplier. An inventory record is a statement of the quantity of materials or goods available at a location. For example, at a distribution centre, records are kept of all the products that have been received in bulk from the factory. As products are selected, or picked, for customer orders, so the records are adjusted. Finally, at the completion of picking an order, a despatch advice will be issued to accompany the goods to their destination. These simple pieces of information will exist at each link in the supply chain for a manufacturing company. Similar information is required in the supply chains of service companies.

Companies use computer information systems to achieve these information requirements. An *order-processing** system is used to carry out checks on the incoming order. Typical checks are to find out whether the order fits within the range of products and services made and to make sure that the customer is able to pay for the goods ordered. If these checks are satisfactory, the order-processing system will instruct a storeman, via a warehouse management system, to pick and despatch the desired products. A *warehouse management system** keeps track of all the goods in the warehouse as they are received, put away, moved and picked-to-order.

Many manufacturing companies have an *enterprise resource planning** system to assist them to purchase and manufacture all the required parts to assemble a complex finished product such as a car or a refrigerator. The basic functions of this system are to schedule sufficient production each day, allowing for rates of manufacture and the order in which components are assembled into the finished product, so that the desired mix of products is produced every day. Many companies involved in distribution use a *distribution requirements planning** system to track each finished product from the factory through levels of warehouses to the end customer. Distribution requirements planning is a technique to manage product flows and inventories by providing planning records that carry demand information from receiving points to supply points and returns supply information to the receiving points. Alternatively, companies use efficient consumer response systems to assist the salespeople to focus their efforts on meeting customer needs fully by coordinating their efforts with their trading partners. For further development of these areas, see Chapter 5.

An important source of information for operators and management is summaries of performance over a period of time. Key performance measures, such as quality, on-time delivery and costs, enable managers and supervisors to check that they are achieving their customers' requirements.

Information needs to be exchanged between partner companies in the supply chain. Historically, this was done by telephone, mail or by facsimile. With the current availability of communications by telephone and the Internet, it is possible to make up-to-date status of orders, production and deliveries immediately available to all the members of the supply chain. *Electronic data interchange (EDI)** is an important means of computer-to-computer communication. It enables instantaneous transmission of documents between companies in the exact formats that each company's database requires.

In this age of electronic information, person-to-person communication is still important to learn about the current situation, to correct wrong impressions and to decide on courses of action. People speak to each other on the telephone, in offices and in meetings. Computer systems cannot be relied upon to carry out tasks automatically without human supervision unless the task is very simple and it is carefully implemented.

1.4 MANAGEMENT AND LEADERSHIP OF CHAINS

Management refers to the attainment of organisational goals through planning, organising, leading and controlling production or service facilities ranging from manufacturing equipment through distribution centres to supermarkets. We use the word 'management' to refer to these activities within one company, or link, in the supply chain. Managers have to take *strategic decisions**, which alter the whole position of the company, *tactical decisions**, which fill out the specifics of strategy, and *operating decisions**, a huge number of short-term decisions to keep the company running properly.

Leadership is the ability to influence people towards the attainment of goals.[5] Although strictly it is one function of management, we will use 'leadership' to refer to the coordination of companies in the supply chain to attain chain-wide goals.

Consider management of the central warehouse of Benetton (see Box 1.1). Managers have planned that facility so that it has the technology and the capacity to respond to customer orders by picking and despatching sweaters. Managers have appointed and trained the workforce. They motivate the workforce and control operation of the warehouse so that distribution is effectively carried out.

In addition to this management of the warehouse, and other chain facilities, the Benetton chain must be led to ensure that all the facilities pull together to get the garments into the world-wide shops. Leadership can be exercised directly in the facilities Benetton owns, such as the central warehouse. Leadership is closer to coordination when Benetton's managers influence the salespeople in the thousands of franchised shops to fit into their overall aim of operating the supply chain.

The leadership of supply chains becomes more complex when one considers the elements of power and trust that may, or may not, be displayed between the various firms in the chain and between each manager in each firm.[10] Few chains have effective leadership at the moment. The most that has been observed is chain coordination.

1.5 SUPPLY CHAIN INTEGRATION AND STRATEGY

An efficient, integrated supply chain plays a major part in the success of the business strategies of its constituent companies. It is now recognised that, in many cases, competition is between supply chains rather than individual companies.[11] Getting the product and service to the end consumer when they want it is critical. Consequently, the partner companies should work closely together to define and execute a supply chain strategy which will both satisfy customer needs and allow them to make an adequate return.

To get full benefit from a supply chain it is necessary to link all the partners involved so that goods and services flow effectively to consumers. This is achieved by working collaboratively with customers, suppliers, trading partners and service providers. The overall aim is to create a flow of products exactly as required by customers, responding dynamically to changes in their orders. First, it is necessary to establish the boundary of the supply chain, how many tiers of suppliers must be included, which service providers are important in chain flow outcomes? Secondly, where will the *decoupling point** be placed, that is the point at which planned production of materials and components changes to exact assembly and delivery of products and services pulled by customer orders? Treatment of planned, or pushed, components is very different from the processing of known customer orders. Thirdly, what physical and human resources need to be built up to provide a capability which will confer distinctive competencies compared to competing supply chains?

Within this integrated chain, managers now need to know the *order winners**. Which parameters are critical in the eyes of customers? Are they quality, speed of delivery or low price? Given the order winners, managers can design the supply chain to achieve them by choice of configurations and policies in each link. This includes *strategic decisions** on policies such as capabilities, quality assurance, response times and degree of customisation of product or service.

An important issue in chain integration is the inherent variability in demand for a product and the variable nature of purchasing, provision and travel times. The chain design should take account of these types of uncertainty to give a robust chain which is capable of the expected delivery time and also responsive to changes in volume, process and mix of orders placed or services demanded.

A new element of supply chain integration is the opportunity, which information systems offer, for firms to be responsive to customer orders rather than to anticipate orders by making goods in advance. For centuries the dominant business model required anticipation of what customers will demand in the future. Manufacturers produced products based upon a market forecast, unordered inventory was held by *wholesalers**, distributors and retailers. *Cycle times** to provide correct stock were long. The differences between plans and results increased costs and risks and frequently led to adversarial relationships between supply chain 'partners'. The availability of low-cost information enables manufacturers and whole supply chains to be more responsive than anticipatory. Time-based competition is used in the responsive business model. Managers share information to improve the speed and accuracy of supply chains. When all partners in the chain synchronise their operations, inventory can be reduced and duplicate practices eliminated. The fewer steps in the responsive process equate to less cost and less elapsed time from order commitment to delivery.

Pulling together the order winners, the centralised information and timeliness of supply, requires supply chain managers and leaders to decide on the policies needed in various functions in each link of the supply chain so that a successful strategy delivers benefits to customers and providers.

Summary

Supply chain integration, for a chain of manufacturing and service companies, requires the major stages in the location, transformation and movement of raw materials and finished goods to be 'bounded', designed and operated very competitively. Using the current limited understanding of the concept of supply chain management, how does a manager in one company work with up- and downstream counterparts to position and tune their businesses for success? There is now strong evidence of the importance of integrated supply chain strategy and management to achieve sustained competitive advantage.

As well as physical movements, the concept of supply chain management needs to be applied to information, leadership and management of constituent firms within supply chains. The concept can be represented by the Double-Bell model which comprises all significant provision and information steps from creation of raw materials to delivery of end products and services to consumers.

A supply network comprises all the product market families going through a focal company (typically a manufacturer or distributor) to end customers. Thus the network comprises a number of supply chains to achieve the desired flow of products to end customers. Each chain can be different from the others to a greater or lesser extent, dependent upon resource availability and economic forces. Widening to various industries providing different goods and services, the range of possible supply chains is huge. The combination of products, lead times and numbers of customers creates a multitude of chains.

Supply chain integration provides an opportunity for you, as future managers of companies along the chain, to work together through shared information to provide and deliver goods and services to customers. Consider a simple supply

(Continued)

(Continued)

chain of one vendor transporting materials to a manufacturer, who transforms them into one family of finished products and despatches these goods to a *distribution centre** for delivery, at the right time, to a retailer for customers to purchase. Assume that the supply chain processes, information systems and services, such as transport, are already well designed to supply those goods at a profit over the costs of operating the whole value chain. You then have three strategic tasks:

- to plan the flow of materials, goods and services from sources to customers along stages of the chain by information exchange, electronic and verbal,
- to perform the necessary physical movements and conversions in the required quantities and at the required times for consumers within acceptable costs, and
- to manage innovations, changes and developments to the benefit of product market families for all companies and to the advantage of all desired customers.

Questions

1. Name the key parts of a physical supply chain in sequence from sources to end consumers.
2. How does a supply chain for a family of products fit into the Double-Bell model of a supply network?
3. Why does the existence of several separate companies along the supply chain make it more difficult to flow materials and products to customers?
4. What does each bell represent in the Double-Bell model?
5. Explain how the supply chain can be considered a series of links and movements.
6. What is the function of information communication systems in running the supply chain?
7. Draw a supply network for a family of products in an industry with which you are familiar. If you do not have a familiar industry, use a case from this book or other literature.
8. What are the two key aims of a supply chain?

Case: Designing a European supply chain[12]

Derek Stuart, Director of Logistics Europe at Shavers Inc., was discussing a new design for Shavers supply chain with the IT Director, Brenda Hunter, and the Distribution Centres Manager, John Beale. In the face of poor customer service and excess inventory, the President of Shavers had charged Derek with the task of overhauling the European logistics with a wide scope.

(Continued)

Shavers Inc

The Shavers company is a long-established company with a corporate brand name that is recognised world-wide. It is a large company with world headquarters in the USA and operations throughout the USA, Asia and Europe. Shavers aims to achieve leadership in male and female shaving and deodorants, anti-perspirants and dental care. The corporate strategy is to run the business on a global basis, maximising the power of Shavers' well-established brands. Shavers' mission, in part, states:

- We sell the same products world-wide.
- We treat all markets the same.
- We package fast-moving commodity products to suit local requirements.

A typical European supply chain comprises product design in Massachusetts, manufacture in England and Germany, and distribution from 13 warehouses to 20 countries. Four hundred and fifty different products are sold throughout Europe, although extra variants were caused by packaging and promotions.

Derek Stuart believed that, despite the company's commitment to a global marketing strategy, there was a lack of integration of its supply chain management, particularly across Europe. Responsibility for logistics was very fragmented with each country managing its manufacturing needs and distribution. A European HQ had been established in London, but decisions on everything from inventory levels to purchasing were made locally. There were 13 distribution centres (DCs) across Europe, all carrying identical stock except that packaging varied locally, plus a number of transport interchange depots. Shavers was not achieving its aim of satisfying its world-wide customers with common products in local wraps in Europe because of poor delivery performance. This lack of customer service reduced competitiveness, revenue and profit.

Current supply chain

John Beale, DC Manager, brought a diagram to explain the concept behind Shavers European supply chain (Figure C1.1). Currently, parts were bought from suppliers in the USA and Asia for manufacture in three European factories. Finished products were delivered to 13 distribution centres where they were packaged for local markets and delivered to customer stores. These stores included chain retailers, wholesalers and pharmacy warehouses. Sales and most logistics decisions were taken in national offices in each country. Figure C1. 2 shows where decisions were then taken across the range of logistics functions. The large number of DCs, with separately planned stock and once-a-month ordering, led to high levels of inventory, typically three months sales cover.

Even allowing for all this inventory, service levels to retail customers were low. Order fill averaged only 78%, and the order cycle time varied from five days to more than 20 days. Service performance was increasingly important as European retailers continued to grow their purchasing power and to place ever-greater demands for service on their suppliers.

(Continued)

(Continued)

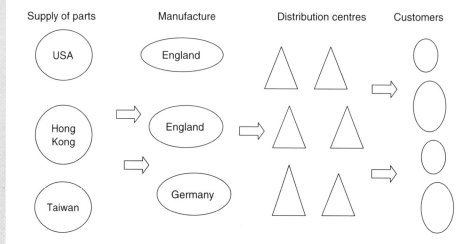

Figure C1.1   **Concept diagram of Shavers supply network**

Each symbol represents goods, information, management and relationships. Except for manufacture, the symbols do not represent all the entities in the supply chain.

Function	Responsibility		
	Europe HQ	National	Local region
Production operations	▸	▸	
Master scheduling		●	
Finished goods inventories		●	
Purchasing		●	
Sales forecasting		●	
Distribution centres		●	
Distribution		●	
Order-processing		●	
Packaging design	▸	▸	
Planning information systems		●	
Systems design and support	▸	▸	

Figure C1.2   **Decision-making responsibilities in Shavers**
(▸ = half; ● = whole)

(Continued)

Many of the markets in which Shavers competed were highly volatile, with high levels of promotional activity requiring special promotional packs. In situations such as this, forecasting was difficult and consequently there was always great pressure placed on manufacturing to make frequent changes to its production schedules. Manufacturing worked on a monthly planning cycle and hence needed to have reliable forecasts to cover the planning period as well as the extended lead times required by suppliers.

A new design

To Derek Stuart, it seemed clear that the global approach to marketing would require Shavers to have a greater degree of central coordination and planning. A European logistics strategy required a number of fundamental decisions to be made at a European level rather than locally. He especially felt that areas of particular strategic importance were:

- finished goods and work-in-progress inventories,
- distribution operations and location,
- supply chain strategy,
- development of forecasting and requirement-planning systems, and
- purchasing.

John Beale held the view that the large number of distribution centres was hindering the achievement of good service levels as well as costing too much. Brenda Hunter, IT Director, saw the need for modern planning and control systems to provide for customer demand by effective scheduling, manufacturing and distribution planning for each product on offer.

The three executives looked at finished goods inventory first. Centralised responsibility for inventory would require the establishment of a European planning function. The task of the function was to obtain sales forecasts from each local market, monitor finished goods stock levels at each DC and develop production plans and stock movement schedules to drive the flow of finished goods to DCs to ensure a high service level.

To start to obtain a better distribution network, John recommended the setting-up of a central European distribution function. This would be required to find the best configuration of DCs and provide input to the proposed business information systems. At that time close working relationships between local business managers and the local DC managers, or transport contractors, made for a difficult transition.

Brenda considered that the planning and execution systems that Derek and Stuart wanted would require the creation of a European business process group. This group would specify, purchase and implement the necessary enterprise requirements planning and web-based systems to give common systems across the whole of Europe. This was the only way, she said, that the integrated logistics management required by Derek could be achieved.

Up to this point all planning had been done in monthly quantities, with the consequence that stocks were at a high level. Once a European-wide forecasting system was installed, Shavers should be able to forecast overall European demand centrally much more accurately than they could by adding up all the local sales forecasts. This would lead to weekly requirements planning, backed up by capacity-constrained master scheduling. The essence of this was that the production of blades and razors in the factories would be driven by accurate, stable, European forecasts while the more volatile packaging requirements were

(Continued)

(Continued)

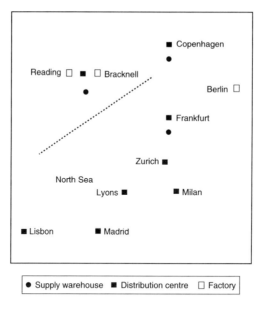

● Supply warehouse ■ Distribution centre □ Factory

Figure C1.3 **Revised European DC network**

driven by national and regional, item-level forecasts (close to real-time demand). Differences between the two would be buffered by work-in-process inventory which, in turn, required the centralisation of inventory responsibility. Although, in reality, there was a close partnership between the European and factory planning teams, the centralisation of control over work-in-process would be a major step forward, which had already been achieved by the corresponding division of Shavers in the USA.

A further plank in Derek's European vision for integrated logistics management was the centralisation of responsibility for all purchasing. This did not mean that purchasing teams within the factories would be disbanded, rather that they now reported to a central executive with a brief to act locally but think European. In his view, Shavers should benefit from significant reductions in purchase prices achieved. This would require standard purchasing systems and projects to reduce inventories of raw material and work-in-process.

Derek sent John Beale and Brenda Hunter away to investigate their areas further.

Distribution

It was apparent to John that, once a European logistics management structure was in place supported by accurate information, there would no longer be a need for 13 DCs. Shavers wanted an order-to-delivery time across Western Europe of two days. John therefore commissioned an exercise which evaluated product flows between the three factories and the markets in all 20 countries. From this work he determined that eight DCs would be required. These were to be located in Bracknell, UK; Copenhagen, Denmark; Frankfurt, Germany; Zurich, Switzerland; Milan, Italy; Lyons, France; Madrid, Spain; and Lisbon, Portugal (Figure C1.3).

The wider distribution area to be served by the German DC provides an example of the reduction in DCs. In Germany, Shavers needed a regional distribution centre located within 100 km of Frankfurt. Its function was to be both a supplier warehouse receiving all production from their largest European factory in Berlin and a regional distribution centre

(Continued)

holding stock and supplying customers in Austria, Belgium and the Netherlands as well as Germany (Figure C1.3). With this facility in operation, DCs can be eliminated in Austria, Belgium and the Netherlands. However, because of the promotional demands of Belgium and the Netherlands, it was necessary to retain cross-docking depots in these countries. These depots will be operated by third-party transport contractors. Here customer orders and promotional packs will be made up from stock delivered daily from the Frankfurt DC.

A similar regional distribution plan will be implemented in Scandinavia. Four separately stocked DCs will be closed and replaced by a new regional distribution centre in Copenhagen, set up and operated by a Danish contractor. All customer orders and promotional packaging for the whole of Scandinavia will be carried out at this facility. At the same time, the rationalisation of divisional warehouses in Spain will enable Shavers to set up a third-party-operated facility south of Madrid.

Shavers originally owned and operated its own DCs. Derek believes the company should move progressively towards more contract operation. The policy is one of concentrating investment in core activities and outsourcing supply chain operations when and where conditions are appropriate. The growth of the third-party-provider industry has ensured that there is no shortage of bidders willing and able to provide a very competitive service in DC operations.

Shavers Europe has used contract carriers for the last 20 years or so, but the role played by third parties in warehouse operations had been mixed. DCs operated by Shavers and those run by third-party operators had worked very well, although warehousing contractors were changed from time to time for reasons of service or cost. However, Shavers' return on capital investment on the one hand, and the expansion of the third-party warehousing and distribution industry on the other, made it increasingly difficult to justify their own DCs. The question was not so much whether they should run their own versus a third-party operator, but the extent to which various logistics management functions and the information systems to support them should remain with Shavers or be handed over to third parties. The policy established by the company differentiates between planning activities, which will all remain with Shavers, and operations functions and systems, which will be considered for placing in the hands of appropriate third parties.

Requirements planning systems

Shavers Europe could not achieve the higher level of customer service needed and obtain the inventory reductions available through the warehouse rationalisation programme without centralised planning and shorter order processing times. After the meeting with Derek, Brenda therefore investigated and purchased an enterprise requirements planning (ERP) system which will provide:

- order forecasting,
- demand management,
- master production scheduling,
- materials requirements planning,
- purchasing,
- factory scheduling and inventory management,
- distribution requirements planning (DRP), and
- delivery recording and invoicing.

(Continued)

(Continued)

This ERP system will provide a real-time view of the whole of Shavers' European business from customer orders to warehouse stocks, from DC stocks to factory replenishment, from order entry to delivery and payment. It will embody weekly production planning by factories and DCs, intranet transmission of information between DCs, depots and factories, and web-enabled visibility for customers, local sales offices and contractors. Although implementing the ERP system at the factories and DCs would be a substantial task, Brenda considers that the longest implementation time will be interfacing ERP and, especially, DRP to every sales office, warehouse and factory around Europe. The DRP operating concept is very simple. Once a week, sales forecasts from each country will be updated and transmitted to the central production and distribution planning office. Real-time data available will include stocks levels by stock-keeping unit (SKU) by location and the status of production schedules from each factory. The distribution requirements planning module will show stocks and movement instructions for replenishment for the current week and 20 weeks into the future for each DC and depot. At the same time, the opportunity was taken to centralise capacity planning and master scheduling at the European headquarters.

Outcomes

Shavers made substantial progress towards achieving a European logistics strategy in the three years after Derek's meeting with Brenda and John. Impressive results had been obtained from the integrated supply chain strategy for Europe:

- Customer service performance greatly improved: order fill rate, which previously averaged 78% in key markets in Europe, had reached 98%.
- Logistics operations costs rose by less than inflation over the period and represented a smaller percentage of sales in all markets.
- Despite an increase in SKUs of more than 50% from 450 to 700, an increased rate of new product launches and more sourcing of components from outside Europe, inventory levels had not risen.
- The total number of logistics employees was reduced in both warehouse operations and planning functions.

In the centralisation of responsibility for finished goods inventory, both Derek and John encountered a great deal of resistance from local business managers. Managers viewed this change as taking away 'their' stock of finished goods. There was widespread belief that service levels would suffer as inventory levels reduced, but experience showed that this was not the case.

Figure C1.4 shows how the location of various responsibilities had changed three years later. Each factory now reports to the Director of Logistics Europe (Derek). European HQ has taken over responsibility for planning and control functions (such as master scheduling), distribution centres and requirement planning. Forecasting and purchasing responsibilities are shared between European HQ and national offices. The move that elicited the most organisational resistance was the setting-up of a European warehousing and distribution function. Derek and his senior managers consulted widely to explain the major management advantages which would flow from this re-organisation. They made many procedural changes to satisfy regional concerns without retreating from the overall plan.

(Continued)

Function	Responsibility		
	Europe HQ	National	Local region
Production operations	●		
Master scheduling	●		
Finished goods inventories	●		
Purchasing	▸	▸	
Sales forecasting	◂	▸	
Distribution centres	●		
Distribution	●		
Order-processing		●	
Packaging design	●		
Planning information systems			●
Systems design and support	◂		▸

Figure C1.4   **Decision-making responsibilities in Shavers three years later**
(▸ = half; ● = whole)

Pitfalls

At this important three-year point, Derek Stuart also reflected on the major issues that had been learned and what things he might have done differently if they were starting the project over again.

After some thought he concluded that the problems could be categorised under chain-wide management, requirement planning systems, people and customer service targets.

i. Chain-wide management

Shavers Europe is still pushing products from factories through distribution centres to supply customers, but this is being done on a weekly cycle. This is a considerable improvement, bearing in mind that the forecasts on which this pre-production is based have improved dramatically and the reduction in inventory enables product to move through the whole of Europe much faster than it previously did.

ii. Requirements planning systems

Although, in theory, the redesign of systems should follow after strategic and operational plans have been developed, in practice changes in technology and the life cycles of large information systems tend to result in hardware and software investments which do not

(Continued)

(Continued)

always follow user requirements. Shavers has undergone during the last eight years a total change from mainframes through mid-range machines and is now moving to a client-server environment. This created a momentum for application software replacement that was not always user-driven. Derek anticipated this would be less of a problem in the future.

Another factor that has affected Shavers' application systems plans within Europe has been the shortage of European software that sufficiently recognised the needs of Europe, necessitating costly revisions. Associated with this has been the lack of investment by certain software houses in support of European customers. The fact that software companies which have not invested are suffering a decline in business as a consequence is of little consolation to those companies who have bought their particular software packages.

Software purchasing decisions are probably the most difficult to make, since it is often extremely difficult for those with authority to understand what they are buying. Conversely, those with the knowledge of the application systems capabilities have generally too little influence on the buying decisions and may perhaps not be involved until a very late stage. This can seriously affect achieving a Class A result. Probably the most significant aspects of systems implementation within the context of European logistics at Shavers has been the performance of international data transmission networks, interfaces and the implementation effort. First, wide area data transmission networks have improved by an order of magnitude. Hence Shavers can be confident that data can be centralised from all factories and DCs and the results of planning decisions can be instantaneously sent to regional centres. Secondly, interfaces between different pieces of software and with EDI and web applications have become far simpler to install and use. Thirdly, installation teams have been allocated to ensure that choices in business process models and data integrity are built to near-perfect accuracy.

Brenda considers that the longest implementation time will be interfacing ERP and especially DRP to every sales office, warehouse and factory around Europe.

Shavers can now claim to have a European data network supporting centralised planning and forecasting in real time.

iii. People

The most common reaction to the centralisation of any activity is the fear of loss of control by local management. In every situation entailing the transfer of responsibility for an operation from that of national or regional managers, there has been resistance. Although this resistance appeared to be irrational and even illogical in the context of a European vision, the reaction is understandable. It is only human to believe that the formula for success in the past will continue to apply in the future, especially when it is proposed that as a consequence of change one's own job and power are diminished. It has, however, been gratifying to see that, after the fact, each step has been embraced enthusiastically and that local management has admitted that their fears were not justified. In retrospect, Derek considered that the most effective means of reassuring managers was a face-to-face discussion to build up trust and understanding.

Overlaid on the top of management issues, such as those discussed, have been those arising from national differences. Despite a strong European business culture and the general acceptance of the advantages of a European Union by senior management, the difficulties in this respect are much greater than had been anticipated. It also has to be said that for an American company working across Europe with English as the working language, it should not be a surprise that meetings need to be longer and there are occasional

(Continued)

errors of communication. Remember that each local manager is working in a foreign language.

Also on the subject of people, European centralisation has created excellent career opportunities for some managers. The gradual movement towards third-party operation has shifted the emphasis from warehouse management skills to those of negotiation and management control and this has been achieved through training and some reassignment.

iv. Customer service targets

Although defined customer service performance targets are a necessary prerequisite for the design of a supply chain, Derek sees them as a pitfall both because of their importance and the degree of misunderstanding which frequently arises between sales management and logistics management. The single most important dimension affecting the distribution strategy is that of order cycle time. That is the cycle that begins with transmission from the customer through order processing, distribution centre consolidation, picking and despatch to final destination. The key to cut order cycle times was to look for ways to streamline order-processing procedures in order to cut processing times, thus freeing up more time for the physical distribution side of the order cycle. This Shavers achieved.

Another very important measure of customer service performance is that of order fill rate. While not affected directly by the warehouse network, it is a prime measure of the effectiveness of the forecasting and planning side of the business. One of the management reporting deficiencies before Shavers redesigned the European supply chain was the lack of any customer service reporting system. Prior to installing a DRP system, Shavers were also unable to utilise forecast error and order fill rate parameters in the setting of advanced stock levels by product family in each DC. This deficiency has been rectified.

Acknowledgement

This case study[12] has been developed from work by Martin Christopher and David Taylor in 1997.

Case questions

1. What changes did Shavers make to integrate its European logistics?
2. What are the pros and cons of centralised distribution for a fast-moving consumer goods company?
3. What is the effect of supply chain design on:

    (a) information,
    (b) organisation, and
    (c) people?

REFERENCES

1   Senge PM (1990) *The Fifth Discipline: The Art and Practice of the Learning Organisation*, Random House, Sydney. p. 127.

2   Dapiran P (1992) 'Benetton: Global logistics in action', *International Journal of Physical Distribution and Logistics Management*, 22(6) : 7–11.

3   Porter ME (1985) *Competitive Advantage: Creating and Sustaining Superior Performance*, The Free Press, New York.

4   Christopher M (2005) *Logistics and Supply Chain Management: Creating Value-Adding Networks*, Prentice-Hall, Harlow, pp. 13–14.

5   Samson D and Daft RL (2003) *Management* (Pacific Rim edition), Thomson, Melbourne, Australia.

6   Harrison A and van Hoek R (2005) *Logistics Management and Strategy* (2nd edn), Prentice-Hall, Harlow.

7   Womack JP and Jones DT (1996) *Lean Thinking: Banish Waste and Create Wealth in Your Corporation*, Simon and Schuster, New York.

8   Krames JA (2002) *The Welsh Way: 24 Lessons from the World's Greatest CEOs*, McGraw-Hill, New York.

9   Saw R and McCullen P (2001) 'What's the 0–60mph time for your supply chain?', in Sadler I, Power D and Dapiran GP (eds), *Integrating Supply Chains and Internal Operations through eBusiness*', Proceedings of the Seventh International Symposium of Logistics, Melbourne, Australia, pp. 223–30.

10   Cox A (1999) 'Power, value and supply chain management', *Supply Chain Management: An International Journal*, 4(4): 167–75.

11   Christopher M (2005) *Logistics and Supply Chain Management* (3rd edn), Prentice-Hall, Harlow.

12   Christopher M (1997) 'Creating a European logistics strategy', in D Taylor (ed.), *Global Cases in Logistics and Supply Chain Management*, International Thomson, London, pp. 38–46.

Logistics in Manufacturing Organisations

2

Strategically managing the procurement, movement and storage of materials, production of *parts and* despatch of *finished products and the related information flows,* into and *through the organisation and its marketing channels* to meet customer needs for goods and service and *to achieve sustained profitability by cost-effective order fulfilment.*[1]

Objectives

- To analyse the functions required in a manufacturing link of a supply chain and design them as a sub-system which transforms materials into goods and relates effectively to immediate supply chain companies, for a specific industry
- To plan effective link structures and trade-offs between functions which would achieve the customer service and profit aims of logistics in a chosen supply network for products using the tools provided
- To consider the parts played by provision, inventory, transport and purchasing in the logistics of a manufacturing organisation
- To examine the more effective use of people to manage and improve the logistics performance of the link, hence satisfying end customers

INTRODUCTION AND ASSUMPTIONS

This chapter describes the supply chain tasks of achieving production flow within a plant so that the materials received are effectively converted into finished products. It includes delivery of parts and material from suppliers and shipment of goods to the plant's immediate customers, commonly referred to as *door to door**. Four sub-sections examine the operations of logistics in one link of the supply chain: order-taking, provision, transport and inventory. Information communication systems are described where they occur, within functions, rather than separately.

A number of tools for analysing supply chains are introduced. These tools include arrangement of functions, inventory management and performance measurement. The majority of the tools are qualitative, such as the effective arrangement of logistics functions, rather than quantitative techniques. We consider many of the quantitative techniques proposed to be less useful in real situations than in gathering strategic information for a management team to make a qualitative business decision. Further analysis tools are introduced in later chapters.

While this chapter mainly considers manufacturing organisations in which input materials are *transformed** into finished products, much of the material can be applied, with a little thought, to many service businesses. Chapter 3 develops the material specifically for service organisations.

In the first half of this chapter, we make some simplifying assumptions about the link studied because it is only part of the supply chain system. Generally the link will comprise one plant owned by one company at a single location. This company link intends to continue its present range of products while making sufficient profit and increasing turnover. Its marketing objectives are to serve current customers excellently while increasing the range of products and market share. The people working for this company are content to make familiar products and services which compete successfully rather than being intent on transforming the company. Similar logistics processes and tasks will be required in other links which supply materials and services or which receive goods and services from this plant. Connecting all the links into a chain is addressed in Chapter 6.

From section 2.6 onwards, we move from existing products to examine the effect of new products and services on this central link of the supply chain. The section on 'Supply development' delves into the new logistics systems which the manufacture of innovative products by new processes will require. Next, a section on 'Departmental links and business strategy' considers the connections of the logistics link with other functions and with the company's overall business strategy. 'Lean management and leadership' looks at the critical human dimensions of managing product flow in a plant involving decisions, tasks, training and steering. Since changes are happening all the time, the last two sections introduce 'Performance measurement and improvement' and the boundaries of a link in a logistics network.

2.1   BRIEF HISTORY OF INTEGRATED LOGISTICS

Logistics was originally used in a military context, meaning all the support actions necessary to keep an army in the field, fighting a war. Fifty years ago manufacturing and service companies did not have a logistics function. Generally, customer service was handled by the sales department. Inventory was managed by manufacturing or sales according to location. Suppliers arranged inbound transport and outbound transport was booked by someone in the sales department.

In the intervening period, many companies have created a logistics function to look after an increasing proportion of movement and storage functions. Typically, logistics manages, or is strongly involved in:

- order-processing,
- purchases,
- inbound transport,

- production plans and schedules,
- inventory management,
- distribution and delivery transport,
- warehouse management, and
- several information systems such as customer response management, materials requirements planning and distribution requirements planning.

For example, an Australian company, which we will call Innovation Plastics (IP), has a Manufacturing Resources Planning system which deals with many of the above functions. IP supplies a range of moulded plastic parts to Ford Australia to assemble into cars. The General Manager Logistics of IP uses this information system to manage all of the above functions except distribution and finished goods inventory. These two functions are not required at IP because Ford only 'pulls', or sends immediate delivery requests for the required car components.

Since logistics is a relatively new function, some companies have moved only part way along this change in organisation structure. It follows that directors and chief executive officers are unlikely to be logisticians. In many cases they lack an appreciation of the potential contribution of the logistics function. Instead they tend to treat link logistics as an area of cost and 'menial' operations which is more often controlled than consulted.

Paradoxically, this move to have a separate logistics function comes at a time when management is moving towards processes, away from functional departments. We favour a company which emphasises processes, such as order fulfilment and new product development, over functional departments looking after production, marketing or logistics.

2.2 LOGISTICS OPERATIONS FUNCTIONS

The general relationship between four key logistics functions in one link, of one company or plant, is shown in Figure 2.1. Some functions, such as order-taking, occur at one position in the plant while others, such as transport, occur in various areas. We can use this simple diagram to review the health of each function and the existence of other functions which may not be necessary. The functions must be examined in each link of the supply chain: if there are five links, there are twenty basic functions. The next four sections describe each of the key logistics functions.

2.3 ORDER-TAKING AND FORECASTING DEMAND

Order-taking comprises the receipt of orders in the supply chain product range from customers, their checking to ensure that they fall within the manufacturing capability and financial guidelines, and the response to customers that goods are available, or can be made, plus a delivery promise and price.

Transmission of an order from the customer is frequently made by facsimile or electronic message and it is often preceded by an order forecast. Checks carried out by the manufacturing company include ensuring that the customer is able to pay, and they

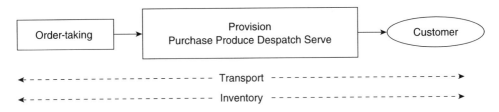

Figure 2.1   **Logistics operations functions**

are frequently carried out by computer program. Once the order has been received, a number of steps are needed to provide the products to customers, that is the adjacent customers in the next downstream part of the supply chain. This is called *provision.*

A tremendous variety of orders exist, according to the type of sale, whether the customer is a company or an individual and whether the product is a commodity or a customised item. Orders typically comprise a number of line items, perhaps 10 to 20 *stock-keeping units** (skus) which the customer requires as one delivery. Even though *forecasting* demand** is not one of the operations functions, it is convenient to include it at this point because it is an early estimate of likely orders.

Although a fast response is the key to good provision of goods, forecasts are important to give the producing firm some information when it cannot make goods in an acceptable period after the order is received. Many companies operate on a mixture of actual and forecast orders. Under current practices, companies which are more distant from the end consumer have to rely on a greater proportion of forecasts and order amendments. A forecast of demand is therefore a critical management tool. The better this forecast is, the better an organisation can prepare for orders, avoiding the costs of over or under provision of goods. So a forecast is calculated, based on previous ordering patterns, and the accuracy of the forecast is *also* calculated. Preferably the forecast is varied according to current commercial knowledge, such as one-off changes due to disasters or industrial action.

Several matters should be considered in deciding the approach to forecasting:

- A single forecasting process should be used for the whole supply chain. This process should be applied at the link adjacent to the customer and the information should be shared with all chain partners.
- A time-series forecast of sales units at an aggregate level is calculated by a forecasting package. The package stores a time-series of sales over the previous 20 time periods. An equation is used to estimate the most likely level of sales in the next period. Equations frequently used are moving average (in which the forecast is the average of a number of previous periods) and exponential smoothing (a weighted average of previous periods in which more recent periods receive more weight). Often allowances for seasonality are also made.
- Management judgement by a number of internal experts from relevant company functions to improve upon the time-series forecast.
- Forecast accountability can be improved by reviewing their accuracy. Otherwise there is a danger that staff responsible for sales will prepare low forecasts, so that they are easier to achieve.

Significant improvement in forecasting requires close collaboration between supplier and buyer. A promising process is Collaborative Planning Forecasting and Replenishment (CPFR).[2] In CPFR both parties enter into an agreement to align their plans. When one party creates the sales forecast, exceptions due to new product introductions, etc. are agreed. This process of forecast and exceptions is followed through into order forecasts and firm orders. CPFR moves away from excessive reliance on past sales data but it has been found to be very labour-intensive.

2.4 PROVISION

*Provision** comprises the *processes** of purchase, produce, despatch and serve. Provision aims to achieve perfect flow by encompassing all the activities required to source *materials** from upstream links, to make products and to deliver them to the premises of the next link in the supply chain. It also includes the services, which each link company requires to carry out these processes, and the concomitant services needed by customers as part of their products, such as training in their use and after-sales service.

First process, purchasing

In the first process, purchasing is the whole relationship with numerous suppliers to effectively obtain all the inputs required to produce the link's output of goods and services. The purchasing process requires:

- appointing a number of companies capable of providing raw materials and component parts,
- placing purchase orders on the appointed companies to deliver quantities of materials sufficient for the manufacturing process. A typical order specifies the materials by a reference number, gives the quantity required and delivery date, and states the place of delivery,
- receiving materials and components on time, and
- evaluating suppliers to ensure that they are achieving promised deliveries.

Many companies negotiate 'blanket' orders with a supplier for a year and then operators tell the supplier the actual quantities and types of materials each day.

The above is the 'running' relationship with suppliers. This 'running' relationship depends upon a supplier discovery process which involves specifying the product needed, finding potential supply companies, working out which are capable of supply and then negotiating a commercial relationship. This discovery process is considered in section 2.6.

Supply has become a very intricate process because of the manufacturer's requirement for very low defect rates, just-in-time supply of components, and the ability for working groups of employees (or purchasing departments) to inform the supplier of the precise types and quantities of materials required.[3] Mass production manufacturers require suppliers to deliver the exact quantities requested, with defect rates in a low number of parts per million, so that the manufacturer is not required to inspect the components before using them. Just-in-time supply entails the manufacturer informing the supplier of the number and types of requirement very shortly (usually hours) before they are to be delivered to the factory.

There is a current emphasis on reducing the number of suppliers with whom a manufacturer deals from hundreds to tens. This can be achieved by the preferred suppliers increasing their range or by their assembling a *module** which incorporates both their own components and those from displaced suppliers. This reduction assists the manufacturer to deal more closely with the limited number of surviving direct suppliers. Manufacturers can now use electronic links, such as EDI or the Internet, to send messages instantaneously and automatically from their factories to suppliers. Planning systems typically provide a module which enables this electronic transfer.

Second process, production

The second process, production, or manufacturing, comprises all the steps required to convert raw materials and purchased components into required forms and to assemble them into a finished product and, by design and quality assurance, to ensure that those products achieve the customer-mandated specification. Production is carried out in a factory where machines convert the materials into the desired product. Quality assurance is achieved by:

- design which provides the necessary product capabilities,
- design for manufacture,
- quality trained operators,
- quality achievement in production by 'zero-defect' practices such as machine capability measurement, quality control charts, quality improvement tools (pareto curves, fishbone diagrams, etc.), and
- total quality management (TQM) philosophy.

From a logistics perspective, important differences in manufacture are whether the product has been made previously or whether it requires engineering design before it can be manufactured. This, and the preparedness of the customer to wait for a product, such as a car, rather than require it to be immediately available, such as food, leads to three different timings of manufacture relative to customer requirements:

- engineer to order,
- manufacture to order, and
- manufacture to stock.

Assume that the product is already designed and it is being manufactured to an order or to stock. Design and engineer-to-order situations are examined later in this chapter. Typically production requires a number of steps which gradually change the materials into all the required components. The components are then assembled into the finished products. This is illustrated in Figure 2.2 in which boxes labelled 'P' are manufacturing processes, ellipses labelled 'A' are assembly steps and a triangle represents an inventory location.

In this stylised production process, there are three manufacturing steps and two assembly steps. The arrows show materials handling between steps. Such handling may comprise movement by a person, a vehicle (such as a forklift truck) or a conveyor.

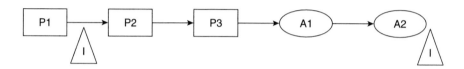

Figure 2.2   **Elements in the production process**

(P = production, I = inventory, A = assembly)

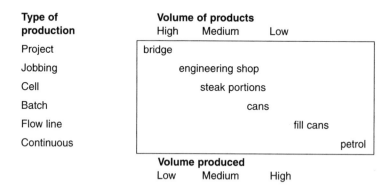

Figure 2.3   **Production responses to variety of products wanted**

The triangles show inventory, or work-in-progress, which can occur between any of the manufacturing and assembly steps. Practical production processes are usually more complex than Figure 2.2 indicates because different steps are used for different products, so there is a network of production steps, rather than the linear situation indicated. Also there are several different types of manufacturing process, ranging from jobbing (in which materials move between separate machines according to the precise work required for an individual product) to flow line (in which materials are moved by conveyors in a fixed route between all the machines required). Production can take many different forms, as illustrated by the case about making sausages (at the end of this chapter pp. 62–8) on a flow line compared to the batch manufacture of sweaters by Benetton (Chapter 1, Box 1.1, pp. 3–4).

Important considerations in production are the batch size passing from one step to the next, the quality attained at each step and the number of different products. Different types of process are needed to make high versus low varieties of product. The results of research by Hayes and Wheelwright[4] are illustrated in Figure 2.3. Ignoring the extremities, this figure shows how a jobbing shop can make small runs of a high variety of products, such as vintage car parts. At the low end of the left-hand scale, a flow line can fill soft drinks into cans in very high volumes.

Whereas manufacture makes or transforms parts, assembly requires a variety of parts to be fitted together. Typically 10 to 100 parts are assembled down a flow line by people and automatic machines. Then the assembled product is packed for protection on its journey to the customer. Packing entails wrapping the product for protection and to keep it in good condition until it reaches the customer, and to identify the product on its journey. Frequently, the product is built into a stack, in a case or on a pallet. This is known as unitising and it helps to reduce handling and errors during transport. *Unitisation** develops sufficient volume of products to be economically transported to the customer or an intermediate warehouse. With increasing frequency, provision includes after-sales service to the product. This was noted above in the automotive manufacturing case.

Manufacturing can take place at one factory or it can be broken into a number of stages at different factories. An example of this is the disassembly process of meat (refer the sausage case at the end of the chapter) which is shared between boning and small goods manufacturing 'factories'. Movements between processes in the factory, called *materials handling**, form an important part of production. Materials handling is described in section 2.5.

Provision information

In this section we examine the key functions of *Manufacturing Resources Planning (MRP)** information systems and the management purposes that they perform. Figure 2.4 outlines the main types of data and information used in provision. A full description of MRP function is given in section 5.4. MRP systems store the product structures and product routes through the plant and quantities required to produce a finished product. The systems also store and collect related data such as costs, inventory, yield and quality.

Key management decision and information recording functions are as follows:

- Driven by a business plan or budget, a resource plan is made for the production processes, the operators and the supply of materials.
- Order forecasts are made and displaced by actual orders as they arrive.
- Sales and operations planning is a procedure by which production, logistics, sales and other responsible managers use the extant data to decide the provision levels for the next month, as a compromise between their varied preferences.
- A *master production schedule (MPS)**, which states the quantities of finished goods required to satisfy orders held or anticipated over 10–15 future weeks, is derived and stored. A production schedule is a list of the end products and quantities to be manufactured over a period of time, such as a week (see Table 2.1). The items are given in the sequence of manufacture. This schedule indicates that, in week one, operators are to produce 17 pallets of sausages beginning with one pallet each of Bratwurst, pork, and honey and soy, and half a pallet of Halal.
- The correct product structure, by which materials and components can be made and assembled into a product, is stored.
- The routes which products must take between various machines are stored.
- *Materials requirements planning (mrp)** is a complicated calculation which converts the MPS into a time-phased list of the quantities of materials, components and sub-assemblies required to make the required products. It draws on product structures, inventory status, manufacturing lead times and routes and checks the availability of capacity to do this.
- Work orders are a document output by the mrp which tells the machine operators what to do. They go ahead and produce components and assemble them into products according to these orders.

Table 2.1   **Production schedule for sausages at Bradley**

Sausage type	Week 1						Week 2	Week 3	Week 4
	Mon	Tue	Wed	Thu	Fri	Total			
Bratwurst	1	1	2		1	5	5	3	2
Pork	1	1		2	1	5	5	2	3
Honey & soy	1		1		1	3	2	1	2
Hungarian		1		1		2	3	2	1
Halal	0.5		0.5			1	1	0.5	
Chicken		0.5			0.5	1	1		0.5
TOTAL	3.5	3.5	3.5	3	3.5	17	17	8.5	8.5
CAPACITY	5	5	5	5	5	25	25	25	25

- Purchase orders, generated by the mrp, tell vendors the quantities of materials and components required to make the products.
- Production activity control to measure and summarise events for managers to review and take corrective action as necessary.

Third process, despatch

The third process, despatch, covers activities of assembling an order of finished goods at the manufacturing plant and movement to the customer's premises. The first physical activity is order assembly, which requires an operator to bring together each line item from areas of the plant and package them on to pallets or into containers for despatch. The operator checks that all the items that the customer requires are included. The complete order is then loaded on to vehicles and transported by a truck driver to the customer. These transport terms are general: vehicles could be rail trucks or aircraft and truck drivers could be train drivers or pilots. The various vehicles may be operated by the manufacturer, the customer or a transport company. In many cases despatch is bulk transport of large quantities of goods, which will require breaking down in the distribution process into consumer quantities. The key piece of despatch information is the despatch advice which informs the customer exactly which goods are being sent in a delivery at a particular time. Other information flows are invoices, and the list of finished goods inventory at the plant.

Despatch is part of the wider process of *distribution*, which follows products from the manufacturer through various journeys and middlemen until they reach the end consumer. Distribution comprises these components, many of which are described in the next sub-section:

- bulk transport from factory to *distribution centre**,
- distribution centres (DC) are product warehouses serving a customer region by receiving, breaking bulk, storing, picking and assembling products to customer order,
- despatch from DC to customer premises, known as *delivery*,
- DC transport covers cross-docking, where goods enter a DC, are repacked and despatched without being stored, and time-slotting, where the truck coming to the

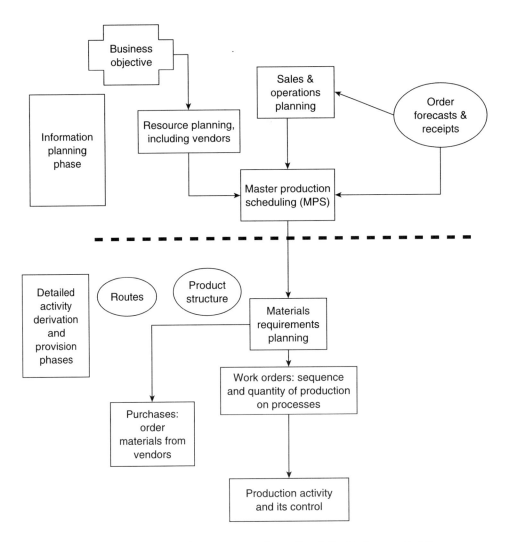

Figure 2.4   **Main components of MRP systems in outline (after Vollmann et al.[5])**

Source: *Manufacturing Planning and Control systems for Supply Chain Management*, 2005 by Vollmann TE, Berry WL, Whybark DC and Jacobs FR reprinted with permission of The Mc Graw-Hill Companies

    DC is given only a short window of time (say 11 to 11.15 am) when his goods will be accepted,
- semi-trailers, or articulated vehicles, loading several destinations,
- transport routing problems (see section 2.5),
- coordinating with 'second tier' customers: product tracking, and
- inventory control and information in distribution, especially *warehouse management systems (WMS)* and *distribution requirements planning* (see section 5.4).

Distribution centres

An important facility for despatch of many retail products is a distribution centre (DC), a type of warehouse, which plays a very important part in the outbound distribution of goods. A DC receives a wide variety of products from manufacturers in bulk and performs these tasks:

- breaking down bulk product quantities into customer-order quantities,
- storage,
- picking to assemble a 'shopping-list' of required goods, and
- fast response to customer order.

A distribution centre typically stores hundreds or thousands of different items in pallet locations arranged in bins along parallel aisles and vertical columns in each aisle. The tasks are achieved by forklift trucks moving pallets around and storemen picking goods from bins with the help of trolleys. In large volume situations, conveyor belts replace trucks to move goods around in cartons.

Distribution centres are frequently linked to factory warehouses and other DCs by distribution requirements planning (DRP) systems. These systems show the stock at each point and the actual or anticipated demand by customers for 8–10 forward periods of, say, a week. The visibility from any point of the whole current picture, and its estimated future situations, enables a high level of customer service to be obtained without excessive inventories being maintained or too many transport movements.

The situation within each distribution centre is managed by a warehouse management system (WMS) which shows the exact current status of each location, the receivals, picking and despatch planned for the current shift and the work status of each storeman or vehicle as they carry out the movement of goods required. The WMS is fed by storemen reading the *barcodes** of each pallet or carton of goods which they move. The overall effect is a very powerful measure of the performance obtained which, if used in a non-threatening manner, can enable the operators to improve their practices.

Fourth process, logistics customer service

The fourth process is service, which refers to all the functions of provision where there is no physical part or product involved. Logistics customer service refers specifically to the service parameters of product delivery and to concomitant services, such as warranty and after-sales service. Many services are necessary to purchase materials, produce goods and despatch them. Consider the training of operators, maintenance of machines, quality advice, cleaning services and technical services provided by engineers or scientists. These are examples of less visible functions, just as important to the provision of the finished goods as the physical components. Information is an important service which is fully developed in Chapter 5. Management itself can be viewed as a service, rather than a control in the modern view of empowered operators (see section 2.8).

Service also refers to a range of intangible 'services' which the customers want to enjoy for their own sake or to complement a physical product which they buy. A customer who has ordered a dining table from a furniture manufacturer wants to know whether it will be delivered on the day promised; a sales manager in Ireland needs to check whether the samples despatched from his parent company in Europe have been delayed on the way; a woman who bought a Ford car three months ago wants it to be checked and serviced.

A useful current view is that almost all manufactured products comprise physical and service parts. A meal in a restaurant comprises both the food and drink and the service of having all the tasks associated with cooking, taking the food to the table and cleaning cutlery and crockery carried out for the diners. Whereas ten years ago car manufacturers sold a car with a restricted repair warranty, now they provide the expected services for a number of years.

Provision dynamics

Provision also has a number of dynamic and performance-enhancing effects. Such effects must be included to get a proper representation of the way in which provision works in practice. Important dynamic effects are queuing, learning curves, and the use of simulation and iteration to get the system of machines, operators, external suppliers and information working well.

Queuing refers to the existence of work-in-progress or unit loads of parts waiting for the next process, or an operator or permission to be completed. In old-style purchasing, manufacturing and distribution managers frequently protected their operational efficiency by inventory or safety stock in warehouses and between processes. Figure 2.2 shows an example with inventory being held between production processes 1 and 2 to lessen the chance that process 2 is delayed. While there are a few situations in which queues are necessary, such as if your raw material comes from overseas, inventory is generally seen as waste, an extra cost which extends lead-times and gets in the way of effective provision. Under lean principles (see section 2.9), providers are exhorted to restrict work-in-progress between machines to a few hours of production. The same applies to deliveries of raw materials and 'bulk' stocks in warehouses and distribution centres except where rapid customer response overrides other concerns.

Learning curves are an important factor in new or modified processes. Especially where people are involved, manufacturing and distribution tasks tend to take considerably longer when first carried out. Research[6] has shown that most processes can be done, say, 12% faster as the number of replications is doubled. This exponential improvement can continue until a change occurs, when a regression followed by further learning improvement is likely to occur. An example of this is building a new ferry for short sea trips. The fourth ferry takes 40 days to build, the eighth takes 35 days, the sixteenth takes 31.5 days and so on.

*Simulation** and iteration are important improvement techniques. Discrete stochastic simulation[5] is a technique for studying the interaction of machines, operators and movement and for training operators and supervisors in effective operating decisions. Basically simulation builds a working, hand or computer, model of a process or processes and operates it in 'pretend' time to familiarise operators with the workings of the systems and allow them to try different methods of operation without taking time and money in the real world. The 'stochastic' or variable part comes from the use of sampling distributions rather than average values for important variable-value parameters. Iteration refers to replication of process improvement through simulation or other techniques until a preferred status is reached.

2.5 TRANSPORT AND MATERIALS HANDLING

Next we consider *transport*, the service operation which moves materials and goods between each process in the link and between links in the supply chain. Transport is examined from the point of view of managers operating the provision link in the supply chain. Many transport companies think that the movements they provide are strategically important to the delivery of goods to customers. Such companies are busy integrating between the various movements so that transport efficiency is optimised. We believe that the importance of this efficiency is limited to a range of resource materials such as grain, coal and timber. For other, more customised, parts and products, transport is simple (e.g. shift a container of toasters from Europe to USA) and many competing carriers are available. For this kind of product, transport is not strategically important to the supply chain. Transport decisions can be taken at an operating level.

The objective is to use information about the task to choose the most appropriate *modes** and types of *transport** for various movements of materials, components and goods in a number of industries. The aim is to obtain cost-efficient transport routes from supplier to factory and from factory to customer. First, we look at external transport modes and types, then materials handling between processes in the factory is examined.

External transport components of the link have changed considerably, with outsourced providers of transport and warehousing services frequently replacing the traditional in-house approach. This is caused by the transport company developing a greater skill in the movement of goods than that which the manufacturer of the products has. The producing company does not see transport as a core activity and therefore uses the transport firm to respond rapidly and effectively to an order.

Movements outside the factory include inbound transport of materials and parts and outbound distribution, or delivery, of goods. We will first focus on distribution, the delivery of finished goods and service from the factory to its customers. Secondly, we examine inbound transport of materials and parts to the factory. Materials handling, the movements between processes in the factory, is discussed in a separate paragraph.

The transport industry is, itself, a complicated set of services. It comprises many modes, many types, which provide different degrees of responsibility, many travel times which affect the price per cubic metre and inter-modal assemblage to achieve economies over long distances. In this section, we examine the types and costs of transport available before addressing the choice of these elements to carry out a particular transport task. Modes of transport, inter-modal assemblage and international transport are covered in sections 3.8 (Freight forwarders) and 4.1, respectively.

Types of transport

We now examine the various types of transport within the modes, and particularly, within the road mode. Types of transport vary according to the regularity and quantity to be moved and the relationship between the producer and the transport company.

Transport can be hired for an individual journey in quantities ranging from a taxi-truck to a semi-trailer. A taxi-truck carries quantities ranging from a few boxes up to a cubic metre. Larger quantities of pallet loads or loose cargo require a truck or a pantechnicon ('pan') towed by a prime mover making up a semi-trailer. In this case the transport company usually charges per pallet or per box.

More permanent arrangements require a contract carrier in which a transport company agrees to move a certain number of loads per week or to provide a truck and driver for several days per week. For example, the movement of meat (see Table 2.2) six miles (10 km) across Melbourne from the meat packer (boning room) to the sausage manufacturer is carried out by a refrigerated vehicle.

Table 2.2   **Examples of journeys by materials and products**

Product/material	Journey		Mode	Type of carrier
	From	**To**		
Confectionery	Melbourne suburb	Distribution centre in Perth	Road	Contract truck
Pig meat	Outer suburb	Inner Melbourne suburb	Road	Hired truck
Pallet of sausages	Inner suburb	Supermarket cold stores	Road	Refrigerated semi-trailer
Steel sheet	Near Tokyo, Japan	Melbourne suburb	Sea plus road	Container ship
Car carburettors	Detroit, USA	Adelaide suburb	Sea and air	Container ship, air freighter
Nissan cars	Durham, UK	Various European companies	Road, rail	Car carrier
Lobster tails	Tasmania, Australia	Los Angeles & London	Air	Passenger aircraft or freighter
Iron ore	Pilbara, West Australia	Japanese steelworks	Ship	Bulk carrier
Wheat	North Victoria, Australia	Port of Geelong, Victoria	Rail	Dedicated train
Beef steak	Meat processor, Hampshire	Various chain restaurants	Road	Refrigerated semi-trailer
Oil and gas	North Sea oil field	Refinery in Scotland	Pipe	Dedicated pipelines

Moving up the scale, a large proportion of product transport is done by *contract distribution** (see *outsourcing**) in which the carrier undertakes to provide all the movement of finished goods from the factory to customer stores. In contract distribution, the contractor quotes its price to provide a stated level of service for all the transport required for a year. When this quote is accepted, the carrier organises the whole goods distribution function. The carrier usually provides a supervisor at the factory who schedules the arrival of trucks and the loading of goods on to them, throughout the working week. He or she also looks after drivers and industrial relations. The journey to the various customers' premises and unloading are also arranged by the carrier. The factory gets a complete service for a known price without any detailed involvement. An example of contract distribution is the delivery of confectionery from a factory in Melbourne to destinations in the city of Melbourne (in contrast Table 2.2 shows that interstate confectionery destinations are handled by contract truck). In some cases, the contract distributor provides warehousing for the products at its site. The more complicated arrangements in which a transport company takes responsibility for an even wider range of logistics tasks is described in Chapter 7.

Historically, most manufacturing companies handled their own transport by their own trucks. This 'in-house' transport is now unusual, but may be retained where a company wants the drivers to carry out an extra task, such as collecting orders or placing the goods on shelves at the destination.

Transport task and decision

It is now possible to decide on the transport required for a particular logistics task. First, define in full the job to be done. This specification must include the quantity, cubic volume, type of goods and any special requirements, such as temperature control, for example moving a pallet of confectionery from Cadbury in a Melbourne suburb to a distribution centre in Perth. Then the choice is:

- which mode?
- which type of carrier?
- what frequency?
- which assembly?
- what price?

Box 2.1 gives an example of this transport decision.

Box 2.1   Specifying a distribution transport task and choosing the type of transport

A confectionery manufacturer, Cadbury-Schweppes in Melbourne, Australia wishes to distribute pallet loads of chocolates, bars and related products to a distribution centre (DC) in Perth, some 2,500 km away in West Australia. How should it move these perishable goods? How much is there and how often? Should Cadbury-Schweppes use road, rail or air? Should it go straight to some customers?

Cadbury-Schweppes chose a chilled contract truck direct to the DC because that ensured that the confectionery reached its destination intact, quickly and for an acceptable cost. So, in this case:

- mode is road,
- type of carrier is long-term contract,
- frequency is probably once a week,
- assembly is simple: one refrigerated truck from door to door, and
- price would be a rate per pallet negotiated between the shipper and the transport company.

Information in transport includes time slots and despatch advice and current location. In addition to the distribution of finished goods, described above, manufacturing companies require numerous raw materials and parts to be delivered to the factory. Modes and types of transport are the same as for goods distribution, but inbound transport has some differences. Historically, the main difference was that responsibility for materials transport lay with the supplier of the materials. This is still generally the case but some industries, notably the car industry, have changed to having the manufacturer arrange transport of parts. Factory-supplied transport is called a 'milk run' because the vehicle tours a number of suppliers, very frequently, picking up the exact number of parts required. The change took place because the factory wants a delivery every six hours, say, but does not want to pay for a complete journey each time. In a milk run, the factory only pays for one journey but gets the parts needed from half a dozen suppliers. In many cases inbound parts are delivered according to a *kanban** system of signalling the exact type and quantity of parts required.

Effective use of transport

Manufacturers aim to get the most economical use of transport by improving the utilisation of vehicles. The basic aim is to fill both the weight and cubic capability of the vehicle on every journey without unduly delaying materials or goods. One refinement is back-loading so that a truck, which has delivered product from A to B, is used to bring some goods from B to A, so that it does not return empty. The return goods could be from the same company or from another. An aim of centralised logistics for a company is to use one fleet of vehicles to carry out as many transport tasks as possible. This applies irrespective of whether the fleet is in-house or contractor-operated. Another method to increase vehicle utilisation is to use an in-house fleet to carry a base load of deliveries which are required weekly, throughout the year. Deliveries above the base are then contracted out to a transport firm.

Wider implications of movement between factories and companies throughout the supply chain are investigated in Chapter 7.

Materials handling

Movements between processes in the factory, called materials handling, comprise a range from handling by forklift truck between discrete processes to the use of conveyors and production lines for higher volume transfer of materials. While the technical details of materials handling technology are beyond the scope of this book, this section discusses several methods to handle materials according to the volume of the movement. Refer to section 2.4 for materials handling in distribution centres. At the lowest volume of flow, the manufacturer wishes to get a few materials or parts from one work centre to another in a jobbing shop or a manufacturing cell. This can be done by hand or by a pallet jack, which takes the weight of the materials on its wheels so the operator can pull the materials between work centres. In batch production, the volume has increased sufficiently to require a forklift truck to move boxes full of parts between work centres. At high volumes with limited variety of parts, conveyors are generally used to convey the huge numbers along the flow line between each machine. In some cases, where the handling has to be more precise, an automatic device, such as a robot, is used to move the parts into the exact position required for the next operation.

2.6 INVENTORY MANAGEMENT

Scope of independent demand stock

The final operations function (see Figure 2.1) is *inventory**: stocks of materials, components and products on the way to customers. Inventory in the link, made in advance of customer orders, serves the purpose of disconnecting the link production facility from its suppliers and its customers. It also separates each process in the provision activity. But each increase in inventory increases the time required for a new order to be delivered to the customer. Consequently materials in inventory are now seen as a mixed blessing: most of the emphasis in *lean manufacture** is to reduce inventory at every point. This is very difficult because managers do not decide the levels of inventory. Levels of inventory result from order forecasts, scheduling and production batch-size decisions. Inventory also results from unforseen consequences, such as order changes and quality failures. They are a consequence, not a direct aim.

Our objectives are, first, to identify the different reasons which require inventory to be held at various stages in a logistics link and hence to explain the quantities of goods that should be held to meet customer requirements, and the implicit costs. Our second objective is to appreciate the role of inventory records and other information in inventory control and management. Thirdly, to identify the impact of modern techniques of inventory reduction on conventional stock holding, especially by lean thinking.[6] Fourthly, we consider the special methods of managing inventories of parts and materials. Inventory levels are strongly influenced by forecast demand, which has been covered in section 2.3.

An important division of inventory is between *dependent demand** and *independent demand inventory**. Where manufacture requires many components to complete a finished product, such as the many thousands of components needed to assemble a car, the inventory of components required can be calculated by dependent demand. In dependent demand, a decision has been made to make, say, 450 cars today. Since each car requires five tyres, an inventory (or multiple deliveries) of 2,250 tyres is needed. There is no room for forecasts or management decisions, 2,250 will be required. The demand for tyres is dependent on the decision to make 450 cars today.

The second type of inventory, independent demand, involves stocks, such as cartons of sausage at a meatworks which are sold to numerous customers from finished stock because the customers will not wait for a batch of sausages to be made. Demand from one customer is independent of demand from another. In this case it may be necessary to forecast the anticipated sales of individual sausage types and have managers decide on the stock levels they will aim to keep. Section 2.3 discusses forecasting demand. This section concentrates on independent demand inventory. Dependent demand inventory is discussed further in section 5.4. A later part of this section examines inventories of materials and parts purchased by the manufacturing link.

Why hold inventory?

Although we argue that inventory should be minimised, there are a number of tactical reasons which tend to require stocks to be held. These inventory purposes vary widely between types of business:

- Inventory is required to uncouple production from customer orders when it is not effective to produce individual products to orders taken.
- Inventory is used to *decouple* (disconnect) fast production processes from slower ones.
- Stocks are used to enable bulk transport from the factory to a distribution centre. Goods are transported by the pallet load and the pallet is broken into individual orders at the centre.

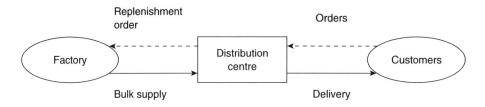

Figure 2.5 **Distribution inventory system**

- Low cost and low volume items, such as nuts and bolts, are held in inventory to save the cost of bringing in supplies frequently.
- Safety stock is a buffer against uncertain demand for products. Sales of products such as ice-cream and beer may vary because of the weather, so a stock is held. A retailer may hold stock because he or she is unsure when a delivery will arrive.
- 'Supermarket inventory' denotes stocks which are available for customers, of various kinds, to pick from without notice. This is a service to the customers. The higher the service level provided to customers, the greater level of stocks that must be held to ensure that level is attained.
- The geographical location of customers relative to producers may require local stock to be held because of the journey time.
- Seasonal inventory is necessary when a product, such as tomatoes, can only be produced for tinned tomatoes at one time of the year. The tinned tomatoes are produced over a period of several weeks and then sold over a year.
- Seasonal sales peaks usually require goods to be manufactured over several months prior to sale. So Easter eggs are produced many months before Easter.

Distribution inventory system via economic order quantity (EOQ)

For simplicity we examine the inventory required at a manufacturer's distribution centre which supplies a range of products to retailers (see Figure 2.5). The situation is *independent demand* in which customers are placing orders on the distribution centre which the centre delivers to them. The centre places replenishment orders on the factory which the factory delivers in bulk to the centre. Here we look at decisions of when to order and how many to order for one product. In the later section, ABC inventory groups and policies for a whole range of goods are examined.

The first step is to look at actual stock movements for the product, which we will assume to be cartons of tissues. Important insights can be gained from looking at daily movements of stock over an extended number of weeks (see Figure 2.6).

Although this step is rare in industry, it is vital to understand the inventory system that we are considering. Looking at the graph of actual stock, you can observe rate of sales, restocking and stock-outs.

*Economic order quantity (EOQ)** is a useful way to approach the inventory decisions of how much to order and when, although its answers must be used with care.[7] The 'sawtooth' graph in Figure 2.7 shows a stylised version of the stock movements for the product illustrated in Figure 2.6. This chart shows how stock on hand starts at the quantity

Figure 2.6   **Tissue carton stock at distribution centre**

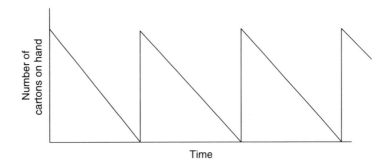

Figure 2.7   **Underlying inventory cycles for working stock for one product**

ordered, decreases as sales are made, increases as an order quantity is received just as stock runs out and then this cycle is repeated. The chart assumes that sales occur at a steady rate and that the reorder period is exactly known, so that the new order is received at the point of zero inventory. A further assumption is made that there are only two costs involved in having inventory, the carrying cost of having valuable product in stock and the cost of placing an order.

What causes these cycles? Assume that there are 200 cartons available at the left-hand side of Figure 2.8. Sales are made at 20 per day so the present stock will be exhausted in ten days. An order for stock will be delivered in two days so we must place an order when the stock falls to 40 cases. We examine the stock on hand and, when it falls to 40 cases, we place an order for 200. The order quantity, 200, is determined by the economic order quantity method, which is explained below, and an example calculation is given in Box 2.2.

The first cost to consider in EOQ is the inventory carrying cost, the expense involved in maintaining inventory. The carrying cost is the interest forgone on the value of the average amount of product held in stock. The value of product in stock is its current (wholesale) price. The average stock on hand is half the maximum, since the quantity fluctuates steadily between the maximum and zero, at the bottom of the cycle. The interest forgone is usually taken as the annual interest rate paid on the company's

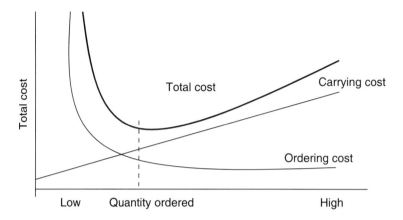

Figure 2.8   **Economic order quantity cost trade-off**

overdraft for the stock value, plus direct costs of storing the goods. Carrying cost increases as greater average inventory is held due to larger order quantities. The second cost is the annual expense of placing orders for that product. The ordering cost is the cost of placing orders a number of times through the year. Ordering costs decrease with larger order quantities because less frequent orders are required.

The economic order quantity is the amount ordered which will balance carrying cost against ordering cost. The minimum total cost occurs at the point at which the carrying cost is equal to the ordering cost, as illustrated by Figure 2.8. This EOQ cost trade-off is a plot of estimated cost incurred for a number of order quantities (x-axis). The straight carrying cost line represents the cost of holding inventory in stock at various order quantities. The curved order cost line is the cost of placing orders on the supplier. Adding these two cost curves together gives a total cost curve which is minimised at the EOQ order quantity. You must consider carefully which *real* costs are used in this calculation for your situation.

Box 2.2   **Example of economic order quantity calculation**

Kleenex Ltd holds cartons of facial tissues at a distribution centre (DC) to serve 20 convenience stores. On average each store sells one carton of these tissues per day. So the demand is 20 per day (d) or 7,000 per year (D), since the stores are open 350 days per year. How many cartons of tissues should the DC order from the manufacturer? Each carton has a cost (C) of $72 since it contains 32 kilograms at a wholesale cost of Aus$2.25 (£1) per kg. The cost of ordering (O_c) tissues is $4.30 per order and orders always arrive in two days (LT). The interest rate (i) paid by Kleenex on its overdraft is 8% (or .08) per year and other costs of holding inventory are deemed negligible.

(Continued)

Then, EOQ = square root of $\dfrac{(2 \times \text{Ordering cost} \times \text{Annual demand})}{(\text{Cost per carton} \times \text{interest rate})}$

$$= \text{square root of } \frac{(2 \times O_c \times D)}{(C \times i)}$$

Inserting the above numbers,

$$\text{EOQ} = \text{square root of } \frac{(2 \times 4.30 \times 7000)}{(72 \times .08)}$$

$$= \text{square root of } \frac{60{,}200}{5.76} \quad = \text{square root of } 10{,}451$$

So the order quantity, the EOQ, is 102.2 boxes

When should the DC reorder? It must order when it has only enough stock to last for two days, when the order will arrive.
Reorder point R = daily demand × lead time   = $d \times LT$
So $R = 20 \times 2$ = 40 cartons

By reference to Figure 2.8, we start at a stock of 102 cartons. When we go down the line to 40 cartons, we place an order for 102 cartons, which arrives in two days, just as we clear the previous stock. Using this EOQ formula gives us the minimum point on the total cost curve in Figure 2.9 (see p. 53).

The distribution centre now knows how many cartons it should order but when should it place an order? An order should be placed when the quantity on hand drops to the amount that will be sold during the lead-time. This quantity was 40 cartons in the above example. This analysis ignores safety stock, which is held to reduce the chance that the centre will ever run out of stock for its customers.

The economic order quantity is widely used by companies to decide the quantities they should order. The answers should be scrutinised carefully, not just implemented automatically. Very many situations could invalidate the EOQ answer. Is another product or a special promotion about to take over from the first product? EOQ is based on a number of small, independent sales which approximate a steady sales rate. Is a customer about to make a one-off purchase of a great number for an event or a festival? Can we order this product by itself or do we prefer to coordinate with other products to reduce joint costs of purchase? Can we get a discount by buying a certain quantity? These very practical issues are considered in the next section, which moves from the ordering of one product to the management of many products in groups.

ABC inventory groups

We now move from the decisions on one product to management of the thousands of products that many manufacturers and distribution centres keep in stock. Good

Table 2.3   **Inventory items grouped by sales**

Product number	Annual number sold	Price per item	Annual Sales	% Total sales	% Cumulative sales	% Total products	Group
1	105	$431.40	$45,300	48	48	10	A
2	626	$51.30	$32,110	34	82	20	A
3	801	$8.99	$7,200	7.6	89	30	B
4	54	$89.80	$4,850	5.1	94	40	B
5	1,160	$1.47	$1,700	1.8	96	50	B
6	63	$15.32	$965	1.0	97.1	60	C
7	127	$6.50	$825	0.9	98.1	70	C
8	71	$9.72	$690	0.7	99	80	C
9	29	$18.62	$540	0.6	99.7	90	C
10	34	$7.95	$270	0.3	100	100	C
Total			$94,450	100			

management requires that these products are divided into groups which have common usage characteristics. This can be done by life cycle, degree of seasonality, usage rate or turnover (usage rate times value) according to the most appropriate measure for the business. Turnover is frequently the best measure. The '80/20 rule' is used to form groups of similar turnover items. Consider the ten items in Table 2.3.

If the product information for all the items held by a company is plotted in a graph of cumulative proportion of sales against cumulative proportion of products, Figure 2.9 results. The 20% of items which represent 82% of turnover are labelled 'A' items, or fast moving. The next 30% of items which represent 15% of turnover are 'B' items and the final 50%, representing only 5% of turnover, are 'C' items. Our analysis frequently turns up 'D' items, whose sales are so low that they should not be in stock at all! Once this inventory grouping has been done, it can be used to manage different groups in different ways. For example, the time spent reviewing the stock available on 'A' items can be much higher than the time spent on 'C' items. *This method is known as ABC inventory control**.

Inventory records and less stock

Companies keep computer records of the inventory that they have for all materials and products at each location. We have seen how this information can be used to decide how much inventory is required. But how good are these records? The majority of companies which we have examined have inaccurate inventory records. Computer records must be updated systematically every time there is a stock movement. Regular checking of physical versus computer records for a proportion of stock will throw light on differences. This regular checking is known as cycle counting because a small proportion of stock is checked each week until every item has been checked. Then the process cycles around again. It is not sufficient to correct the errors found. The reasons for the errors must be identified and the errors prevented from recurrence.

A major aim of logistics managers is to reduce the holdings of unordered stock because it gets in the way of delivering products to customer orders, as well as costing money to acquire and carry. So our third objective in this section is to identify the impact of modern techniques of inventory reduction on conventional stock holding,

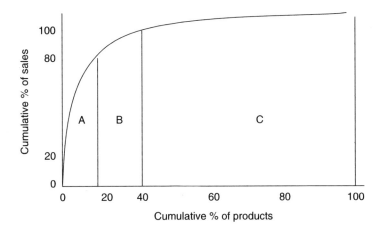

Figure 2.9   **Pareto analysis of inventory items**

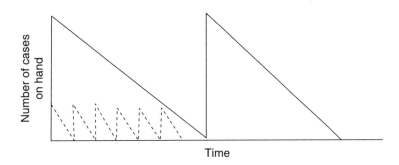

Figure 2.10   **Inventory cycles for traditional and JIT/lean for one product**

especially by the lean philosophy. Figure 2.10 shows how the saw-tooth model we used above for traditional inventory management can be modified to drastically reduce the amount of stock required. Under the *lean** philosophy,[6] derived from just-in-time, inventory is regarded as a type of waste. The large saw-tooth represents a monthly stock cycle, which was very prevalent in poorer industries in the 1990s. If this high stock cycle is replaced by the small 'dotted-line' quantity, then enormous savings in quantity of stock on hand can be made. But will this lead to higher ordering costs and stock-outs? It need not. The cost of ordering items is drastically reduced by automatic ordering and frequent review will prevent stock-outs. There is a consequent reduction in *safety stocks** which will be discussed next.

   Safety stock can be used to increase customer service levels where resupply times are longer than customer delivery expectations at the cost of a larger inventory investment. Effectively there is an extra stock below the x-axis in Figure 2.10. When working stock runs out, the provider simply dips into the safety stock to continue supply to customers.

The amount of safety stock required in a given situation is related to the number of standard deviations of variation in sales, above the mean, for which stock cover will be provided.

Another important method of reducing inventory is to require suppliers to manage stock on behalf of a manufacturer or a retailer, known as *vendor-managed inventory (VMI)**. In VMI the supplier tracks product sales and inventory levels at their customers, sending products only when stocks run low. The decision to supply is taken by the supplier based on the ability of the stock available to satisfy market demand, allowing for the lead-time to resupply.

The success of VMI depends upon a close relationship between, for example, retailer and manufacturer. The overall aim is product availability at the retailer. Both parties need to use appropriate performance measures. The supplier needs to know real-time demand at the customer.[8]

Parts and materials inventory

Inventory of spare parts is very different from stocks of products being distributed because there is no order or forecastable demand for the spares. They are held as an insurance against a possible future breakdown which will require such a part. Some possible approaches are:

- estimate annual demand from that of a similar part which has been in use for some time on a car or an electrical appliance,
- if the part is inexpensive, buy a large number,
- if the part is important, say a drive shaft of a vehicle, and cannot be obtained in the future, buy a number related to the numbers of that vehicle sold in that area, and
- if the part is very expensive and not too bulky, hold a few at a central location and airfreight them to the location when required.

The last four sections covered the major operational functions in each link of the supply chain. An important piece of analysis is to check the sufficiency and sparing design of each function.

2.7 SUPPLY DEVELOPMENT

This section looks into the design of the focal company in a supply chain for new and existing products from a functional or tactical view point, filling in matters already in train. Figure 2.11 shows how product and supply chain development is best considered as a separate cycle. In the figure, provision is split, loosely, into market development and manufacturing components. It delves into the logistics changes required to operate effectively with the introduction of new products and new processes. A new product may have a different size of package, or outer, which requires negotiation with marketing or modification to pallet storage. A new process in manufacture could have a range of logistics impacts such as inventory or hours of service implications. The more proactive or strategic approach to design a whole supply chain, or one link therein, to cater for new products or novel processes, is covered in Chapter 8.

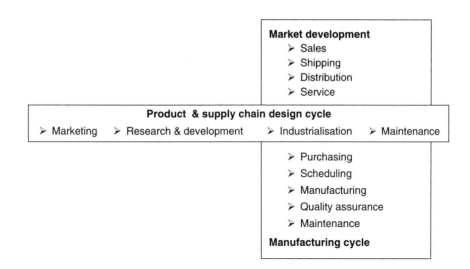

Figure 2.11   **Relationship between design and provision cycles (after Jouffrey and Tarondeau[9])**

Product design is an earlier step in the overall business than the order-taking and provision processes described above. It requires marketing to specify the general form of the new product. Then a team of product designers works with process and manufacturing engineers to identify how the new product will be manufactured and to purchase and commission the machinery required. Suppliers will be discovered and developed to deliver the exact materials and components required. Production managers and administrators join this team towards the end of its work until the new product is launched on to the market.

At the same time the whole supply chain must be designed, or altered, to fit the new product: to enable its effective provision and distribution to customers. The 'start from scratch' approach to this is considered in Chapter 8. Here we consider tactical changes to supply, provision and distribution which will do the best job without investing in new facilities and systems or the experienced people to operate and manage them.

The introduction of a new product may have a major or a minor effect on the logistics operations required in the company. If a manufacturer of hair shampoo changes the designs of its plastic containers, this is not likely to make a serious impact on the logistics of materials into the factory or distribution of shampoos. However, if a computer manufacturer decides that its new models will be delivered within 48 hours of receipt of a customer specification (as Dell did a few years ago), this will turn the supply chain inside out. So logistics managers need to keep close enough to the design of new products, and new manufacturing processes to make them, to respond with appropriate changes to the logistics system.

Consider the case at the end of this chapter, 'Sausages made to order?'. The introduction of many new types of sausage has caused the inefficiencies in batch production which the operations manager seeks to remove. Each single introduction is a minor change but the move from 'one type to nine varieties' requires a major change to logistical operations. The managers concerned with logistics need to review production scheduling methods, and *make-to-order** rather than to stock and transport to the customer.

For a major change, consider the changes being made by the European automobile industry as a result of the '3-day Car Project'.[6] Studies in the mid-1990s showed that European car companies took, on average, 30 days to make and deliver a car against a new order placed. However, the manufacture of that car took only 25 hours. The difference is partly due to inventories of parts and finished cars, but mainly due to the time taken to pass the order between the various players and to get the car into a production schedule. This situation does not fit within the 'one link of the chain' emphasis of this chapter. But it does show a major redesign of the car manufacturing logistics as a result of the introduction of new methods of handling customer orders.

Each car company is aiming to receive orders quickly from the dealer, schedule them rapidly on to the production line and deliver the complete car to the dealer for the customer in five days instead of the previous 30 days.

In reality there is a continuum between manufacture to stock and new design of product and process. The continuum is the degree to which customers' requirements have to be taken into account before manufacturing and assembly can take place. Mass vehicle manufacturers which have engineering changes to product several times a day illustrate the deleterious effects of getting this wrong. This adversely affects training, product quality, reworks and productivity.

Midway in this continuum is 'engineer-to-order', in which customers want products to be varied to meet their needs. Because this variation is not part of the standard range, the order must be referred to a manufacturing engineer. He or she specifies a change to the production process for this individual order, which is then manufactured. This situation is unusual across the spectrum of manufactured products. It rarely occurs in food or consumer goods. It is more frequent in jobbing shops, producing small numbers of metal components. An example is the manufacture of varied buckets for a range of earthmovers.

The location of manufacturing processes relative to suppliers and markets is an important factor. This varies according to the value of products and their perishability.

Finding new suppliers

The purchasing process, (see section 2.4), first process, requires firms to discover suppliers of particular materials, components and services. Major steps are:

- specifying the material or service needed,
- finding potential supply companies,
- working out which companies are capable of supplying the material effectively, and
- negotiating a commercial supply relationship, including lead-time, price, quality and quantity.

2.8 DEPARTMENTAL LINKS AND BUSINESS STRATEGY

Bureaucracy hates change…
is terrified by speed
and hates simplicity.[10]

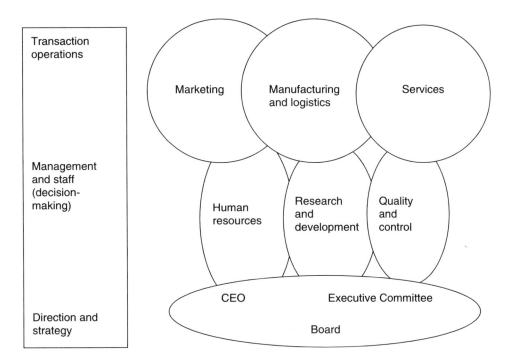

Figure 2.12   **The structure of a company showing the main departments (after Mintzberg)**[11]

(CEO Chief = Executive Officer or President)

How do supply chains fit within the overall organisation of one company? Supply networks are responsible for the majority of resources in the company but, for many reasons, the company is not organised as part of a family of chains. Rather it is arranged into a series of departments working under a business strategy developed by top executives and approved by the Board. Figure 2.12 is a simple model of a firm, based on Mintzberg's work.[11] This model shows three levels of activity from transaction operations at the top, through management and staff decisions in the middle to direction and strategy at the bottom. Direction is put at the bottom because, in more modern, effective firms, it supports management and technical staff, who in turn coach and enable supporting operations to provide goods to customers.

This model is equally applicable to distribution companies, such as supermarket chains and quasi-manufacturing service businesses, such as maintenance shops. The important topic of the type of organisation structure which the firm adopts is delayed until section 6.5 when it can be considered in the context of the whole *supply network** (i.e. a set of supply chains) of the businesses. Each circle contains a number of actual functions, depending upon the size and industry. For example, key services are accounting, engineering and information systems. Marketing includes sales, merchandising and market development.

The relationship between the management of logistics and the other departments within the overall organisation of one company (see Box 2.3) could be the subject of another book. In another sense there is no single answer: the answer is contingent upon the industry, the management style, the strategic direction, the geographical dispersement and the place of the business entity (firm) in its group. This area is covered in section 8.3.

Box 2.3   Innovative organisational structure at Becton Dickinson

Becton Dickinson, a global manufacturer of medical products, has created a new operating division called BD Supply Chain Services. The role of this unit is to integrate and more effectively manage all the company's supply chain processes and their interaction with Becton Dickinson's operating divisions. BD Supply Chain Services has forged a clear, competitive advantage for the company. Profitable growth, cost minimisation, and capital efficiency are influenced everyday by the best practices adhered to within this new division.

(Source: Tyndall and colleagues[12])

The most important point in tactical management of the whole firm is the requirement for its strategy and processes to have priority over department responsibilities, parochial preferences and executive power bases. The thesis that a company is a link in a business supply channel implies that all departments, not just purchasing, manufacturing, logistics and distribution, should work, predominantly, for the development and provision of new and existing products.

Link strategy

Recently, forward-thinking managers have realised that strategy is needed at a functional level as well as the overall business strategy of a complete *strategic business unit** Functional-level strategy is profoundly determined by the managers closer to the activities and can be viewed as emergent[13] rather than imposed from above.

A lot of energy has been expended on wide audits of the logistical activities of companies. The view taken, then synthesised from an all-encompassing audit, is less important than product-group strategy derived by a group of responsible managers. For example, when a smallgoods company sells bacon to another company for making pre-prepared meals, this is an entirely different distribution route from bacon sold to a supermarket chain for fresh retail consumption.

2.9 LEAN MANAGEMENT AND LEADERSHIP

> The final test of a leader is that he (or she) leaves behind him in other men the conviction and the will to carry on.[14]

We now consider the roles of the operators, managers and directors who steer and carry out activities in links in the supply chain. We argue that successful chains occur because trained, motivated, dedicated people ensure that a near-perfect flow of goods is delivered to the end customers. The managers of such chains aim to train, steer and guide the operators.

Management of logistics in a firm is an evolving process since this perspective on companies and their partners has only recently been developed. Consequently, many companies are arranged according to functions such as marketing, operations and finance. Supply chain management has responsibilities which cut across functional boundaries.

This situation can be addressed by forming logistics as another function comprising the parts best managed under a senior logistics manager. Alternatively, processes and committees can be put in place which enable coordination between the various functions to achieve the flow of planning information and goods.

The biggest body of work on the management of supply chains is that on lean thinking leading to a *lean enterprise*.*

Lean management

Womack and Jones[6] developed the following five principles through which *lean thinking** can be applied to a value stream, the name they use for a single-product supply chain:

- specify value by a single product as seen by the end customer,
- identify the value stream for each product,
- make value flow without interruption,
- let the customer pull value from the producer, and
- pursue perfection.

Lean management* requires a team of managers, representing all companies in the supply chain, to meet and be trained by consultants in lean value stream analysis. The team then maps each step in each process that the product goes through from source to consumer. They then consider a future supply chain, from which waste has been removed. Finally they implement an *action plan** to reach an agreed future state, in which waste has been removed, people reorganised and unnecessary processes have been dropped. In later work, more managers from the companies will analyse and improve the supply chains of further products, continually moving towards a perfect state.

Leadership

Here we quote from five lessons of FD Roosevelt's presidency of the USA, as reported by Axelrod.[15] We believe they apply equally to leadership of supply chains as to national and international policies:

- *Purpose and policies.* FD Roosevelt responded in actions so that a perfect social programme was one in which it was impossible to tell where theory stopped and practice started.
- *Contact.* 'All policy is human policy', so the leader must keep in contact with his/her people and inform them of the true state of the business.
- *Persistence.* Leaders never lose hope. They do something to survive. Things go wrong, but a committed leader never abandons the enterprise by allowing it to ride with the prevailing current. For each circumstance, plans are drawn up and policies determined.
- *Motivation.* An excellent way to motivate employees is to provide them with a choice. 'Either we go down this path with these consequences, or we choose a

better path with superior outcomes.' Leadership plans must be built from the bottom to the top. Any plan which focuses on one at the expense of the other must be rejected. To an individual, an effective leader comes across as one who is speaking directly to him or her while also addressing the collective enterprise.

- *Progress and prediction.* A leader is a guide. He/she tells not only how far we must travel but also how far we have come.

Teams and support

We believe that supply chain and logistics practices should be formed by teams of operators and advisers under the direction, coaching and 'listening' of managers. The key idea is that supply chains, and their parts, cannot be managed by individuals, however talented. Effective chains demand teamwork in design and in operation.

For a fuller development of people improving supply chains, see section 8.2.

2.10 PERFORMANCE MEASUREMENT AND IMPROVEMENT

Supply chains should be managed so that products and services flow from source to destination, where the customer receives her or his products. This management needs to be very effective to make a profit for all organisations concerned while meeting customers' needs on time. This requires reduced waste (rejects, time, extra efforts, etc.) and greater customer effectiveness. To improve the efficiency of our supply chain we need to measure how well we are doing and make chain-wide improvements. It does not matter how well we go at any point: it is the 'system' efficiency and effectiveness that count in meeting customers' needs.

Link goals

Each link in the supply chain has its own goals which should be consistent with the customer supply goal of the whole chain. There is a current emphasis on reducing the number of suppliers with whom a manufacturer had to deal from hundreds to tens. This assists the manufacturer to deal more closely with the limited number of surviving direct suppliers.

Performance measurement and profit control

An important part of management is performance measurement which must comprise physical and financial measures of business achievements.[16] The tendency of businesses to rely on purely financial measures is being addressed by the use of the Balanced Scorecard.[17] This is very important in logistics areas where customer service and delivery performance are more crucial than dollar turnover figures. Logistics must be seen as a function which can increase turnover and profit, rather than as a cost centre to be controlled.

It is also essential to view logistics in the firm as contributing to business profits. Logistics has a main objective of satisfying customers by excellent delivery of correct products but immediately behind this objective comes the need to operate profitably. Businesses have mainly viewed logistics as a cost centre. This approach is not conducive to allowing logistics to invest in new facilities and information systems. Consequently, logistics should be seen as a profit centre which can, in conjunction with other functions, increase turnover and hence justify an optimal level of expenditure.

2.11 LIMITS OF THE LINK NETWORK

The meat-processing case in this chapter describes a supply chain with three important suppliers, two transport service companies and six main customers. This is assumed to be the limit of the network of companies that must be considered to make decisions about the link. In practice there were 95 suppliers, 46 service companies and 220 customers which the meat processor, Bradley, had dealings with during a year. Students need to make a similar simplification in examining the main link in their supply chain. This is quite independent of the need to consider suppliers to your suppliers and customers of your customers. These and other wider aspects will be addressed in Chapter 7.

No analytical formula can be given to decide the limits of the supply chain network for study purposes. Students should consider which suppliers, distributors and service contractors make a significant difference to the chain they are studying from the perspectives of the end customer and the major partners in the chain, who are endeavouring to operate profitably.

Summary

This chapter describes the supply chain tasks of achieving production flow within a plant so that the materials received are effectively converted into finished products. It includes delivery of parts and material from suppliers and shipment of goods to the plant's customers. It introduces the great variation between the key logistics issues for clothing, sausages and cars while all fit within the same framework. The history of integrated logistics documents its rapid development over the last 30 years. We examine four main drivers of logistics in one link of the supply chain: order-taking, provision, transport and inventory. Information communication systems are an integral and enabling part of each of these drivers.

After looking at the *operations* of one link, the chapter reviews some wider link issues. 'Supply development' delves into the new logistics systems which the manufacture of innovative products by new processes will require. Next, 'Departmental links and business strategy' considers the connections of the logistics link with other functions and with the company's overall business strategy. 'Lean management and leadership' examines the critical human dimensions of managing product flow in a plant involving decisions, tasks, training and steering. Since changes are happening all the time, the last two sections introduce 'Performance measurement and improvement' and the boundaries, for planning purposes, of a link in a logistics network.

Analytical tools covered are the arrangement of operations functions, forecasting demand, transport selection, inventory management, supply development and performance measurement.

Questions

1. For your chosen organisation within its supply chain, revise the link structures and trade-offs between functions so that they better achieve the firm's customer service and profit aims for an existing product group.
2. Repeat question 1 for a new product.
3. Recommend the improved use of people to manage a production, or distribution, company to improve its logistics performance for end customers and stakeholders.
4. You have the task of managing inventory at a car spare parts warehouse. What principles would you use to buy inventory? How would you segment the 70,000 parts for more specific control?
5. For a product you know, explain how you would make the transport decision for its distribution: (a) in one country, and (b) world-wide.

Case: Sausages made to order?

Introduction

At 11am Paul Liddy, Operations Manager of Bradley Smallgoods, sat down at his desk. He has been at work since 6am, checking that all the meat-processing lines are operating to schedule. He has talked to his supervisors, his main meat supplier and his largest customer, Safeway supermarket chain. Paul's thoughts turn to possible improvements since Bradley's profit is too low.

Bradley, a meat-processing company in Melbourne, Australia, has employed a series of continuous improvement techniques over the last eight years in an attempt to change from being production-driven to having a strong customer orientation. While this has improved the industrial relations environment and working conditions, it did not improve the return on assets employed until last year, 1998. A loss was made in 1997 as a result of having to recall smallgoods after a food poisoning outbreak, although it was later proved that Bradley was not responsible for the food poisoning. The improvement in profit in 1998 was more due to a fall in pig meat prices than enhanced market or operations strategy.

Paul's main long-term objective is to streamline operations so that customer service levels will increase and costs will be reduced. At the top of his list of desirable improvements is: 'making sausages to order'. While studying last year, he was impressed by the concept of replacing inventory of perishable goods by manufacture to order. He knows that, typically, 22% of sausages are sold at a discount, because not enough orders are received for the many varieties in stock. It has been difficult to achieve change in the past but Paul believes that the necessary changes could be made at Bradley. How will his supplier, Apollo Meats, and his major customer, Safeway supermarkets, react to his proposal?

Background

Bradley purchases boned pig meats and processes them into a range of cured, preserved and fresh meat products known as smallgoods. Formed in 1947, it is the subsidiary of a large food-processing company. Bradley has an annual turnover of Aus$110 million from

(Continued)

sales of 14,000 tonnes of product and employs 440 people. Although selling into national markets and having some exports, its sales are predominantly made in the state of Victoria. Bradley sells to three market segments, 60% of its output going to supermarkets, 20% to delicatessen shops and 20% to other food manufacturers.

Management at Bradley is in transition due to the appointment of a new General Manager at the end of 1996, and a new Operations Manager, Paul, in May 1997. The General Manager restructured Bradley's senior management and totally reorganised the operations group under Paul Liddy. In operations, this reorganisation comprised the appointment of six new managers to manufacturing and logistics positions and retrenchment of the majority of factory supervisors. Bradley is now progressing towards self-directed work groups, including shop-floor team leaders as part of the unionised workforce. Consequently, Paul's operations and logistics team at Bradley includes both new appointees and managers who had been there for many years. It comprises 11 managers, as shown in the partial organisation structure, see Figure C2.1.

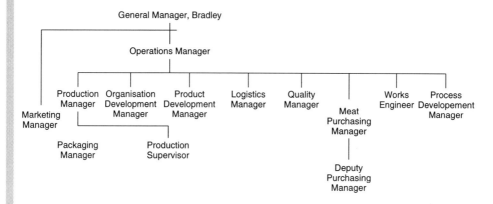

Figure C2.1   **Partial organisation chart**

Bradley has been making fresh sausages from meat trimmings, grain and seasonings filled into a casing for almost 50 years. Originally the company made only one kind of sausage. Pork sausages were primarily sold through corner shops and delicatessens, delivered in refrigerated vans. Total weekly sales were very regular – 20 tonnes per week. Given steady sales in one product, it made sense to make sausages in runs of five tonnes, loaded into 16-kilogram boxes for distribution.

More recently many other producers have started making sausages with very cheap ingredients, 'to throw on the BBQ'. These inferior sausages are sold in supermarket meat counters at $3.99 per kilogram. At the same time customers of the deli counter in a supermarket, where prices are up to $12.99 per kilo, want a variety of sausages such as bratwurst, pork, honey and soy, beef and tomato, and chicken. When Paul last counted there were 14 varieties on offer and Bradley make nine varieties themselves.

(Continued)

(Continued)

The present supply chain

The supply chain starts on a piggery in northern Victoria where the pigs are grown to the appropriate age. Bradley buys, say, 2,000 pigs which are slaughtered and dressed at an abattoir adjacent to the piggery. Their carcasses are delivered to western Melbourne where Bradley employs Apollo Meats to bone them. Apollo's butchers separate the various cuts of meat and trim all meat from the bones. This meat is refrigerated and delivered twice a week to Bradley, 10 kilometres away, in large plastic boxes. Bradley buys various spices and other additives. It obtains packing from a local branch of Sealed Air Corporation. This comprises sausage casings and packs to receive the links of sausage.

Figure C2.2 shows Bradley's sausage manufacturing process:

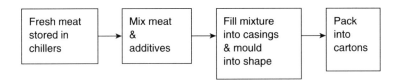

Figure C2.2   **Processes in a smallgoods factory**

Bradley distributes sausages from its chilled store at the end of the production line. Distribution to Safeway comprises mainly full pallets with some 16 kg boxes picked for the lower volume varieties, such as Halal sausage. Transport from Bradley to Safeway's cold store is achieved by 'pans' (pantechnicons) pulled by a prime mover, carrying a load of 28 pallets weighing about one tonne each. Bradley hires a transport company to deliver these pans to the cold store at the Safeway distribution centre in a narrow time slot.

Safeway is the largest supermarket chain in Australia, with 150 stores in Victoria. Its central meat buyers, working for Gwen Davies, the senior buyer, purchase sausages from Bradley by the truckload on a two-day lead-time. Bradley keeps pressing for a week's notice of requirements, but Safeway buyers prefer to order at 4pm on Monday for a Wednesday morning delivery. Faced by large swings in sales both through the week and according to the weather, their response is to postpone ordering until the last possible moment. Safeway's customers are the full range of people who use its many Victorian stores. Some of them buy sausages to keep in the freezer until needed. The majority buy sausages for a particular occasion, such as a barbeque.

The overall supply chain is depicted in Figure C2.3.

Information flow

Safeway places orders for sausage varieties twice a week. It estimates its requirements a month in advance but without any commitment, so these estimates are very little use to Bradley. Bradley has a weekly requirement that Apollo processes a number of carcasses for delivery every two working days. This number is changed without notice when Bradley so wishes, on the Friday before a working week.

(Continued)

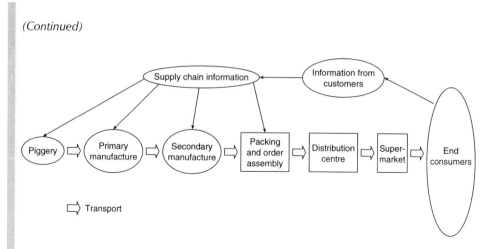

Figure C2.3   **Links in the integrated supply chain for smallgoods products**

Production scheduling is carried out at Bradley using a stand-alone spreadsheet. The scheduler uses this sheet to plan production four weeks ahead, but there are daily changes to the schedule as customers' exact needs are obtained.

The only computer information Bradley has on the stocks of sausages is the financial value of the pallet loads in its despatch store. To find out stocks of individual varieties, sales staff have to ask the store person. Safeway has detailed information about its sausage stocks at its cold store but does not share this with Bradley. Delivery information is compiled from the loads assembled in despatch.

Delivery performance and profit

Mikhail, Bradley's production supervisor, knows that getting meats in is not a problem, since the trimmings are a by-product of the thousands of carcasses processed each week. Schedules for production quantities of the nine varieties of sausage are drawn up by Chris, production scheduler, one month ahead and firmed up on the Friday before the week of manufacture. Typically, the two most popular sausages are made twice a week, three more varieties made every week, and the four others once every two weeks.

Table C2.1 shows a typical sausage production schedule. With use-by dates just eight days after manufacture, this requires some juggling and significant price reductions to clear stocks when orders do not match stock on hand.

Paul's improvement project

Paul knows from experience that Bradley management takes an autocratic view of changes. However, he felt that the recent reorganisation and the emphasis the General Manager was putting on increased profit would improve his chances. In the past matters would be investigated internally and then announced to suppliers by a phone call with a confirmatory fax. Safeway were apt to treat Bradley in the same way. Paul feels he would resolve this production problem more effectively if he consulted his supply chain partners at the outset. He arranges a meeting with Gwen of Safeway and Brian of Apollo Meats for 10am on Friday.

(Continued)

(Continued)

Table C2.1   **Scheduled production of sausage – produce to stock (tonnes)**

Sausage type	Week One						Weeks		
	Mon	Tue	Wed	Thu	Fri	Total	Two	Three	Four
Bratwurst		5				5	5	5	
Pork				5		5	5		5
Honey & soy			3			3	3		3
Hungarian	3					3	3	3	
Halal			1			1	1		1
Chicken					1	1	1		1
TOTAL	3	5	4	5	1	18	18	8	10
CAPACITY	5	5	5	5	5	25	25	25	25

After discussing current performance, Paul introduces his ideas, saying: 'I have a proposal for a change in the production of sausages. I want to move from making sausages in large batches in advance, to making exactly the varieties and quantities you want when you order them.'

Gwen was interested. 'That sounds like a good proposition. We would get fresher sausage, provided you can react quickly to our afternoon order. We could not tolerate any drop in delivery performance. Already we have seen 8% of deliveries miss the required time this year.'

Brian had a problem. 'My boning room is not set up to deliver meat exactly when you want it. I only operate one crew of butchers, so I need to arrange my production schedule a week in advance.'

Paul acknowledged his concern. 'I see my proposal as a major change which we will have to think through to suit all our situations. If we could achieve this change, it would provide a major increase in margin for our company. Bradley intends to share any gains with you after paying for any extra costs you incur.'

Paul sought their agreement to a study that he would drive. He suggested they meet again in two weeks to examine the study and deal with any sticking points. After further discussion, Brian and Gwen agreed to this course of action.

Two weeks later

At the next meeting, Gwen brought her order clerk, Rachel, and Brian was accompanied by his boning room supervisor, Zoltan. Based on the studies Mikhail and Chris had done, Paul tabled a typical schedule (see Table C2.2) that would result from his proposed just-in-time production of sausage. To achieve this would require Safeway to order what they wanted more frequently from Bradley. Paul suggested an order every four hours would help him.

Result of study

In mid-April Paul, Mikhail and Chris summarised their investigation findings (see Table C2.3). For various performance measures at Safeway, Bradley and Apollo, the study

(Continued)

Table C2.2   **Scheduled production of sausage – just-in-time production (tonnes)**

Sausage type	Week One						Weeks		
	Mon	Tue	Wed	Thu	Fri	Total	Two	Three	Four
Bratwurst	1	1	2		1	5	5	3	2
Pork	1	1		2	1	5	5	2	3
Honey & soy	1		1		1	3	2	1	2
Hungarian		1		1		2	3	2	1
Halal	0.5		0.5			1	1	0.5	
Chicken		0.5			0.5	1	1		0.5
TOTAL	3.5	3.5	3.5	3	3.5	17	17	8.5	8.5
CAPACITY	5	5	5	5	5	25	25	25	25

Table C2.3   **Study results**

Item	Current	Proposed
Safeway		
Ordering pattern	Twice a week	2 times per day
Average order size	3 tonne	0.4 tonne
Delivery performance	92%	97%
Shelf life on receipt	8 days	14 days
Bradley		
Production process	Make-to-stock	Make-to-order
Ability to fulfil order	78%	98%
Loss on discounted sausages per week	£1200/$4400	£110/$400
Number of sausage batches per week	~4	~10
Apollo		
Shifts operated per week	5	5
Shifts boning for Bradley	2	5
Cost of 15 minute downtimes	0	£60/$165

findings show the current situation and the expected achievement if the recommendations are adopted. Notable changes are the increased frequency of Safeway ordering, the increased number of sausage batches and the extra shifts needed at Apollo. This would make considerable improvements to delivery performance into Safeway's distribution centre and order fulfilment while delivering significantly reduced losses on discounted sausages.

Reactions to the proposal

Gwen, the Safeway buyer, accepts the main results of the study. She agrees that orders could be placed every four hours during the working day, with the benefits of getting fresher sausage and fewer delivery failures. However, she says she cannot predict the size of individual orders. Her biggest problem will be to get her superior and store managers to accept Paul's proposals.

(Continued)

(Continued)

Brian, from Apollo Meats, is quite negative about his ability to bone some carcasses for Bradley during every shift. Zoltan has told him that traceability and cleanliness would be compromised by changing from boning for a food service company, such as Best Cut, to Bradley products during every operating shift. He would probably have to stop the entire operation for 15 minutes and he could face an industrial dispute from the boners. They would lose earnings because of the piece-rate pay system.

Paul has explained the study's proposals to his General Manager. The General Manager is entirely in favour, and has promised his enthusiastic support. He will tell all staff what is happening at the weekly management meeting and at the next employee meeting in the canteen. Unfortunately, Bradley's shift supervisors were not convinced when Paul took them through his proposal. They could see problems in changing over, which they didn't want to do during the Easter period, in two weeks' time. More seriously, they could not envisage the real savings in their area to be obtained by make-to-order processing. A lot of their work is related to the batch of sausages made. So, they say, more batches equal more work.

Paul's next step

Paul feels disappointed that his initiative has met with such a mixed reception. He has the General Manager's permission. Should he push ahead with the move to make sausages to order when the Easter peak is past? Perhaps he should carry out a further study involving his supervisors so that they would feel part of the recommendation? Maybe Bradley needs the help of a change agent who has been through this before?

Paul resolves to think carefully about the effects of his plan on supply chain partners before proceeding. He is reliant on Apollo for his meat supplies at the moment, other suppliers could be obtained, but it would be better to try to negotiate a compromise acceptable to the boning plant. Will Gwen be able to get the other Safeway managers' support? And will the actual size of Safeway orders fit Bradley's capacity to make to order?

Case questions:

1. Can you identify Bradley's supply chain and justify the steps you include?
2. What are the three most important supply chain issues for Paul to address?
3. What should Paul do? Why?

REFERENCES

1   Christopher M (2005) *Logistics and Supply Chain Management:* (3rd edn), Prentice-Hall, Harlow. Quote modified by author as shown in italics (page 4).
2   Smaros J (2003) 'Collaborative forecasting: a selection of practical approaches', *International Journal of Logistics: Research and Applications*, 6(4): 245–58.
3   Sanchez-Rodriguez C, Hemsworth D and Martinez-Lorente AR (2004) 'Quality management practices in purchasing and its effect on purchasing's operational performance and internal customer satisfaction', *International Journal of Logistics: Research and Applications*, 7(4): 325–44.

4   Hayes RH and Wheelwright SC (1984) *Restoring Our Competitive Edge*, Wiley, New York.
5   Vollmann TE, Berry WL, Whybark DC and Jacobs FR (2005) *Manufacturing Planning and Control Systems for Supply Chain Managment* (5th edn), McGraw-Hill, New York.
6   Womack JP and Jones DT (1996) *Lean Thinking*, Simon and Schuster, New York.
7   Braglia M and Gabbrieli R (2001) 'A genetic approach for setting parameters of reorder point systems', *International Journal of Logistics: Research and Applications*, 4(3): 345–58.
8   Whiteoak P (1999) 'Rethinking efficient replenishment in the grocery sector', in J Fernie and L Sparks L (eds), *Logistics and Retail Management*, Kogan Page, London.
9   Jouffrey F and Tarondeau JC (1992) 'A methodological framework for the formulation of an industrial strategy', in CA Voss (ed.), *Manufacturing Strategy: Process and Content*, Chapman and Hall, London.
10 Krames JA (2002) *The Welsh Way: 24 Lessons from the World's Greatest CEOs*, McGraw-Hill, New York. p. iii.
11 Mintzberg H (1983) *Power in and around Organisations*, Prentice-Hall, Englewood Cliffs, NJ.
12 Tyndall G, Gopal C, Partsch W, Wolfgang P and Kamauff J (1998) *Supercharging Supply Chains*, Wiley, New York, p. 26.
13 Mintzberg H and Quinn JB (1991), *The Strategy Process* (2nd edn), Prentice- Hall, Englewood Cliffs, NJ.
14 Lippman W (1945) *New York Herald Tribune*, 14 April, in Creswell J and Leinter A (1996) *The Hutchison Dictionary of Business Quotes*. Helicon, Oxford, p. 96.
15 Axelrod A (2003) *Nothing to Fear: Lessons in Leadership from FDR*, Penguin Portfolio, New York.
16 Ramos MM (2004) 'Change in the logistics management style through performance indicators: a case study', *International Journal of Logistics: Research and Applications*, 7(4): 313–24.
17 Kaplan RS and Norton DP (1996) *The Balanced Scorecard*, Harvard University Press, Cambridge, MA.

Logistics in Service Organisations, Customer Service and Transport

3

Objectives

- To consider how supply chains serve consumers by providing goods and services
- To use the tools provided to understand how supply chain concepts help service organisations to respond to the outcome and perception needs of customers
- To explore how a service business chain may attain superior operational performance within the desired strategic direction
- To examine one particular service industry, freight transport, which is widely used in many service and manufacturing supply chains
- To understand the assembly of different modes of transport, terminals and depots into cost-efficient transport routes between various supply chain links
- To make supply chains secure against the risk of disruption

INTRODUCTION

This chapter brings into clear focus the need for supply chains to deliver the market promise of products and services for end consumers. Also it broadens business logistics from the traditional association with manufacturing industries into service industries. Supply chain concepts are important in most service industries although there is a wide range from personal services, such as banking, to mass services, such as retail stores. Service organisations, with the exception of professional services, require materials and goods to provide to customers or to use in their service operation. Service firms require sophisticated information communication systems to receive data and information to assist in making numerous decisions. Such firms need management coordination and strategic leadership along the supply chain to ensure that all their components pull together in providing services.

Delivering the products desired requires distribution centres to store goods close to customers. Next the chapter examines the freight transport services required to move materials and products between facilities. Finally, it considers how supply chains can be made secure against disruptions.

Tools are provided so that students can measure the extent of service that a supply chain proffers to its customers. The tools cover both manufacturing and service supply chains. They comprise customer service levels, classification of service businesses, choice of supplier relationships, distribution centre choices and analysis of freight transport.

3.1 SERVING CUSTOMERS

Building on Chapter 1, this section looks at the *raison d'être* of supply chains, providing services and goods to selected groups of customers. The main aim of every chain is to supply the particular needs of end consumers perfectly.

The marketing perspective is the view of the whole supply chain from the position of the end consumer, the person or company which consumes the goods and services provided by the chain within its wider network. There is a danger in logistics operations of focusing on the job at hand and losing sight of the essential aim to give the customer what he or she wants. According to Doyle:

> Marketing is the philosophy that integrates the disparate activities and functions that take place within the network. Satisfied consumers are seen as the only source of profit, growth and security.[1]

Within supply chain marketing, *logistics customer service** is the process of providing goods, information and services to customers in a way that both creates customer satisfaction and is cost-effective to the supplier. Readers must be careful to distinguish between this *logistics* customer service and *sales* service, which they receive whenever they go into a supermarket. Sales service consists of attending to the customer's every need in the local situation, such as the store, answering questions and helping the customer to 'feel good' about the purchase. Logistics service is primarily about providing and delivering products and services to the consumer.

In this twenty-first century, customers have rising and fast-changing expectations. The job of the supply chain is to satisfy those needs. The market segment of customers to be served is chosen by the marketing function of the focal company. 'Marketing'[1] as a separate discipline is beyond the scope of this book. However, the work of logistics, in each link of the supply chain, is to accept the marketing strategy of the company responsible and to address the task of supplying goods and services when and where they are required. The 'company responsible' may be the distributor rather than the focal company in the supply chain.

Logistics operators need a lot of information about the end customers whom they supply. What quality of goods and services, how quickly, how many sizes, where, what price and so on. Since a supply chain is responding to the needs of a whole cohort of customers, this information boils down to 'flow-creating criteria'[2] which are developed in detail in section 6.2. For a retail product, such as a vegetable, these criteria may be size, freshness, price and availability. For an assembled product, such as a car, important criteria may be power, shape, colour and particular features. For a customised service, such as a haircut, criteria may be availability, style, safety and perception. For a commodity service, such as an air journey, they may be departure time, safety, price, space available and meal service.

3.2 CUSTOMER SERVICE LEVELS AND LOGISTICS FUNCTIONS

Once 'flow-creating criteria' have been determined, we must set the levels of service we will provide to the sets of customers whom we serve. Remember the very different types of supply chain shown in Table 1.1, section 1.2. (see page 14). For each specific chain the general criteria must be translated into specific service levels such as:

- availability of 99.8%,
- weight of at least 500 grams,
- shelf life of seven days,
- price $1.30,
- arrival on time of at least 95% of flights,
- bill correct on 99% of occasions, and
- personal service without hassles for 98% of bed-nights.

The idea of logistics service levels was developed by Peter Gilmour.[3] Service levels are individual to each business and each supply chain. Single company service levels are well understood by many firms but chain-wide service levels are rarely set or measured. The required customer service level must be established for the most important aspects for a range of products.

By means of a survey of a range of manufacturing companies, Gilmour found that the nine most important aspects of customer service were:

- on-time delivery,
- order accuracy,
- price,
- no product damage,
- ease of order placement,
- customer enquiry handling,
- quality,
- availability, and
- order status information.

The relative importance of each of these aspects varies according to the company and product or service concerned.

Some marketing managers put around a myth of '100%' service levels which must be dispelled. A typical statement might be: 'We want to provide the goods immediately 100% of the time, in perfect quality at minimum price.' Perhaps these 'perfections' can be achieved, but only at excessive cost. Figure 3.1 shows the usual situation. Clearly the economic aim point is a little below 100%. Beyond this level, the extra benefit to customers is vastly outweighed by the huge extra cost of inventory, hours of opening, staff training and salaries, etc. The exact service level to be attained must be separately decided for the flow-creating criteria for each group of services or products.

A graphic example is the aircraft company wishing to set the acceptable failure rate, or in-service level, for the engines on its planes. The higher the failure rate, the greater the chance that a plane would crash with considerable loss of life. Some years ago it was suggested that a customer's life should be valued at £0.5 million for the decision on how good an aircraft engine should be. This approach would probably not be acceptable today!

Once realistic customer service levels are determined, they must be measured. In a supermarket, how often is a product not available on the shelf? In a garage, what proportion of repairs is completed on time? In a hotel, how long must you queue to pay your bill? If a product is ordered online, what proportion is successfully delivered to the

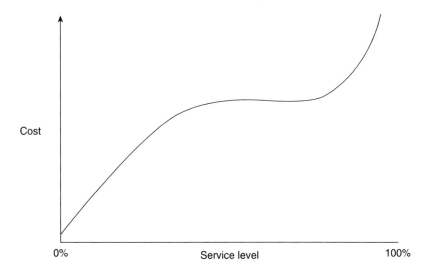

Figure 3.1   **Cost Of 100% Service**

customer? Our experience shows that many organisations do not measure the customer service level achieved. It is important that you define and measure customer service in the supply chains you investigate.

A question frequently asked by students is: which company functions are logistics and which are marketing? Consider the following functions:

- order forecasting,
- order processing,
- product inventory,
- customer service,
- distribution,

- delivery transport,
- sales,
- promotion,
- production scheduling, and
- relating to the customer.

We argue that logistics must have an input into all of these functions, except product and service promotion. The extent to which logistics manages these functions, rather than marketing, varies between companies. Modern organisations are designed to get the best business processes for the customers rather than to operate with functions in distinct departments. Therefore the debate over which function belongs in which area is not so important.

3.3 A SPECTRUM OF SERVICE BUSINESSES

*Service businesses** form a wide spectrum from mass service, in which most of the service operation is completed before the customer appears and there is little contact with the customer, to professional service, which is based on the personal skills of the people providing the service. An example of mass service is a petrol station. Examples of professional service providers are accountants and doctors. In mass service the 'back office' (actions without the customer present) dominates the process whereas in the 'front office' the interaction with the customer takes place. Among mass service companies the supply chain may be just as complicated as in manufacturing firms. It may contain all the elements of the 'Double-Bell' model (see Figure 1.6, section 1.1, page 10) if the centre ellipse is considered to be a product distribution centre.

Alternatively, a single consultant providing advice to managers may have no logistics requirements beyond purchase of a computer and use of road and air transport. There are many more parameters which distinguish service businesses, such as the amount of customer contact, the extent of order placement by the Internet and the extent of customisation of the service. Consequently, the supply chains required are very varied.

Johnston and Clark define a service business as follows:

> *Service organisations** integrate value-adding activities in terms of outcome and experience by delivering a service product to customers by configuring resources and processes to create that service.[4]

A useful way of approaching service business is to see it as comprising a business proposition plus a customer perception of service. The proposition is provided by the organisation while the perception comes from the customer. The service concept is defined in terms of the service product, the constituent parts that form the service, the outcomes and the experience, including the 'servicescape'. A *servicescape** is the surrounds, excluding the service product, which create an atmosphere in which the service is delivered. The service supply chain, then, is the set of processes which:

- procure materials and goods for the service operation,
- transform the customer, or the customer's object, with the goods, and
- deliver the transformed goods or object to the place where the customers want them.

Several service business factors are in contrast to manufacturing business:

- amount of customer contact,
- lack of ability to stock the service,
- importance of customer perception, and
- ability to be, in some cases, delivered electronically.

The case 'Serving motorists' at the end of this chapter illustrates a mass service situation in which the staff undertake a considerable variety of purchasing before the customer arrives. Customer contact is very limited. In some cases motorists just 'swipe a card' to pay for their fuel and drive away without any contact with the console operators. Motorists expect to get straight in front of a fuel pump and have immediate access to all the accessories, food and drinks in the shop. Their perception of the service station is 'created' by its branding (e.g. BP green, Shell yellow and red) and 'met', hopefully, by the rest of the servicescape inside the station and shop.

A good classification of service process is into mass service, service shop and professional services.[5] This classification uses six service operation dimensions:

- equipment versus people focus,
- length of customer contact time,
- extent of customisation,
- extent to which customer contact personnel exercise judgement in meeting individual needs,

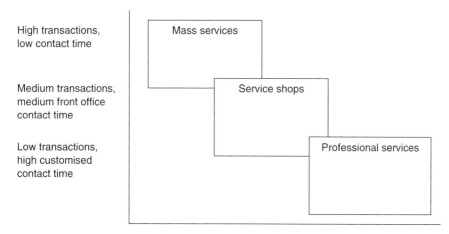

Figure 3.2   **Model of service processes (after Silvestro et al.[5])**

- source of value added, front office or back, and
- product or process focus.

Figure 3.2 shows how the following three classes compare on these dimensions:

- *Mass services** have high customer transactions with little contact time and low customisation. The offering is product-oriented and back-office dominated (e.g. retail whitegoods, petrol station).
- *Service shops** form a class midway between the two extremes. They have a medium number of transactions, medium customisation and medium front-office contact time. There are both process and product elements in the offering to customers (e.g. transport company).
- *Professional services** have few transactions and a highly customised, process-oriented contact dominated by front-office work in which considerable judgement is applied (e.g. management consultancy).

The foregoing enables you to classify the service business you are analysing. This class then identifies which areas will be more important to the supply chain. For example, if you are investigating a supermarket, it falls into the 'mass service' class. Its focus is on the effective provision of groceries, with a very high proportion in stock, with limited customer contact and no customisation of the service offering.

3.4 WHY ARE SUPPLY CHAIN CONCEPTS IMPORTANT TO SERVICE BUSINESS?

The underlying concept of a supply chain is to design and manage a path from original suppliers of materials to delivery to end consumers, which will meet their needs very

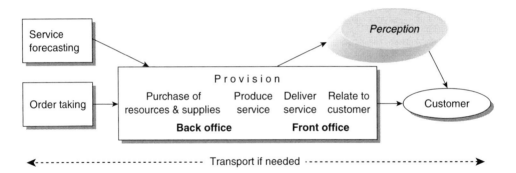

Figure 3.3   **Functions in the service supply chain**

effectively, while the organisations in the chain make a profit. The emphasis is on a series of movements and operations which do this.

So a *service supply chain** is defined as:

> The relationship and coordination of a number of organisations to create, develop and deliver a service product to a particular group of customers. The service chain creates value by the coordination of purchased goods and services with a suitable transformation operation and service delivery. Delivery may include passing goods or transformed objects to the end customers so that they perceive that the service is attractive and they are likely to use it again.

By analogy with Figure 2.1, a service chain has the functions shown in Figure 3.3 for the main organisation involved.

This concept applies to most service businesses. Fuel stations, supermarkets and hospitals require extensive supplies from near and far. Customers loathe waiting, so storage of capacity or goods is essential in all these services. Design is critical both to give the customer the service he or she wants on demand and to generate a return for the operating organisations.

Because the service does not necessarily include a product, some services place less importance on supply chain processes. Professional services have limited application of the supply chain concept for this reason. Because of the need to supply the service as the customer turns up, most services require a chain which anticipates demand extremely effectively.

Let's look at a supply chain for a petrol station, a mass service operation(see Figure 3.4).

Consider how the concept of service logistics can be applied to a petrol station. The design of the service process is evident from the establishment of a site manned by trained people to assist customers. The medium-term demand estimate leads to the number of station operators available and the fuel and food supplies at the station. Fuel, food and other goods are only available because of the relationships with many suppliers. The main customer focus is on those requiring fuel, while passing on the road, and purchasing convenience items or accessories during their brief visit. Delivery has two components. Customers serve themselves with petrol and other goods and then pay an operator for them. The petrol station is a mass service operation because it has a high

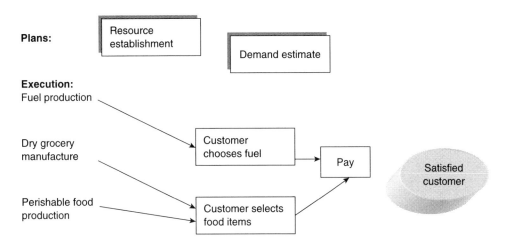

Figure 3.4   **Service supply chain for a petrol station**

number of low-contact transactions. Limited customer loyalty may be generated by the servicescape, the fuel price or the variety of goods available. To explore this situation further, refer to the case at the end of this chapter.

An important design step in service processes is providing flexibility to customers. Since customers have to be present in many service operations, either because they are acquiring goods or because the service is performed on them, the service has to be delivered flexibly when the consumer wants it. The flexibility may be timing at any hour of the day, customisation to give exactly the service desired, or electronic access to place orders or receive intangible products. This flexibility has manifold implications for the firms upstream in the supply chain. For example, the ability to provide men's, women's and juvenile haircuts has implications for the shampoos, scissors and razors which the hairdresser requires.

3.5 CUSTOMER AND SUPPLIER RELATIONSHIPS

A service business provides a less tangible product than a manufacturing business, hence the relationships with customers and suppliers must, in many service chains, be stronger. Relationships vary from partnerships and joint ventures at the intense end to short-term contracts and transactions at the low, uninvolved end.[4] We will deal with relationships to customers and suppliers separately because they have quite different implications in services.

Customer relationships

The service provider, in the service chain, needs to have a closer relationship with its customer than a manufacturer because it is supplying an intangible product and it is reliant on the perception of the customer as to the adequacy of the service. For example, when a garage carries out maintenance on a car, the owner has to trust the mechanic and other garage processes to do all the required maintenance and not more. Since the customer knows less about the car than the mechanic and nothing about checks carried out, he or she may have a good, bad or indifferent opinion about the service supplied. This opinion may be realistic or unrealistic. The garage's aim is to create a realistic expectation, 'my car will function properly, barring unfortunate occurrences, for the next 5,000 miles', and deliver against it while making a margin on the capital and variable costs expended on that maintenance transaction.

Events, known as 'moments of truth',[4] are occasions when the customer finds out about the service. The example here could be the size of the bill when he or she returns at the end of the day expecting to pay $200 for a service and being asked for $580 because the brakes needed lining and two new tyres were fitted. Alternatively, a driver might be called by the garage service scheduler to tell him that he cannot have his car back for a day because the garage is awaiting delivery of a cylinder head gasket which must come from a parts warehouse interstate. The garage may not be 'at fault' in either of these situations, but the customer may be livid. The garage needs to prevent the driver from getting the wrong expectation. Many garages insist on speaking to customers before any maintenance is carried out in excess of that agreed when leaving the car. The garage could also tell the owner that his model is quite unusual and, therefore, unexpected need for parts could delay service completion.

With the best service system in the world, some service failures will occur. In this case the provider should undertake service recovery. Recovery requires that the service fault be put right and, frequently, some extra recompense be provided so that the customer feels that the service organisation cares about her business. Airlines frequently provide free meals or accommodation when flight delays would cause the traveller extra expense. Fuller coverage of this area of service perceptions is beyond the scope of this book. You are referred to *Service Operations Management*.[4]

Supplier relationships

Figure 3.5 shows the typical stages in a service supply chain. Johnston and Clark[4] suggest there are four kinds of relationships:

- standard supply chain,
- management through intermediaries,
- supply partnerships, and
- make-it-yourself.

In the *standard supply chain*, products and materials are purchased by the service organisation from numerous suppliers to obtain all the inputs required to produce the link's output goods and services. The purchasing process requires:

- appointing a number of companies capable of providing the products required,
- placing purchase orders on the appointed companies to deliver quantities of products sufficient for the service process, and
- evaluating suppliers to ensure that they are achieving promised deliveries.

In *management through intermediaries*, a *service organisation* (the distributor in Figure 3.5) provides a service, such as cleaning or telephone maintenance, over a wide area:

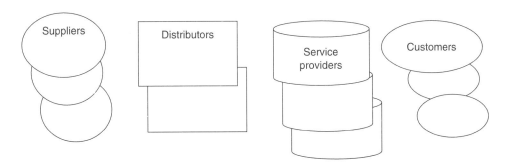

Figure 3.5   **Many organisations together provide a service to customers**

a state or a country. The *service distributor* licenses other intermediary firms to deliver the service product in a part of the geographical area. For example, the distributor could be a telephone company, called 'Phonecom'. *Service providers* are electrical tradespersons who, using parts from Phonecom's suppliers, visit individual houses to repair phone and network faults.

*Supply partnerships** refer to an alliance between two, or more, service firms to work together to deliver a service to a group of customers. For example, a separately-owned shop within a departmental store.

In *make-it-yourself*, the service operation decides that the required product or service process is best made or provided within the operation. For example, most car service garages rely on separate firms to stock and deliver the spare parts that they need very quickly after the need is established. A garage decides to stock a range of parts so that it can operate the spare part service itself. It sets up a store adjacent to the service workshop, purchases the auto spares it expects to need and trains the mechanics to select their own parts as required.

Consider which of these relationships is the most appropriate for your service business. A supermarket will typically have a standard supply chain to source its products. A restaurant will manage its urgent requirements for small amounts of high-quality foods by employing a food service company.

3.6 SERVICE PERFORMANCE AND INNOVATIVE STRATEGY

The first step in service business is to establish the needs of the segment of customers that it desires to serve. These needs must address:

- the product, if any,
- the customer transformation, and
- customer perception.

Then a service strategy is formed by following the stages illustrated in Figure 3.6.

The first stage is to understand the *business goal* that the service firm is aiming for. The goal is usually to achieve a number of market and financial targets over several years. A service company may aim to increase its market share by 40% over the next

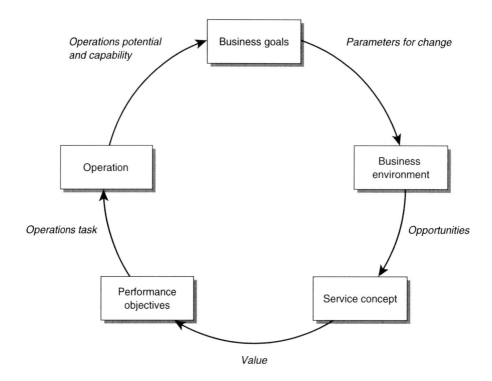

Figure 3.6   **Key stages of a services strategy (adapted from Johnson and Clark[4])**

Source: *Service Operations Management*, by Johnston R and Clark G, reprinted by permission of Pearson Education Limited, copyright 2001, 2005.

three years while achieving a return on assets of at least 12% after tax. A service mission is often used to define and limit the business area in which the firm operates. A service mission is a succinct statement that encapsulates the nature of the service business. For example, Club Med's mission is to provide a fully-paid holiday package where the customer makes her arrangements and pays the bill in advance in return for a well-managed programme in which she doesn't have to worry much about money, transport, food, activities or clothes.

The second stage is to analyse the *business environment* in which the service firm operates. The opportunities available to a service station will differ according to the car-owning population in its area, the disposable income to buy drinks and groceries, and the extent of nearby competition.

The third stage is to identify the *service concept*, the clear statement of what it offers customers and what employees are endeavouring to achieve. The service station concept is to provide readily accessible fuel supplies and the opportunity to pick up convenience items at the same time.

Fourthly, *performance objectives* predicate the particular tasks which operations must implement to satisfy service consumers and hence attain the firm's business goals. The service station's objectives revolve around selling at the right price to maximise sales of petrol and having sufficient grocery items in stock to satisfy all customers without investing in excess inventory. Service performance objectives are also addressed in section 3.2.

Finally, the service *operation* is carried out every day for all customers. The service operations manager is responsible to see that all the elements come together seamlessly so that customers get exactly what they want and costs are controlled so that an acceptable return is made.

3.7 DISTRIBUTION CENTRES

A major factor in the effective delivery of goods to customers is the use of distribution centres (DCs) to briefly store goods close to customer locations.[6] This section examines the key tasks carried out by DCs and assembles the strategies which affect DC design and location.

A distribution centre is a warehouse for finished goods *en route* between a manufacturer and a set of customers. Its main function is to provide speedy access to a range of products. This is achieved by receiving goods in bulk and sorting them into customers' exact requirements. DCs are generally sited close to major highways on the edge of cities. Their storage racking and truck access are designed to achieve the following major tasks:

- Receiving involves unloading goods from trucks and putting them into pallet racking.
- Storage involves bulk inventory on racks and live storage in picking locations, so that individual cartons from a pallet load can be retrieved to satisfy a customer order.
- In-store handling moves pallets and cartons between receiving, storage and despatch locations in the DC. Handling may be carried out by mobile equipment, such as forklift trucks and reach trucks, or by captive equipment, such as high-rise cranes or conveyors.
- Picking is the selection of all the cartons in a customer's order from the racking so that they are moved to one point for despatch.
- Despatch is the consolidation of the picked orders into one load to be taken by truck to the customer's premises.

The decision to design a DC and place it in a particular location is based on four strategic factors[7] (see Figure 3.7).

1.   The decision regarding how many DCs to have depends upon the speed of customer service required, risk factors, economies of scale achieved by fewer DCs and the reduction of total logistics costs. These pressures act in different directions with greater numbers of DCs generally reducing transport costs but multiplying the cost of operating the warehouses. In practice, cost pressures tend to favour centralisation, with real-time information being used to prevent customer service from suffering.

2.   DC location tries to take advantage of closeness to customers while considering the availability of resources such as labour, correctly zoned land and buildings. In

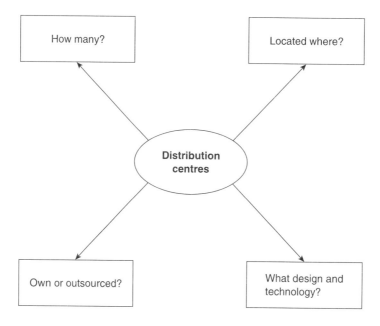

Figure 3.7   **Strategic distribution centre decisions[7]**

practice, there are very few locations to choose from and DC parks tend to grow on major roads near big cities.

3.   Should the company own or outsource the DC? This is a complicated decision which is reviewed in section 7.5.

4.   What design layout and technology should the DC have? This decision includes the layout of storage racks and the use of conveyors and mobile equipment to move goods around. Research shows that a high level of technical development does not guarantee better performance.[8] So the decision must take account of the flexibility to cater for demand changes, the risks involved in getting the intended throughputs, industrial relations implications and the financial justification for major capital expenditures.

Putting all this together is very difficult since the DC has a life of at least twenty years whereas it is very difficult to estimate the future demands on the DC even five to ten years in the future. Nevertheless, these factors provide a framework for analysis.

3.8 FREIGHT TRANSPORT SERVICES AND CONSOLIDATION

Section 2.5 introduces logistics transport from the point of view of the focal manufacturing company in the supply chain. It covers effective transport decisions. This section examines various modes, for different transport tasks over specific journeys to obtain economic and effective service. A method to analyse freight transport efficiency is suggested. Currently, few manufacturing or distribution companies conduct their own transport; more frequently they outsource transport, distribution storage and related activities to freight transport companies. This section takes a freight industry view of transport, including consolidation, inter-modal transfers and international freight forwarding. It examines freight forwarders, service companies which specialise in knowledge of a wide range of overseas transport methods and the detailed information and documentation to make them work, without owning the methods themselves. The section also covers special services such as air, refrigerated, bulk, reticulated, and temperature-controlled goods.

More extensive arrangements, such as contract logistics, and '3PL' (*third-party logistics**) and '4PL' providers (management of a series of transport movements often carried out by 3PL companies along the supply chain) are becoming more important. Inter-modal transport considers the exchange of packaged products between modes of transport, such as from road to rail, from rail to sea or from air to road. Such goods exchange requires terminals and storage depots. Inter-modal transfers are needed to move lobster tails from Tasmania to Los Angeles; after being packed and consolidated into a refrigerated air container, they are transferred from road transport into the hold of a ship across the Bass Strait to Melbourne. After another short road journey, the lobsters are loaded into the airfreight plane which will fly them from Australia to Los Angeles in California. Transport around the world is needed for firms like Ford, Benetton and Nike when parts or modules are made in one country and assembled into products in another. This is further developed in Chapter 4.

Transport means the movement of goods between each link in the supply chain. This component of the supply chain has changed dramatically over time, with outsourced providers of transport and warehousing services replacing the traditional 'in house' approach. Globalisation, reduction in trade barriers, and just-in-time manufacturing have led to freight companies such as Toll, Pickfords, UPS/Fedex and Linfox achieving economies of scale and scope that enable them to 'partner' with manufacturers and others in the supply chain.

Modes of transport

Road is the prevalent mode of transport within cities and, for general goods, between cities. The basic road transport service comprises loading a number of pallets of materials or products on to a semi-trailer (or articulated lorry) at a dock at the providing premises. The vehicle drives the load to the receiving dock at the destination and the goods are unloaded by forklift truck. The operators provide a 'door-to door' service which is easy to access and they respond to customers' actual needs. Road caters for most sizes of load and it carries medium cubic volumes: more than air, but less than rail or sea. It is carried out by private operators with strong competition. In Australia the existence of 'owner drivers' helped to decentralise road transport and lower its price in the past. Australian research shows that road tends to be cheaper than other modes for distances less than 300 kilometres. Hence road is the only mode of transport within cities and urban regions. Examples of road and other modes of transport are given in Table 2.2.

Long-distance road transport attracts different prices according to the speed with which freight is delivered. With a haul of, say, 800 kilometres, there will be one price for next-day delivery and a lower price for delivery in 2–3 days. This is particularly important with lower quantities of goods that cannot command a full vehicle over the entire route.

Rail is an excellent mode of transport for large quantities and long distances, say 300–2,500 kilometres, provided products fit within height and width restrictions. Most national rail systems have one gauge, the width between the two rail lines. In Australia rail's ability to transport freight is reduced because there are different gauges in each state. A growing standard gauge links the New South Wales railways with interstate capital cities. Because the state government owns railways in each state, they have tended to cater parochially for local industry and crops rather than assisting national production and trade. State management tends to be narrow-minded in providing services. Coupled with strong unionism, this makes the railways unresponsive to customers' freight needs in Australia. This is now being addressed by the development of a national freight service but it tends to lag behind road transport in infrastructure and door-to-door service.

In Britain the railways achieved a single gauge one hundred years ago. Major strides have been made in updating the speed of trains and the rails and signalling that make this possible. However, the short distances involved and the service requirements of shippers mitigate against the use of rail for freight. By far the greatest quantity of freight, both within Britain and to and from the European Continent, is carried on road by articulated vehicles.

Rail transport is good at the line haul from station A to station B and its cost is frequently cheaper than road. However, the transport required is from factory AA to customer BB (because most do not have rail connections). Therefore in getting from factory AA to station A, from station B to the customer BB, rail frequently becomes more expensive and slower. Freight forwarders, such as Toll Holdings and Fedex, have improved this situation by contracting whole trains to provide next-day delivery in interstate capital cities but at a premium price, as noted under road transport.

Air is a rapidly growing means of freight transport in all parts of the world. Cargo is placed in the belly of passenger planes and in dedicated air freighters. Its high cost per tonne-mile can be borne by high value and perishable goods, such as computers and seafood. Access to air is restricted by the location of airports but goods move very quickly, from airport to airport, and have a smooth trip. Products have to be small enough to fit into limited rectangular containers. Air freight has similar potential problems to rail transport because of the need for delivery to and from airports at either end of the flight. These end delivery problems are much fewer with air transport, because the operators are used to providing better service and the high value goods are not sensitive to extra costs. More firms are using air for part of their transport because of the ability to deliver to customers faster and reduce inventories. Air is particularly suitable for small perishable foods such as lobsters, salmon and gourmet cheese.

Sea provides a very low cost per kilometre for bulk and container cargo to overseas and some local coastal destinations. It tends to be cheaper than other modes for journeys over 2,500 kilometres but it is difficult to access, especially from far inland locations. Bulk cargoes include oil, grain, ores and fertilisers. The development of regular container ships plying between the main ports on each continent has made this an excellent means of transport. The container can carry most products, using refrigeration for food cargoes. Sea container travel tends to be quite slow, due to centralising containers at the port chosen by the shipping line, and the movement of vessels between many ports of loading and several ports of unloading. Hence travel times from start to destination are about a month. Sea transport between Australian ports has been hampered by conservative attitudes in maritime unions.

The use of *pipelines*, or reticulation, is only possible for liquids, gases and electricity. It requires a large capital investment to permanently link two points for one product. That pipeline then provides a low variable cost per tonne moved. A typical use of pipelines is to convey crude oils from a landing point to a refinery and the refined products to the oil terminal for retail sale. Pipelines are very reliable.

The various types of transport within the modes are examined in section 2.5.

The flow of materials is driven by orders from the next link down the chain, or from the end customer in more advanced supply chains. Industry is moving from a situation in which such movements were monthly bulk deliveries to frequent (at least daily) deliveries to the exact requirements of manufacturers and retailers. The movement requires a mode of transport and a schedule, so that deliveries for numerous customers can be met without an unreasonable level of resources. Close links along the in-bound supply chain are fostered so that all the related goods required to assemble a number of refrigerators, cars or pizzas are delivered at once. When many suppliers are located within an hour's drive of an assembly plant, the manufacturer may use a 'milk-run' in which a truck collects exact quantities and types of part several times a day and delivers the whole collection to the precise location where the parts are required for assembly into finished goods.

Material and product flows are made possible by electronic information which orders, specifies and updates the types, quantities and timings. Some of this information is from manufacturers to suppliers (e.g. among physical locations), while other information is between manufacturers and their transport companies. Transport companies are predominantly required to move a set of goods from A to B according to a fixed time slot, but they are increasingly taking over wider responsibility for warehousing, picking and consolidating shipments. This information topic is further developed in Chapter 5.

How can you check that a company's use of transport is efficient? Work by McKinnon and Ge[9] studied the opportunities for improving transport efficiency in a supply chain. They examined the movements of 3,600 vehicles from 53 fleets over a 48-hour period. The survey of road transport in the food supply chain in the UK was done by recording data in Excel workbooks for that period, so that each fleet was exposed to similar trading conditions and road traffic levels. Movements comprised factory to distribution centre, DC to supermarket and local depot to small retailers and caterers. McKinnon and Ge measured five key performance indicators (KPIs): vehicle loading, empty running, fuel efficiency, vehicle time utilisation and deviations from schedule. Analysis of the KPI data revealed wide variation between industry subsectors attributable to both differences in the nature of the operations and failure to achieve best practice.

Next, consider the complex process of assembling a transport choice for any type of goods over any route in the world.

Freight forwarders

Most manufacturers use *freight forwarders** to advise of the particular routes and transport methods to convey products to any part of the world at any time of the year. Freight forwarders are service companies which specialise in knowledge of a wide range of overseas transport methods and the detailed information and documentation to make them work. They will not be fazed by a pallet from Birmingham to Alaska,

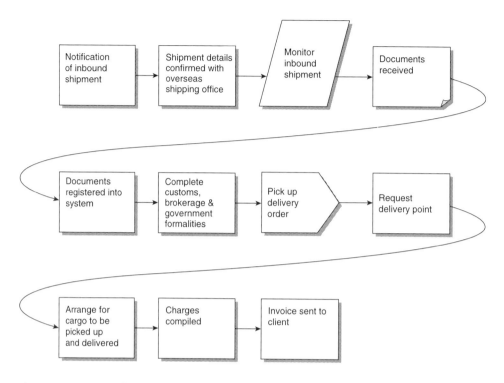

Figure 3.8   **Import freight information flow**

or a container from Suzhou, China to Milan, Italy. Many freight forwarders provide a pure service, they give advice and make arrangements without owning the transport methods themselves.

> Freight forwarders can be thought of as travel agents for cargo shipped to overseas locations. They employ highly skilled staff who search for the most economical and speedy means to ship cargo. The myriad of documentation requirements and government formalities are commonly handled by forwarders.[10]

International freight forwarders, such as Excel, carry out this service task of assembling transport for any type of goods over any route for manufacturers and distributors. The freight forwarder (FF) is, effectively, an outsourced company transport department which assumes total responsibility for the goods after, say, manufacture in the eastern USA. The FF frequently has access to the manufacturer's internal data so that it knows what loads and destinations to expect as early as possible. The FF arranges actual movements over each mode required, insurance, export and import documents and bank credit, acting as the agent of the manufacturer. Effectively, the FF is a transport provider coordinating activities between all the separate transport and shipping companies along the multi-country route that the cargo takes. Figure 3.8 illustrates the part played by a freight forwarder by showing the tasks it undertakes with a typical import consignment.

Table 3.1   **Freight forwarder services**

PO Management	Sea & air operations	Brokerage	Invoicing
Customer service	Cartage	Track and Trace	Consultancy
Supplier management	Performance measurement	Documents	

(PO = purchase order)

Consider a large UK-owned freight forwarder, which we shall call All Freight (AF). It employs 60,000 people in numerous locations in 120 countries. Its main services are air freight, sea freight and brokerage, but All Freight also provides consultancy and third-party services (see Table 3.1).

With clients who provide a low volume of business, All Freight provides a commodity service. It helps the client with all the required elements from Figure 3.8, but gives them a standard service in which the contact is low and the service is not customised to the client's specific needs.

A small group of consultants within All Freight specialises in serving its largest clients. These clients place over 1,000 shipments per year with AF. AF then treats them very differently. It appoints an account manager to handle their business. It spends large amounts of staff time to understand the company client. AF produces a service which is very detailed and specialised to suit that client's business. Consultants in contact with the client exercise a high degree of discretion in altering the service to suit their precise situation. They also have a number of back-office staff who can do analysis on the client's routes to find out the best method of transport. Rather than being static, the consultants handling large client companies are proactive in looking for tailor-made solutions and apply a continuous improvement philosophy.

Time-slotting and transport innovation

Time-slotting is a distribution centre (DC) requirement that the transport company presents its load at an agreed time of day. Usually there is a window of 15 minutes. If the truck arrives at a different time, its cargo may not be accepted. Time-slotting enables the DC to smooth the task of unloading a large number of local and import container loads.

An important innovation, which is rapidly spreading through the transport of all retail goods, is product tracking. Product tracking gives a permanent record of the manufacturing and supply sources of each product sold through its whole supply chain. The aim is to use records to pin-point the farm of origin, batch of manufacture, etc. of each cargo in case there is any problem with the use of the product. Such tracking can be achieved by barcodes, by electronic records or by microcomputer chips.

Many other areas of innovation in transport are driven by the truck having online access to full information about the product, the customer and the location to which delivery is required. This enables fast solutions to a series of problems such as:

- Where is the delivery required? – solved by global positioning systems.
- Do we have all the items required in the order? – solved by computer access to the original order.
- Customer does not have cash to pay – solved by the driver carrying credit card facilities.

- Customer is not expecting this load – solved by advance shipping notices.
- Immediate proof of delivery – receiver signs on to electronic pad which captures this delivery for anyone, anywhere who needs to know.

For further development of this area, the reader is referred to a book on transport.[11]
    For transport and materials handling in distribution centres see section 3.7.

3.9 LOGISTICS SECURITY

Having looked at service logistics and freight transport, we now consider a very important service facet of supply chains: are they secure against all kinds of risks or are they likely to be disrupted?

Effective supply chain management requires certainty in the delivery of products and services. Information is used to maintain this certainty in the face of random variation and occasional major potential disruptions. Managers use the physical processes of transport and storage to meet exact customer demand with the least amount of disruption and uncertainty. The removal of inventory buffers and minimisation of activities, to reduce cost, increase supply chain vulnerability. Approaches such as lean thinking, synchronised deliveries, reduced number of stocking locations, and Quick Response threatens the supply chain with failure if there is disruption.[12]

In the wider scene, greater product/service complexity, outsourcing and globalisation create increasingly complex, dynamic supply networks.[13] Such networks are more susceptible to disruption.

Disruption can arise from many sources: process or transport breakdown, labour unrest, acts of nature, the need to recall product, theft and the threat of terrorist activity. It can also be caused by risks to information such as computer failure or attack by viruses.

The three important stages to protect the supply chain are to find out what risks are likely, to estimate their chance of occurrence and to find out how significant a loss would be. Table 3.2 is an example of how to analyse a business situation to find risk exposure and the possible losses that could result. The constructed situation is close enough to a supply chain and it shows the different risk exposures of two players in the situation.

Building upon this analysis, we can assess the likelihood of each risk and the size of the resulting loss. Losses can come in many areas, such as financial, performance, physical, psychological and time. Investigation of one food company showed that theft cost $20 million per year. Also security consultants investigated a pharmaceutical factory in the middle of the night. They found a sterile production zone with the doors chocked open and everyone smoking. The company concerned could lose its export licence.

The solution that the companies in the chain should adopt will be a combination of the following measures. First, standard procedures should be designed and followed 24 hours per day every day of the year. Strong procedures to protect valuable and attractive items can reduce shrinkage considerably. The official standards of the country provide a good overall guide to the content of those procedures. Secondly, all operations employees should be trained, motivated and consulted. Such people who are on the spot are an essential line

Table 3.2   **Example of different aspects of risk**[14]

Benefit	Exposure	Event	Consequence	Business impairment	Magnitude of loss
1. Driver of Taxi	Parking illegally	Parking ticket	Fine	Increased costs	Range from minor to major
	Speeding	Caught by camera	Fine	Increased costs	
	Running a red light		Loss of points or licence	Possibly cease trading	
	Faulty products fitted to vehicle	Fails annual test	Vehicle off road	Temporarily cease trading	
2. Customer CEO can work in transit	CEO uses taxi to attend meeting	Taxi involved in crash	CEO misses meeting	Business lost	Range from minor to major

of defence and resolution. Thirdly, security procedures should be developed between the chain partners. It is no good waiting until an opportunistic attack occurs and then suing the other parties jointly responsible. Clearly, the actions are contingent on the types of product and service being delivered. Security procedures will vary widely between the supply of food, banknotes, computer software and car components.

In short, we think that supply chain companies should carry out some contingency planning. A plan which considers all the known significant risks enables hazard reduction to be carried out. There is still a possibility that disruption could occur. A pre-prepared contingency plan will give staff the best chance of disaster recovery. Strategic planning for supply chains is further developed in section 8.4. Security is one of the policies which should be included in that work.

Summary

The primary aim of all supply chains is the provision of goods and services to customers. This aim must be made precise to the particular products. It should be aligned to the marketing strategy of the focal company. Then the specific service level, such as delivery in full on time or correct invoicing, should be measured and positively controlled. Measuring service levels is one example of a number of tools provided for students to analyse particular supply chains.

Supply chain concepts are very important in service organisations for inventory of goods, for the use of information, and for coordinating companies in several links along the chain. Service companies require sophisticated information communication systems to receive data and information to assist in making numerous strategic and management decisions along the supply chain. This chapter explores the outcome and perception needs of service customers and the necessary responses of service organisations via supply chain design and execution. This response encompasses both operational performance and the strategic direction adopted by a service chain.

(Continued)

(Continued)

The choice of type and location of distribution centres is considered, in line with their importance in providing customer service. One particular service industry, freight transport, is widely used in most service and manufacturing supply chains. Freight transport is a complex industry, especially as supply lengthens across countries, seas and continents. Transport involves receipt of goods, unitisation for a long haul, short-term storage, breaking bulk and delivery to the eventual customer. Such transport can be the very essence of the product, as when grain is transported across the globe, or it can be a mere commodity item which the shipper rarely considers, such as in the movement of clothing or tinned food. Freight forwarders assemble different modes of transport and terminals into cost-efficient transport routes between the source manufacturer and the end consumer for specific products. Finally, all businesses are susceptible to disruption. The security of modern supply chain operation requires that risks are identified and reduced so that disruption, from all causes, is minimised.

Questions

1. Why are supply chain concepts of such importance to service firms? Consider hospitals, supermarkets, garages and airlines in your answer.
2. Describe the main functions of each of the steps in the supply chain, which enable the finished service to be provided, for one of the service organisations in question 1.
3. Service supply chains differ from manufacturing chains in the frequent need to have contact with the customers and to enable them to have a good experience. Explain this with some examples.
4. Given question 3, name some of the main service factors which are improved by actions upstream in the supply chain. For example, the range of spare parts at an automotive distributor improves the ability of a garage to finish car maintenance on time.
5. How are different modes of transport and terminals assembled into cost-efficient transport routes between the various links along supply chains for specific products?

Case: Serving motorists

A year ago Tony Adams bought the franchise of a Melbourne service station which sells fuels from the company 'Combined Fuel' (CF). He has built the business up to a Aus$3.2 million annual turnover. Although he is pleased with this success, he wants to improve this turnover and increase his profit margin.

The service station supplies petrol, diesel and liquid petroleum gas (LPG) to its customers. These fuels are provided by Combined Fuel Pty Ltd (name disguised), one of the biggest petroleum product suppliers in Australia.

(Continued)

As well as fuel, the service station sells almost 4,000 grocery and related items in five areas:

- oils and vehicle accessories,
- groceries, confectionery, magazines and newspapers,
- hot and cold food and snacks,
- dairy products and cold drinks, and
- cigarettes.

Tony has already made many improvements to the business, and he believes that more can be made. Once motorists turn off the road, how can he and his staff improve the service to them? How can they understand their customers better? How can they make sure that the food, fuel and service that they want are readily available? With the large number of products they sell, are their current supply chain processes adequate and efficient?

He knows that it is important to involve all his staff in a review of current ordering and supply systems. After all, they are the ones dealing with customers every day. Tony has already invested in customer service training for all his staff. He has also ensured that they receive training in the business's information systems. New staff are given thorough training as part of their induction, and regular staff are kept up to date with technology changes.

Let's meet the members of Tony's staff.

The staff

Tony employs two full-time shift managers responsible for staff and supplies during their shifts. Mary is the day-shift manager, who places all fresh food and other purchase orders requested by the night-shift manager, Peter. Peter decides purchase quantities and restocks the range of products from the store, helped by an operator. Both are capable and experienced managers. Tony works the extra two day-shifts and night-shifts, so that he has a good hands-on knowledge of the way the service station operates. During the past year, he has come to know and trust all his staff.

Tony also employs eight console operators. Ravi and Serena are senior operators who have worked at the station for several years. The operators are mainly casual but work over 30 hours most weeks. Each new operator is trained to work the console, to handle customers effectively and politely and to replenish food and other stocks from the warehouse. He or she is also trained to deal with difficult customers and to look after the security of cash and products.

Now let's look at how these staff operate the service station, 24 hours a day, seven days a week.

The service station

Motorists come to the service station for petrol, oil or other vehicle accessories. The station has a daily turnover of about 15,000 litres in total across the five fuels. Tony sets the selling price for his station. The volume increases when the petrol prices are low, and decreases when the petrol prices are higher. This means that a rapid response is required to frequent changes in the wholesale price. Fuel sales depend considerably on how quickly the new prices are adopted.

(Continued)

(Continued)

Groceries, food and other items are also a 24-hour service. Most customers also buy other products because the service station is more convenient than having to make another trip to a supermarket, newsagency or fast-food shop. Some come regularly to buy groceries, hot or cold foods, or cigarettes. Tony decides the pricing of these products.

Fuel supplies and delivery

Tony's fuel supplier, Combined Fuel (CF), owns the franchise of 100 service stations through-out Australia, 43 in the state of Victoria. CF has an annual turnover of $400 million. It does not refine any of the petroleum products it sells, but buys the processed fuels from other companies, such as Shell and Mobil, in bulk and sells them at its service stations at competitive rates. CF chooses suppliers on the availability of fuel and the price offered.

Combined Fuel does not have its own fuel tanks. It keeps a central inventory of fuel bought in bulk and held in suppliers' reservoirs. This fuel is directly transported to the service station by CF's fleet of petrol and gas tankers. It takes great care to follow safety regulations to protect its fuel in transit. The system ensures that Tony's station has sufficient stock for at least two days' custom in its underground storage tanks. As there are 18 fuel pumps in total, the delivery time is kept to a minimum. The pumps must work accurately without any breakdowns.

Fuel orders for Tony's station are automatically generated by the CF computer system after studying the daily sales and stocks in inventory reports. This software responds to entries made by the console operators to generate the entire delivery schedule automatically. Tony believes Combined Fuel does a good job of delivering fuel to his station.

Fuel quality and pricing

CF's procedures may save infrastructure cost of central fuel tanks, but its quality control over the petrol is reduced. Tony therefore feels that he has very little control over the quality of the fuel delivered to his station. Motorists require fuel to be in stock and available at all hours. Tony's operators carry out periodic checks on the cleanliness and quality of petrol. Tony decides to review whether these checks are adequate or whether improvements can be made.

While fuel delivery is not Tony's decision, its selling price to motorists is. CF changes its wholesale prices frequently, so that Tony has to respond quickly to remain competitive. Retail prices change several times per day and the fuel sales depend considerably on how quickly the new prices are adopted. Unless prices are competitive, many of the passing motorists will go to other stations, regarding petrol as a commodity which can be bought wherever the price is lowest.

For example, if the price charged to Tony drops from 129.5 cents to 125.5 cents per litre, he will lose a lot of business until he drops *his* price. Conversely, if the price increases and Tony's station is slow in responding, it may sell a lot of petrol without making any profit.

Information systems

The service station uses Combined Fuel's information system which manages inventory. CF has an enterprise resource planning (ERP) system which runs the whole fuel delivery needs for Tony and the other CF franchised service stations. The system handles stocks, orders and delivery of all the station's fuels, keeping account of quantities as well as prices.

This ERP system uses the same database in CF's different departments, at various stages in different links so that all departments communicate electronically with each other. Any

(Continued)

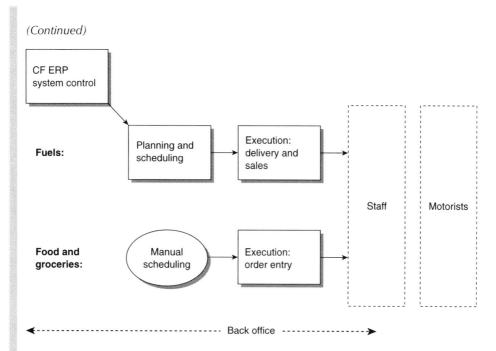

Figure C3.1   **Service station flow of information**

modification or changes once made at one point are automatically reflected in all other modules. This is all done in CF's head office in Melbourne. Once the number of litres of petrol and other fuels sold is entered in the system, ERP arranges the delivery of a tanker load of the required fuel without the station placing an order. It also does the banking and sends a daily performance sheet to the station. Tony has checked that fuel is delivered to the service station accurately on 98% of occasions.

The ERP system manages the inventory at Tony's station for all fuels, keeping account of the many price changes. At the day's end a console operator connects to the main office through a modem. Then he or she enters all the sales details for the day. The operator also has to enter the quantities in the underground tanks after 'dipping' them by hand to the nearest 50 litres. Frequently, these readings do not match pump sales readings, which are recorded electronically.

Tony has drawn a picture of the flow of information (Figure C3.1), which they use to compare the highly automated fuel system, for both plans and deliveries, with the food and grocery information. Food and grocery sales are automatically recorded, but Tony and his shift managers do plans and orders 'by hand'.

Other service station products

There are currently 3,850 items of food, drinks, groceries, newspapers and magazines, cigarettes and car accessories in the service station. Sales of these products are recorded in the ERP system (Figure C3.1), but all other functions must be carried out separately. Making order-quantity and timing decisions on such a large number of products is very labour-intensive, in contrast with the fully-automated buying and delivery of petrol. It becomes even harder with perishables such as milk, fresh food and newspapers.

(Continued)

(Continued)

Inventory management

Tony is concerned that, in the service station's food area, no specific purchase system or schedule has been designed. The track of the entire food inventory is kept manually, with errors often encountered. Purchase orders are generated as and when required. For dairy products, papers and magazines, stocks are purchased daily and the purchase orders are revised according to the day-to-day requirements. All groceries are purchased from the local wholesalers, low cost being the only selection criterion.

Since food store stocks and inventories are not monitored by Combined Fuel, no particular attention is given to inventory management. Station sales often suffer big losses because of unavailability of certain products. Occasionally the day manager, Mary, has had to buy stocks at higher rates. Wastage of the items due to expiry dates is approximately 5% of perishable products. There is obviously room for improvement here.

The service station is not involved in the transport of groceries. Tony relies on the supplier to provide the necessary transport and pays for the transport along with the product's cost. Tony needs to check whether transport costs could be reduced. Would savings be made and efficiencies achieved by the service station having its own small delivery truck?

Review of the service station operations

Tony has already made a list of the areas he has identified where improvements can be made. He then asks for written suggestions from his casual staff, and lists these suggestions along with his own observations.

He then arranges two review meetings with his two managers and the two senior console operators. They discuss all the items on the list, rejecting some as not workable or worthwhile, and allocating priorities for considering other suggestions. Mary and Peter, Serena and Ravi know one another well enough to enter into robust argument, and all are surprised at how much progress is made in a short time.

At the end of these meetings, Tony is able to list all the improvements agreed upon, and circulates a copy to all his staff. Each change in procedure is given a timeline for implementation, and Tony apportions responsibility to various members of staff for completion and signing off. It has been agreed to assess progress in three months' time.

Studying the customer requirement is a fundamental element of analysing a supply chain. Once those needs are understood, the supply chain can be tailored to suit specific requirements. Tony told staff he thinks a good definition of a supply chain for a service station is: 'Service logistics management is coordinating information and the delivery of petrol and other products while "enabling" station operators to give customers the service that they want.' Okay, they all said, but *what do we actually do?*

Tony asked his staff to prepare a chart of the physical flow of products in the whole network supplying goods and services to the service station. Although Tony only has the franchise for one service station, he wants to consider the whole supply chain in which he is involved, from sources of products to delivery of service to customers. Figure C3.2 shows the physical flow of products in this network, including all the links between suppliers, distribution centres, and the sales to end customers. Important areas are fuel stocks and pricing, purchasing of food products, transport to the station and satisfied customers. Tony and his shift managers will take responsibility for monitoring all parts of this supply chain. He will approach various suppliers to achieve greater efficiency and profitability for both suppliers and his service station.

(Continued)

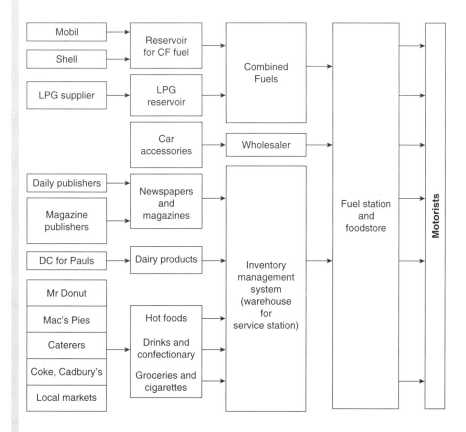

Figure C3.2   **Supply chain for service station**

Improvements to operations and profit

Here is a list of the proposed improvements identified by Tony and his staff, with some extra context for clarity.

Customer Service.   Customer needs are fundamental to designing and operating supply chains. In this petrol station all staff are aware of the importance of the welcome and effi-cient service offered to customers. This includes promptness, courtesy and building a rapport when dealing with every single customer, to encourage return business. Once cus-tomers are won, they are more likely to visit the service station again. A system is intro-duced so that any incidents of unsatisfied customers are reported to the shift manager on the day they occur. Whenever problems arise, senior staff will assist operators immediately.

(Continued)

(Continued)

Staff training and satisfaction.   Tony has already introduced customer service and information technology training for all his staff. He reviews this with all his staff, and sets out a schedule of training to ensure that everyone receives adequate education and support. Each console operator receives an initial two weeks' training in customer service and use of the console, banking and computer systems. Managers and senior operators attend a range of management and computer training courses in their paid time. Tony received some feedback that all members of staff appreciated being consulted, and enjoyed having some input to the success and profitability of the service station.

Fuel sales.   The five different types of fuel are needed to suit different customers' needs. Tony's station relies heavily on information sent to Consolidated Fuels. Much of the data is automatic, as when a sale is recorded from a barcode. His managers have worked hard to ensure that manual entries have next to no human errors. Staff have been trained to 'dip' the fuel tanks more accurately, and this has paid off. The loss compared to CF's figures has been halved. Ravi undertakes to review the frequency and accuracy of these 'dip' measures, to see whether further savings can be made. Tony considers that by talking to various CF contacts and attending franchise-holders' meetings, he could learn a lot. Staff consider that the real gain on fuel sales will come from increased patronage as the food and grocery sales and helpful service convince customers to return.

Fuel pricing.   Motorists want fuel at a competitive price. Mary is keen to introduce an automated system to respond to cost changes by Combined Fuel and competitors. Currently, pump price changes by local service stations are discovered by telephone. The station manager judges when to change price and does it manually. Mary makes two suggestions for improvement: either Combined Fuels should operate a central computer system to change retail prices at all their 43 Melbourne service stations simultaneously, or Tony's service station should implement an ERP software tool for the console operator to enter competitors' prices. This tool would then suggest what price change the station should make, and its timing. Mary agreed that this method could be cumbersome and prone to delays and errors.

Review of computer systems.   Tony agreed that Mary should undertake a review of the information system. A different automated purchase system should be designed and that system should be integrated with the existing ERP system. This would increase discipline in the system and result in proper accounting and report generation for future reviews. He also agreed that the station's food products should have fixed suppliers, so that they could be integrated with the station's supply chain by sharing the information database and by working towards the common goal of customer satisfaction. Profits can thereby be increased and the workload reduced.

Product range.   Almost every member of staff has complained of the complexity of dealing with so many product lines. Although these products provide nearly half the profits for the service station, they have a much lower turnover than the fuels. These products provide a huge amount of work in ordering, receipt, unpacking in the store and putting on the shelves, promotion and sale. Tony has agreed that the 3,850 products can be profitably reduced. Serena is asked to go through the whole product range to identify which items are the best sellers, and list those items which can be removed without upsetting customers. Where possible, one or two brands only of each product are to be retained. Peter agrees to explore whether the purchase of a small delivery van would save on delivery costs.

(Continued)

Wastage.   Operators carry out periodic checks of food and grocery articles sold, to ensure that out-dated items are thrown away. Staff are congratulated that the wastage of fresh food due to expiry dates has been reduced to 3%, and overall to 5%. Serena undertakes to check whether still less wastage can be achieved. She proposes to put the food and grocery items on to the station's computer so that the inventory can be monitored more effectively. By agreeing to reduce the number of products carried, this task will be easier.

Product pricing.   Staff understand that the station's prices are higher than at supermarkets. The service station is manned 24 hours a day, when many competitors are closed. Motorists are obviously happy to pay extra for this service and convenience, and generally make impulse purchases. Tony will undertake a review of non-fuel prices to get the right balance between volume of sales and profit margin.

Tony's overall picture

After these changes, Tony felt that he and his staff were making definite progress, and his staff enjoyed having some input to the success and profitability of the service station. They appreciated being consulted and requested a review every six months.

Tony wanted to ensure that a continuing search for improvements was built into the service station's operations so he wrote down three questions for regular reference (see below).

Case questions

1.   How can supply chain concepts help Tony run his business?
2.   What do service station customers want?
3.   What changes should Tony make to information systems and goods delivery?

REFERENCES

1   Doyle P (1994) *Marketing Management and Strategy*, Prentice-Hall International, New York.
2   Hill T (2000) *Manufacturing Strategy: Text and Cases*, Palgrave, Basingstoke, in which supply chain 'flow-creating criteria' are developed as 'Order-Winning criteria' in a manufacturing context.
3   Gilmour P (1993) *Logistics Management*, Longman Australia, Melbourne.
4   Johnston R and Clark G (2005) *Service Operations Management*, (2nd edn), Prentice-Hall, Harlow.
5   Silvestro R, Fitzgerald L, Johnston R and Voss C (1992) 'Towards a classification of service processes', *International Journal of Service Industry Management*, 3(10): 62–75.
6   Stephens C and Wright D (2002) 'The contribution of physical distribution management to the competitive supply chain strategies of major UK food retailers', *International Journal of Logistics: Research and Applications*, 5(1): 91–108.
7   Dapiran GP (2005) Lecture notes for Masters students, Monash University, Department of Marketing, Australia.
8   Frazelle EH (1996) *World-class Warehousing*, Logistics Resources International, Atlanta, p. 103.

9   McKinnon AC and Ge YL (2004) 'Use of a synchronised vehicle audit to determine opportunities for improving transport efficiency in a supply chain', *International Journal of Logistics: Research and Applications*, 7(3): 219–238.

10   International Trade Line, 1992, *Journal of Commerce*, Baltimore County Chamber of Commerce, Baltimore.

11   Coyle JJ, Bardi EJ and Langley RA (2000) *Transportation* (5th edn), Thompson South Western, Mason, OH.

12   Dapiran GP (2005) Teaching notes (unpublished), Monash University, Department of Marketing Australia.

13   Harland C, Brenchley R and Walker H (2003) 'Risk in supply networks', *Journal of Purchasing and Supply Management*, 9: 51–62.

14   Brenchley R (2001) 'Trust, power and control in trans-organizational relations', *Organisation Studies*, 22(2): 337–65.

International Logistics
(with David Taylor)

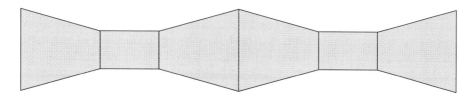

This diagram represents a generic international supply chain by two 'Double-Bell' models, each from sources to customers, linked by a decoupling point.

Objectives

- To study the international dimensions of supply chains from strategic and operational points of view and the concomitant risks
- To examine the methods of organisation, information communication and transport required by international commodity supply chains
- To analyse and understand a 'transnational commodity' supply chain which has stages in different, distant parts of the world
- To introduce the impact of culture, language, nationality and external issues, such as government policies, on international supply chains

INTRODUCTION

Many of the products which we use, such as cameras and socks, require an international supply chain. The international dimension may enter from the locations of customers, manufacturers or suppliers. In the widest sense, supply chains are global, with significant presence in different countries and continents at various stages. This international dimension adds complexity of culture, language, nationality and distance. Although more operational than strategic, transport and information become more complicated. This chapter examines the strategic choices used to construct international supply chains, the positions of suppliers relative to manufacturers and distribution centres relative to end customers; this is one of several tools provided, which can be used to analyse international chains. The chapter also examines the operational point of view to decide which information system will be used to combine orders and which suppliers will provide components.

The type of product required has an important influence on the international supply chain. Region-specific products have to be designed and manufactured for a particular part of the world. For example, in 1998 the Honda Accord had two body designs, one for the USA and one for Japan and Europe. In a truly global product, such as Coca-Cola or McDonald's hamburgers, no modification is necessary for the country where it is sold. There is then a further split in global products into those, like Coke, which require regional manufacture and bottling, and those that are distributed in the same way throughout the world, such as Benetton's woollen garments.

The economist would say that international supply chains are assembled from international trade and concentrate on the movements of goods between countries. She or he would further say that, over the last 25 years, there has been a rapid increase in the globalisation of industry and markets. This has led to a great increase in international trade as countries lower their barriers to imported products. In international logistics we take a different perspective. International logistics conjures up a vision of materials and parts flowing from suppliers via manufacturers to customers located anywhere in the world and information systems driving supply and distribution networks that span the entire globe. Ubiquitous products such as cars comprise components made in many locations and assembled in countries which use ocean shipping to distribute to agents and dealers throughout the world.

It is evident that the management of global supply chains, and the international operations which they require, have not always kept pace with the growth in trade. Hence many international chains operate inefficiently, causing higher costs and poor service levels to the customer. Often the only way to keep customers along the supply chain satisfied is to put in place high levels of inventory. One of the big challenges facing managers responsible for global chains is to try to reduce levels of inventory while maintaining, or improving, the level of service.

There are concerns that the current era faces greater risks in international trade due to extremes of climate and terrorist activity. The initial response of many supply chain managers is to put additional inventory at strategic points in the chain. Thus, the management of international chains is an important issue for many companies.

Global supply chains are made more complicated by uncertainty and difficulty of control. Uncertainty arises from longer lead-times and lack of knowledge of risks and local market conditions. Coordination becomes more complex because of additional language and currency transactions, more stages in the distribution process and local government intervention through customs and trade barriers. Additionally, there are many instances in which a truly global logistics system is not necessary, and where 'internationalisation' is a more accurate description. Internationalisation certainly is an increasing feature of the majority of supply chains. International sourcing of component parts and international markets for finished goods are extending as world trade increases.

Our response is to talk about a range of supply chains but to concentrate on one type of chain, which we call 'transnational commodity'. A *transnational commodity supply chain** is defined as one in which manufacture of finished products is carried out in several countries, suppliers of materials and components reside in many global locations and customers for common products are located in many parts of the world. An example is the footwear chain at the end of this chapter.

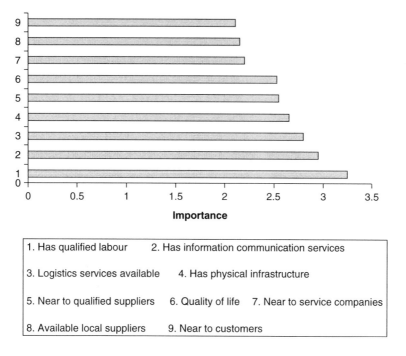

1. Has qualified labour   2. Has information communication services

3. Logistics services available   4. Has physical infrastructure

5. Near to qualified suppliers   6. Quality of life   7. Near to service companies

8. Available local suppliers   9. Near to customers

Figure 4.1   **Relative importance of international location factors[1]**

Source: *Logistics Management and Strategy,* by Harrison A and van Hoek R, reprinted by permission of Pearson Education Limited, copyright 2002, 2005.

Figure 4.1 supplies a ranking of factors important in the choice of each facility location along the international supply chain from a study by van Hoek and colleagues.[1] It is notable that qualified labour and information communication services are considered the two most important factors.

Hence this chapter looks, first, at the strategic reasons for the development of international supply chains; secondly, at the decisions that are made harder by distance, nationality and location around the globe; thirdly, at the risks inherent in global chains; and fourthly, at the organisation and information communication, and hence the people and transport, that are required to manage the supply chain. The particular issues raised by international commodity sourcing, manufacture and distribution are covered fifth, since these are important and different from international chains for niche products. Sixthly, we focus on the reasons for international sourcing. Finally, a number of external issues, which have major impacts on transnational chains, are considered, including government, cultural and infrastructure issues.

4.1 STRATEGIC DRIVERS AND IMPLEMENTATION REQUIREMENTS

This section examines the strategic reasons for the development of international supply chains in general prior to focusing on important elements of strategy for a 'transnational commodity' supply chain.

As trade becomes more global, it is clear that global operations and supply chains are becoming increasingly significant. Compared to domestic supply chains, international chains can provide a wealth of additional opportunities if managed effectively. Four forces are driving the trend towards globalisation. First, global market forces comprise pressures created by foreign competitors and opportunities created by foreign customers. There is an increasing demand for products as a result of the Internet. The web provides the ability to purchase goods in one country that will be delivered in another without leaving your home. As Ohmae[2] points out, 'people have all become global citizens, and so must the companies that want to sell us things'.

The second force is the technology required by the products themselves. Various components and technologies are available in different regions of the world. To use these resources quickly, firms need to locate research, design and production facilities close to these regions. It is also useful to be close to suppliers so that they can help in the design process. The same logic applies to collaboration. It is useful to locate joint facilities close to one of the partners.

The third global force is cost, which often forces global location decisions. The low cost of unskilled labour has been a decisive factor in determining factory location. Studies have shown that, in many cases, the cost of unskilled labour was more than offset by the increase in other costs due to operating in a location remote from customers and headquarters. Now costs of skilled labour, such as computer programmers, and sources of materials are key determinants of location.

The fourth global force is political and economic. Such forces are caused by exchange rate fluctuations, regional trade agreements and trade protection mechanisms.

In response to these forces, even the largest global company needs to prepare for managing its global supply chains. Important implementation requirements are:

1. Products should be designed so that they can be modified easily for major markets and can be manufactured in various facilities. It is dangerous to have an 'average' product which will not suit any market. Rather, the companies need a base product which can be readily adapted to several markets.
2. In purchasing, it is advisable to have one central management team responsible for buying important materials from vendors around the world.
3. Manufacture should have excess capacity in place so that production can be shifted between different facilities as conditions warrant. Effective communication systems must be available so that central management knows the current status of factories, suppliers and inventory.
4. Demand management, which is often carried out regionally, also needs to be reviewed centrally.
5. Order fulfilment requires a centralised system to be in place so that regional customers can receive deliveries from the global supply chain just as efficiently as from local firms. The system will turn customers off if it is cumbersome and less than fully effective.

What is a transnational commodity supply chain? A chain is a transnational commodity (TC) if it has manufacture of finished goods and components in many countries and it sells to customers in most parts of the world. The commodity goods it makes are not customised and are generally price-driven because of the existence of competition. Figure 4.2 shows an example, the physical supply chain for shoes and their components.[3]

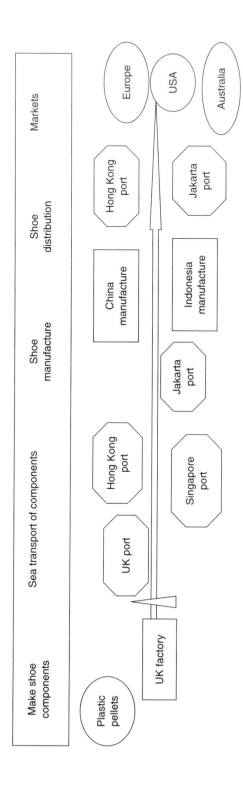

Figure 4.2 **Transnational commodity supply chain for shoes**[3]

(NB: 1 Figure simplifies distribution channel from manufacture to customers.
      2 Figure does not show the transport between each stage nor all the inventories (triangle shape) held.)

The strategy for a supply chain must address the key functions to source, manufacture and distribute products, knowing the requirements of all intended customers. Key functions vary between chains for different products involving different technologies, value densities and life cycles. The following generic functions, very appropriate to most TC supply chains, should be analysed in any study of such a chain:

- customer requirements,
- economic positioning of manufacture and assembly,
- information availability,
- management complexity,
- pipeline, and
- geographical location and transport.

Customer requirements

The first driving force for a transnational commodity supply chain is the needs of its end customers. The number of different products can be single digit for electronic goods and hundreds for clothing or footwear. The 'clockspeed' at which new products are designed and introduced, and new technologies are brought into service, is part of the customer requirements. Other areas are quality, delivery, features and price. Collectively, customer requirements provide the aim of the whole supply chain. Companies in the chain can inform, manipulate and excite customers but, in the end, they must win orders from them.

Economic positioning of manufacture and assembly

Competition between open economies drives some manufacture and assembly areas into low-wage countries. There has been a proliferation of manufacture of electronic components and clothing in countries such as Thailand, China and the Philippines. This prevails in the limited areas of manufacture in which direct labour is a significant cost of production or assembly. It may be done for many other reasons, such as dual sourcing of supply and moving away from restrictive labour practices.

Information availability

Information is the transaction end of the communications needed to manage the TC chain. It comprises the ability to move order information quickly and transparently up the supply chain so that production and pipeline inventories can stay very closely linked to customer demand. It includes the ability to develop new products among supply chain partners and quickly implement the inclusion of those products into all chain processes. When the chain extends across numerous countries, languages and time zones, this is a major undertaking. To have automated updates of products, while retaining the ability to review performance, is a complex information design goal.

Management complexity

The supply chain management task described in Chapters 1 and 2 becomes an order of magnitude more complex when many countries and languages are included. Management complexity may come from the following:

- The executive, who understands the TC supply chain, does not speak the language of local supervisors and operators.
- Each extra country of operation adds an extra set of laws and customs regarding product regulation, transport limitations, occupational health and many more areas.
- Limited knowledge of the operations of processes in other parts of the world adds uncertainty to decisions in one part of the international supply chain.
- Management establishes a factory in a low-wage country, partly due to local incentives to provide jobs there, and then finds that the available workers lack some of the skills required.

A likely retreat from these management complications is a command structure from headquarters of the focal chain company or an external marketing focus. Unfortunately, this retreat is the antithesis of supply chain management. Integration has been lost, as has the opportunity to manage the international chain using the knowledge available in all its parts.

Pipeline

Materials, parts and products in the pipeline to supply end customers are a vital strategic choice, affecting everything else. The pipeline is measured in terms of days of use of these inventories at current rates of sales. Normally international pipelines for commodities are many times longer than for single country supply chains. There are many reasons why pipelines should be short, especially customer responsiveness, cost and quality. This immediately creates a tension in TC chains.

There are also more *decoupling points** in TC chains, typically two or three. A customer order decoupling point is the point in the goods flow where forecast-driven production and customer order-driven production are separated. In other words, the decoupling point is the place at which products are designated to a particular customer. A domestic supply chain has the one decoupling point between actual orders received and parts made in anticipation of orders.[4] An international chain may have at least two more points:

1. One is at the point of assembly of goods. If this is a great distance from the market, production must anticipate real orders from the distribution decoupling point.
2. One is at the point of manufacture of components. Again time and distance from the assembly point may require manufacture in advance of good information about overseas assembly.

Geographical location and transport

The final strategic driver is geographical location and the transport between all the production locations and all the customer positions on the globe. Every extra location in the progression of materials and products towards the customer adds an overhead to the whole international supply chain. An example of this is clearly seen in the Shavers' European distribution strategy, the case in Chapter 1. The director of European logistics centralised Shavers' distribution into eight warehouses from the 13 operated previously. He did this while improving order cycle times and order fill levels.

The addition of ocean transport into the moves of commodity products along the supply chain adds strategic complexity. Freight forwarders and land and sea transport become necessary. This is discussed further in the next section.

4.2 CHALLENGES OF DISTANCE AND LOCATION

For many commodity products, supply chain companies deliver to customers in most parts of the globe to gain economies of scale and to spread the investment in new products. Even if manufacturing were carried out in one location, there would be complexity of distribution to each continent, each country and through each distributor to the retailers.

Extra challenges are added by multiple points of manufacture, distant sourcing of components and supply from the farm, mine or oil well. The importance of location of each supply chain stage varies between products. The practical solution is to define the chain according to its significant steps. This could lead to one or more 'Double-Bell' models. Recall that the Double-Bell model comprises all the suppliers that are important to the manufacture of the group of finished products, the point(s) of manufacture and the distribution stages to all end customers for those products.

Decoupling points may vary the Double-Bell model. The Shavers case (Chapter 1) asserts the primacy of distribution, the right-hand 'bell'. It suggests that, for personal care items, it is sufficient to design and operate the distribution network for a whole continent, given several manufacturing sites. The transnational commodity chain for shoes (Figure 4.2) is best represented as two Double-Bell models. The first is the manufacture of shoe components from leather and synthetic materials and their distribution to factories in Indonesia and China. The second is the manufacture of shoes from those components and their distribution throughout the world.

The leader at the front of this chapter shows two Double-Bell models. This is suggested as a typical representation of international supply chains for commodity items. There is no fixed reason for having two models. The extent of the supply chain depends upon the aims of the companies operating the chain and the number of decoupling points along it. This decoupling could be caused by a supplier having major interests in other goods so that it is not willing to cooperate with the interests of the particular product chain.

An important part of the challenge of distance is the government, language and culture of the people running the business in each location. This can affect supply chain planning and operation in a multitude of ways. For example, negotiations are required with local partners and governments in setting up transnational commodity international chains. This is an extra impost and makes it harder to change the chain at a later date. Communications between people with different languages is very difficult. You may argue that English is the international language of business and numbers are universal. However, it is unlikely that the operators of a shoe assembly line in Indonesia

Table 4.1   **Contrast in logistics support in different world regions**[6]

	First world	Emerging	Third world
Infrastructure	Highly developed	Being developed	Not sufficient to support advanced logistics
Supplier operating standards	High	Variable	Typically not considered
Information system availability	Available	Support systems not available	Not available
Human resources	Available	Available with some searching	Often difficult to find

speak English. Operators are the front line in understanding customer order schedules and reading descriptions of shoe component sizes and styles.

Shipment by sea is at the heart of TC supply chains because that adds minimum cost to the low-value components and goods moved around the globe.[5] The price for this low cost is a slow and somewhat erratic means of transport. A typical solution is to hold large stocks of products in the distribution centres. A more creative solution, which limits expensive inventory, is to ship most goods by sea and to use air transport to replace items that have unexpectedly run out. Provided good information is used, the air–sea freight combination is capable of reducing this problem. This dual means of transport was first used by car manufacturers between sister companies 20 years ago. Now, it is believed to be quite widespread among commodity supply chains.

Part of the challenge of location is the existence of great contrasts in infrastructure and information systems in different parts of the world. Research by Simchi-Levi and colleagues[6] divides the world into three main regions. Table 4.1 indicates the different levels of support that may be expected in each group of nations. First world refers to the developed nations of western Europe, the USA and Japan. Third world refers to countries in Africa, South America and Asia. Emerging includes Thailand, Brazil, Taiwan and Eastern Europe.

International distribution is much more complex than domestic distribution due to complicated documentation and the need to have multiple carriers according to destination and transport mode. Consequently, many companies use freight forwarders for low-volume or infrequent destinations. A freight forwarder is an agent who will hire a number of carriers to ship any quantity to any destination.

4.3 RISKS OF INTERNATIONAL SUPPLY CHAINS

The world is converging towards commodity products in many product areas, such as sports footwear, personal computers and televisions. This engenders a vast market for such products. Companies can realise economies of scale in marketing, production and distribution. However, the global supply chain brings some risks for its partners. These should be analysed and steps taken to minimise them.[7]

Foremost among the risks is movements in foreign exchange rates between the countries in which various parts of the chain operate. There can be an increase in the value of currency in the countries where the components are sourced or goods are manufactured. Customer reaction or competition in the country of sale may not permit prices to be raised to recoup the change in operating costs.

There is a risk that sub-contracting manufacture to a company in another country may create future competitors. For example, in Japan Toshiba manufactured copiers for 3M, but now Toshiba is a major supplier under its own brand name. Similar dangers exist with foreign governments. Some of the expertise given to Chinese partners has enabled them to set up in competition with the original owner.

Governments also pose a threat to global supply chains because of local protectionism. For example, in 1986 Taiwan had a $16 billion trade surplus with the USA as a result of products manufactured by local subsidiaries of US companies such as GE and IBM. The US government imposed trade restrictions on Taiwanese products. Taiwan was forced to increase the value of its currency and this removed the cost advantage of manufacture in Taiwan.

There are health and hostility threats that require trade routes to be altered and prevent managers from visiting certain areas. Recently, we have seen the SARS crisis, the Gulf Wars and many smaller geopolitical upsets. There are also transport breakdowns due to strikes and extreme weather that can cripple movement for weeks or months in particular areas. All these risks underline the need for managers to think carefully in advance about the kind of risks to which their supply chains are exposed and prepare contingency plans which can be quickly activated. Techniques which can remove uncertainty from an international supply chain include total quality management, business process engineering and Six Sigma.[7]

4.4 ORGANISATION AND INFORMATION FOR COMMODITY SUPPLY CHAINS

Imagine you are responsible for redesigning an international supply chain for men's and women's shoes. Leather is made from skins, then leather and synthetic materials are made into components which are assembled in a number of countries into a wide variety of shoes. The finished shoes are distributed throughout the world. In undertaking this redesign, you analyse the organisational aspects and the provision of information at the points where decisions are made.

Organisation

Organisation comprises the extent of management at each point in the supply chain, the leadership exercised in each company and the decisions taken. Management is generally considered to comprise planning, organising, operating and controlling, or improving. Leadership in an international supply chain may be exercised by a focal company or by several companies, perhaps one for each decoupled part of the chain. For example, a powerful manufacturer of leather components might lead inbound logistics to the shoe manufacturer, while a powerful marketer leads and controls the distribution of finished shoes to world-wide customers.

A key organisational issue is the balance chosen between local autonomy and centralised control. Centralised control can take advantage of some of the strategies

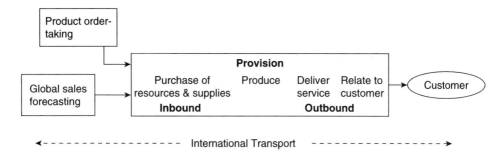

Figure 4.3   **Overall functions in part of a TC supply chains**

outlined in section 4.1, but in many cases local autonomy makes sense. Sometimes local managers may be tempted to follow local conventional wisdom, but may be missing opportunities derived from knowledge of the global supply chain. For example, when Smith Kline Corporation wanted to release a new decongestant 'Contac 600' in Japan, it was advised to use 1,000 distributors in line with local practice. This would have given little contact between Smith Kline and the individual distributor. Instead it chose 35 wholesalers, remained in close contact with all of them and was very successful with this new product. This is a good example of achieving global coordination but ensuring products suit local markets by devolving control to local operations managers.

There are a large number of potential organisational issues and the most important ones will vary according to the type of supply chain. Recall the key functions in an integrated supply chain. Figure 4.3 catalogues the critical functions which apply to each decoupled part of an international supply chain. Some of the organisational issues, which have been found to be important, are:[1]

- The strategic positioning of management relative to major stages in the supply chain. For example, if the purchase of the correct grades of steel, leather or plastic sheet is important, decisions and control should be made at a receiving warehouse near to the location of suppliers.
- Central planning of product movement and inventories along the distribution channel. Shavers' experience in Europe showed that such planning can both reduce inventories and distribution costs while improving service levels, such as the order fill rate.
- Conversely, local finished goods inventories of commodity items should be managed by the supervisors of the distribution centre or transport point at which bulk loads of products are split into deliveries to customers.
- The management of flows according to the Pareto principle, in which different styles of management are used for fast- and slow-moving products.
- Focused factories and warehouses, whose managers have total responsibility for resources and the provision of goods within their section of the product range.

Information communication

Many of the above organisational issues are strongly impacted by the information moved to places at which decisions are made. Some of the general restrictions, such as the need for central planning of product distribution, can be overcome if sufficient correct data are provided to local planning and execution points. Hence the proliferation of functions at the headquarters of the focal company can be reduced unless each provides a benefit to customers or chain profitability.

There are a large number of potential information communication issues and the most important ones will vary according to the type of supply chain. Recall our classification of information in an integrated supply chain, reproduced here as Figure 4.4 and containing some pieces of information for each major stage in an international supply chain. Some key information communication issues are:

- product orders should only be forecast once, or once per decoupled part of the chain,
- provision and supply upstream should be dependent on finished goods required,
- preparation and communication of export documents such as bills of lading, licences, credits and insurance,
- planning and implementation of the information communication systems used for parts,
- inventory levels and unitisation (batch) sizes,
- separate management of different material and product streams according to volume, value and substitutability,
- point of final packing,
- radio frequency identification and its use, and
- services provided alongside products.

We adapt Chopra and Meindl's model[8] into five basic supply chain stages (see Figure 4.4) and four decision phases. The five stages contain the following information for one 'decoupled' part of the supply chain:

- Supplier information. The materials and components available for purchase, their stock availability, lead-times and prices. International purchase order status and supplier performance analysis.
- Manufacturing information. Data such as the product range available from factories in particular countries, in what batch sizes and lead-times at what cost and what location. Cost of fast supply.
- Distribution information. For a varied set of middlemen and forwarders, what is to be transported, to what distribution centre, by what mode, at what price? How important are the delivery times and how much buffer stock should be held?
- Retail information. Similar to distribution, but more local and detailed involving items such as packaging, promotions and local features or preferences.
- Demand information. Who is buying what products, at what price, where and what quantity for each country and culture? Forecasts of future product types and demand.
- Orders and long-term trends for existing and new products.

We argue that the same four decision phases, planning, execution, 'inter-company' and strategic analysis used for domestic supply chains apply to TC chains. The extra complication of different governments, cultures and languages is introduced in section 4.6. The planning phase involves medium-term plans, for a period from a month to a year, for capacity, inventory, deliveries and budgeted cost. The *execution** phase records

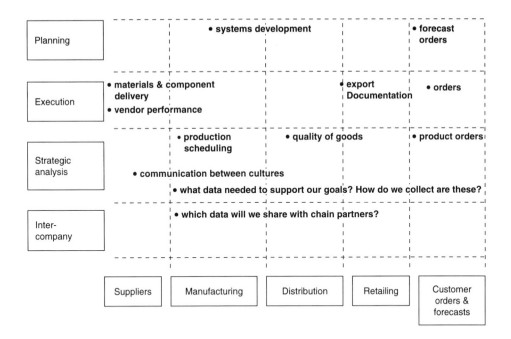

Figure 4.4   **An international information framework**[8]

transactions with short time frames through material and product flow and the myriad controls imposed by ports, customs and banks. Strategic analysis is the complex and confidential (between partners) use of information from other phases to model future situations and hence support strategic decisions. *Inter-company* is the permission to move information between separate firms which are situated in different countries where managers speak different languages.

This section provides concepts to analyse the organisational control and information communication of international supply chains to improve the strategies of individual chains. For further consideration, refer to the case 'Shoes go global' (pp. 115–22) and Chapter 5.

4.5 INTERNATIONAL SOURCING

A major factor in international logistics is the dramatic increase in international sourcing of components and products from low-cost countries such as China, Thailand and Malaysia. A corresponding effect in services is seen in India, which provides software and call-centre services to western countries. This section explores the reasons behind such international sourcing and establishes some guidelines for choosing which components are most appropriate to source overseas.

The primary reason for overseas sourcing is to reduce the cost of wages in manufacturing. This particularly applies to goods like clothing and footwear and functions such as assembly, where there remains a strong manual involvement. Firms adopting this strategy frequently fail to assess the wider logistical implications of such a move, which may outweigh the manufacturing cost effect. Secondly, having suppliers in low-cost countries increases the competitive pressure on domestic suppliers. Thirdly, placing

Table 4.2   **Overseas sourcing guidelines**

Criteria	Domestic sourcing	Overseas sourcing
Product life-cycle length	Short	Long
Product variations	Many	Few
Labour content	Low	High
Intellectual property	High	Low
Transport cost	High	Low
Product value per volume	High	Low
Import constraints	High	Low
Transport uncertainty	High	Low
Supply lead-time	Low	High

Source: *Supply Chain Logistics Management*, 2006, by Bowersox DJ, Closs DJ and Cooper MB, reproduced with permission of The Mc Graw-Hill Companies.

component business in a low-cost country may be a way of establishing a local presence which allows sales of finished products. For example, the US and Japanese automobile industries source components from China and Thailand and they sell cars in those countries.

Table 4.2 lists sourcing criteria which have implications for the decision to source a component overseas rather than in the domestic country. A high or a low score on each criterion influences the decision between local and overseas sourcing. There is no simple answer on which components and products should be purchased in each way. An analysis of the total effect of the decision on the firm and its supply chain is needed to make an informed choice.

4.6 EXTERNAL PRESSURES

External pressures refer to impacts on transnational commodity supply chains from outside the industries directly involved in each constituent country. A separate book could be written about this area! The treatment here introduces some of the key pressures exerted by cultures, languages, governments and the extent of national development.[9]

A good first example of external pressure on a supply chain is that exerted by people's choice of colours in clothing. Different cultures have different colour preferences and dislikes. Some of these are fixed, like the Buddhist need for saffron robes, others change slowly, like western businessmen's colours of shirts. Still others change in response to fashion, in which the current colours and styles reflect both internal and external pressures.

A different example is the restrictions placed on shipping meats, such as pork, between countries. Pork is a very contentious meat because, first, most of the world's Muslims do not eat any pig meat. Secondly, the world's pigs are very prone to disease, which spreads very quickly when they are kept in confined pens. The country which produces the most pork, China, exports none due to domestic consumption and lack of export clearance. A country, such as Australia, which has a low level of pig disease, places heavy restrictions on imports from other countries. Currently, Denmark and Canada are the only two countries allowed to sell pork meat to Australia and this has only been allowed for four years.

Government

Governments place a whole range of restrictive practices on international supply chains, for example tariff barriers, security regulations, customer regulations, currency restrictions or specification of product standards. Dealing with these restrictions not only causes additional cost but also can cause significant delays to product movements.

Culture, beliefs and language

Cultural differences can strongly affect the way international subsidiaries interpret the goals and instructions of the global enterprise. Beliefs, values, customs and language are very different between western, Asian and Latin American countries. Language is much more than just the spoken word: it includes expressions, gestures and the context required to make sense of the words. Language has a strong effect wherever information must be transmitted across borders. Examples are packaging, information booklets and export documents.[10]

Beliefs or specific values vary widely from culture to culture. For example, America and Germany value 'efficiency' in ways that some cultures do not. People in some cultures, that have less exposure to western materialistic business precepts, may have a less serious attitude to a late delivery. Customs vary greatly from one country to another. Care must be taken not to offend local customs, such as serving particular meats and planning work during festivals. Festivals and holidays place limits on supply chains for some products in most countries.

Recent investigations by Huang and colleagues looked at the importance of intercultural competence in British import/export managers dealing with Chinese companies.[11] Huang et al. believe that intercultural business competence comprises relational competence, conflict resolution competence and commercial competence. Their studies showed that effective overseas outsourcing requires employees to develop intercultural competence. In the early stages of a business relationship managers see intercultural business competence as very important. However, mature business relationships are associated with strong skills in conflict resolution, so all staff need to be informed of the Chinese way of dealing with conflict.

Level of development

Building on the differences in infrastructure found in different world regions, the level of development typically found in each region can be contrasted as follows. In first-world countries, infrastructure is highly developed. Highways, ports, communications and information systems are all up to modern standards.

In emerging nations, supply chain infrastructure is not fully in place. These nations have national transport policies in place but the focus of infrastructure may be solely on exports, not helping imports (e.g. China).

In the third world, infrastructure is generally insufficient to support advanced logistics operations. Roads are in poor shape, warehousing is not available and distribution systems are non-existent. Specific decisions must be considered carefully in case things taken for granted in western countries do not exist.

Summary

This chapter examines the international dimension of supply chains from strategic decision-making and operational points of view. The international dimension may enter from the locations of customers, manufacturers or suppliers. In the widest sense, supply chains are global, with significant presence in different countries and continents at various stages of manufacture and distribution. This international dimension is an enormous complication which adds complexity of time, culture, language, nationality and distance. Nations are classified into first world, emerging and third world with some general implications for the supply chain. Transport and information become more complicated as does the management of the global supply chain.

The key driver for global supply chains is the enormous market available for commodity products throughout the world. Other drivers are low costs of production in certain countries, which leads to international sourcing, and the need to set up operations in a country to gain sales access to its population. Such potential gains bring risks in terms of foreign exchange exposure and the danger of copying of proprietary knowledge.

The chapter focuses on one type of supply chain, called 'transnational commodity', which has the manufacture of finished products carried out in several countries, suppliers of materials and components residing in many global locations and customers located in many parts of the world. An example is the footwear supply chain case at the end of this chapter. A number of tools are provided to analyse such chains: How healthy are the key functions? How appropriate are the organisational and information structures? Which components are best sourced overseas? And can the chain stand up to foreseeable risks?

Questions

1. What are the main differences between international supply chains and those imited to one country or continent?
2. Give an example of a 'transnational commodity' supply chain. Describe its main features.
3. How is information communication different in international supply chains from domestic chains?
4. By means of an example, discuss the impact of culture, language, nationality and government policies on an international chain.

Case: Shoes go global[3]

Texon International plc is one of the world's leading suppliers of shoe-making materials. At the Texon executive committee meeting, Peter Halliday, the Export Director said:

Our export business to East Asia is progressively being threatened by the growth of global shoe 'specifiers', such as Nike and Adidas. Our shoe components, made in Britain, are world-class in quality and cost ex-factory. By the time they have been shipped to the shoe manufacturers in several East Asian countries, they are late and expensive. Adidas is exerting pressure on us to establish factories in these countries, close to the shoe assemblers. This poses problems of capital cost, ability to operate to our required standards and uneconomic loads.

I want your permission to investigate the supply chain in depth. I believe there will be many areas which could make significant improvements in the distribution from Britain to the Asian countries.

Peter Halliday was given the go-ahead to establish a supply chain project to research and improve all the functions which contributed to some aspect of the international supply chain. How had this problem arisen?

International supply chain context

For 20 years there has been a steady drift of manufacturing activity to the low labour cost areas of the world such as South East Asia. The main driving forces for this drift are the development of global markets, global cost forces, technological changes, as well as political and macro-economic influences. This movement has created complex global supply chains for both the distribution of finished products from South East Asia to Europe and North America, and for the inbound supply of raw materials and components into South East Asia from the west.

Over the same period there has been significant globalisation in the shoe industry led by Nike, Adidas and Reebok in the sports shoe market. Globalisation has occurred in terms of branding, marketing and manufacturing. These large brand-name companies are referred to as 'specifiers' because they specify design. They do not own manufacturing facilities but employ a range of sub-contractor manufacturers who may be based anywhere in the world. Because shoe manufacturing is labour-intensive, the specifiers have looked to the low labour cost areas of East and South East Asia to assemble their shoes.

There are four important parameters to consider in an international supply chain:

- physical product flow through manufacturing, warehousing, transport and distribution,
- information systems for planning, order-processing and scheduling,
- organisation and management control structures of the supply chain, and
- production and communication of the documentation necessary for international shipments and the payment transactions required.

The Texon supply chain

Peter Halliday's task was to evaluate and improve the supply chain for products supplied from one of Texon's UK factories to shoe manufacturers in China, Indonesia and Vietnam

(Continued)

(Continued)

and thereafter shipped to a brand leader in the world sports shoe market. Texon International plc has headquarters in Leicester, the heart of Britain's traditional shoe manufacturing region. As a leading supplier of the components required in shoe making, its products comprise linings, insoles, adhesives and fastenings. From main manufacturing plants in the UK, Germany and the USA, Texon's products are supplied to shoe assemblers all over the world with an increasing proportion of them in South East Asia and China.

Texon's current supply chain suffered from problems with inventory, variability of orders, and a long cycle time from orders placed until fulfilled. Total inventory at various places from Texon's factory in England to the shoe assemblers amounted to 3.5 months of sales. Orders varied by a factor of six times, with major changes from week to week. A typical cycle time for processing and transport was 52 days, nearly two months.

Supply chain mapping

The starting point for the project was the establishment of a supply chain project team, comprising four Texon staff drawn from sales, logistics, information technology and operations management. Peter Halliday, the Export Director, had ultimate responsibility for generating sales in the Asian countries. He had many years of experience at Texon. Mike Murray, the Logistics Planning Manager, was responsible for scheduling production and contracting transport and warehousing for the entire journey required. As the Information Technology Manager, Liz Newby looked after systems for scheduling and control and for producing the complex documentation required to permit the movement of products between various countries and obtain payment. Finally, Daniel O'Donnell supervised production at the Texon factory in the North of England which made the plastic coils used in shoe manufacture. Advising the project team was David Taylor, a senior researcher from the Lean Enterprise Research Centre at Cardiff University.

David's task was to train team members in the 'Five Lean Principles' (see Figure C4.1) set out in *Lean Thinking*[12] and help them to apply the value stream management (VSM) technique to Texon's exports. The 'lean' approach aims to remove waste to achieve better customer satisfaction in terms of quality, cost and delivery, and to help suppliers to respond more flexibly to rapidly changing customer needs. VSM analyses individual products to specific customers. This was the first time that VSM had been applied to a supply system which extended some 10,000 miles across the globe.

Derive the current state map

The first step in VSM, identifying all the steps and times taken and inventory held, is known as a 'current state map'. The first draft of this map was therefore constructed in the UK from the knowledge of the team backed by telephone calls and emails to people along the supply chain to fill in data gaps or to verify the team's perceptions. The team chose the product 'T26', a coil of shoe lining specified by Adidas in the production of various ranges of sports shoe because it was the biggest single export product. T26 was a synthetic shoe lining material manufactured in Texon's UK Teeside factory and produced in coils one metre wide and 100 metres in length. Texon's output was split between China taking 54% with 16 manufacturers, Indonesia 22% with 10 manufacturers, and with Vietnam and Thailand taking the balance.

Figure C4.2 shows a simplified structure of the international material flow system.

(Continued)

The five principles which are fundamental to the elimination of waste:

- SPECIFY what does and does not create VALUE from the customer's perspective and not from the perspective of individual firms, functions and departments.
- IDENTIFY all the steps necessary to design, order and produce the product across the whole VALUE STREAM to highlight non-value-adding waste.
- MAKE those actions that create VALUE FLOW without interruption, detours, backflows, waiting or scrap.
- ONLY MAKE WHAT IS PULLED by the customer just-in-time.
- STRIVE FOR PERFECTION by continually removing successive layers of waste as they are uncovered.

Figure C4.1   **The five principles of lean thinking**

Team members examined product flows first, and then information flows. The T26 product was manufactured exclusively in the UK Teeside factory. A batch production system was operated with varying batch sizes. Mapping the production processes showed a six-day production lead-time of which three hours was value-adding time, for which the customer would be prepared to pay.

Sea freight of T26 involved Texon contracting Cheverton Freight, a UK freight forwarder, who collected the product by truck from Teeside and moved it to their warehouse adjacent to the port of Felixstowe in southeast England. There T26 would be consolidated with other products to make up full container loads and moved through the port on to a vessel. The time from collection at the Teeside factory to the boat sailing was typically seven or eight days.

All Texon product destined for South East Asia was then shipped to Singapore, a scheduled 17-day sea passage. In Singapore, Texon sub-contracted warehouse space from Nostra, a third-party warehouse operator. Approximately three weeks of stock was kept in Singapore across the whole range of Texon products, but in regard to specific products, including T26, the amounts varied from nil to 12 weeks. Nostra were responsible for managing stocks and picking and despatching orders for South East Asia and East Asian customers. Onward transport to regional manufacturers was again by sea. The Singapore freight agent collected product from the Nostra warehouse, arranging port clearance and booking sea freight. Normally product destined for China was shipped to Hong Kong as the port of entry and for Indonesia to Jakarta. At each port a local freight agent was employed to arrange port and customs clearance. The final leg of the journey was in most cases organised by the Texon port agents. Then local shoe manufacturers, Texon's customers, took possession and collected their product from the port, triggering invoicing. The time line at the bottom of Figure C4.2 shows the overall time components spent in inventory was 50 days, over seven weeks.

Figure C4.3 shows the information system structures that Liz Newby, the Information Technology Manager, had mapped. Five echelons were involved in transmitting demand information from the ultimate customer Adidas to the Texon manufacturing plant. Adidas

(Continued)

(Continued)

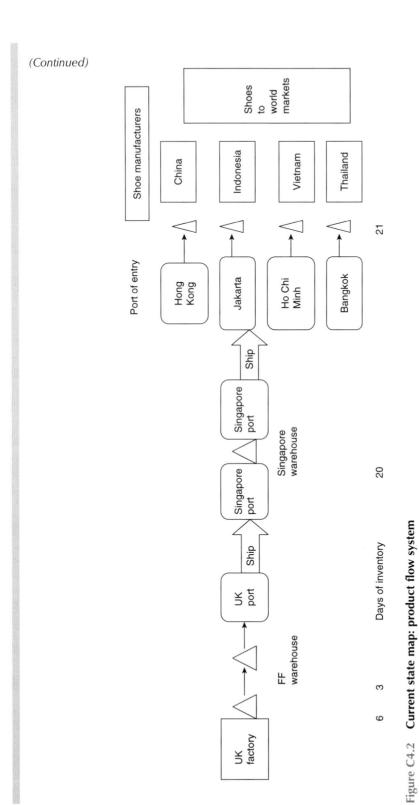

Figure C4.2   **Current state map: product flow system**

(Continued)

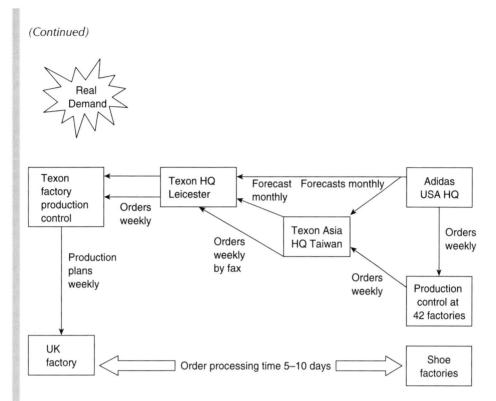

Figure C4.3   **Information flows in the current state**

headquarters in Seattle generated forecasts and orders in terms of the number and type of shoes required. The 42 manufacturing companies each had their own planning and purchasing departments that would generate orders for the T26 shoe material based on Adidas demand, together with their internal production planning, inventory management and purchasing policies. Texon had a South East Asia regional sales headquarters in Taiwan which took orders from the manufacturers and placed an amalgamated order and forecast on Texon UK sales office at the Leicester headquarters. The UK sales office reviewed the situation and placed weekly orders with the UK factory in Teeside. In total, the time to transmit orders from the Asian manufacturers to the UK factory was a frightening 5–10 days because of batching of information handling processes at Texon's Taiwan and Leicester offices.

Once the current state map of product and information flows had been developed, Mike Murray, the Logistics Planning Manager, was dispatched internationally to follow the processes and check on what happened in practice.

Issues uncovered

The team members responsible wrote up the issues uncovered by the VSM project for Peter under the four international supply chain parameters.

(Continued)

(Continued)

Mike found that the key issues in the physical flow of products were:

- There were large amounts of stock in the system, 50 days average demand, but much of the stock was a long way from the customer. It was unable to help service levels to the customer.
- There were many non-value-adding steps in the chain. For example, the warehouses at the factory, at the UK freight agent and in Singapore all added cost, interrupted the flow of product from factory to customer and did little to add value.
- Why was the majority of product destined for China trans-shipped through Singapore when there were direct shipping services from the UK to Hong Kong?

Mike's favourite anecdote concerned a directive from Texon head office to field warehouses in South East Asia to reduce stock. One warehouse manager had hit this target by delaying the call-in of product into his warehouse after ships had docked at the local port. Inventory in the port incurred high demurrage charges, but these were hidden in an overhead charged to head office rather than to his warehouse. The local manager had met his targets but at greater overall cost to the firm.

Liz Newby identified the following problems in relation to demand information management systems:

- There was a lack of a systematic and coherent basis for forecasting and activity planning. Three sets of forecasts were produced by Adidas HQ, Texon Asia headquarters and the Texon HQ in Leicester. A graph of the last 20 months shows that these forecasts did not correlate with each other and, worse, that none of them was a good predictor of eventual demand.
- There were many points at which demand or forecast volumes could be altered, thus creating demand amplification in which small changes of orders at source are exaggerated when they pass through multiple hands.
- The result of demand amplification was highly variable demand on the Texon factory, which in turn created difficulties for purchasing, resource planning, production planning and stock control.
- There was no single individual or even department responsible for managing the complete supply chain.

Mike Murray studied in detail the planning and control of the movement of product along this chain. His analysis, using Figure C4.2, indicated that many organisations and individuals were required to control product movement and no one person, function or company had control of the whole supply chain. The Texon Logistics Department at Leicester HQ had the widest span, but even it covered only half the chain, from the output from the Teeside factory to the Singapore freight forwarder.

Liz also investigated the three categories of documentation required to operate the supply chain:

- documents relating to international transport such as bills of lading,
- documents relating to customs clearance such as certificates of origin, and
- export licences and international payment such as letters of credit.

Various departments and companies along the chain had responsibility for producing or processing these documents and frequently delays or mistakes held up the physical movement of product.

(Continued)

Overall, the result was a long pipeline lead-time (52 days), high inventory holding (50 days or more) and poor customer service (73% of orders delivered on time).

Future operations

With this detailed knowledge of the current situation, Peter Halliday and his team next proceeded to consider the improvements that could be achieved in the following year using these lean principles:[12]

- To create stability and regularity in production and transport processes.
- To compress the time from order placement to receipt of goods by the customer.
- To reduce demand amplification effects along the chain in order to more closely link the amount produced to customer demand, developing a 'pull' system.
- To respond to real changes in customer demand and requirements in this 10,000 mile chain.
- To reduce the amount of inventory in the system and for the remaining inventory to be in the best place in the supply chain to support the customer.

Daniel O'Donnell, the production supervisor, suggested that they should smooth weekly production volume to the average of 40,000 m². Production could be achieved by devoting the first 11 shifts in the week from Sunday afternoon to Wednesday midday to T26. This established a rhythm to pump product into the international pipeline at the rate of average demand. A flow system was developed in the factory so the product moved from one process to the next without any delays or inventory. At the end of the line, product was loaded direct to a shipping container.

The weekly output of 40,000m² filled two TEU (twenty-foot equivalent) containers. These were transported directly to the UK port, eliminating the non-value-adding steps of warehousing at the factory and the freight forwarder's depot. Since half the demand came from China, one container per week was shipped direct from Felixstowe to Hong Kong, using the regular UK to Hong Kong shipping services. To serve the other markets of Indonesia, Vietnam and Thailand, the second full container load was dispatched each week to Singapore where it was deconsolidated and trans-shipped to those countries. The third-party warehouse in Singapore was replaced by a literal 'cross-docking' operation.

Safety stocks were established at the local ports of entry managed by local freight agents. For example, two containers (40,000 m²) of stock were located in Hong Kong. This represented three standard deviations of demand as a first measure to develop local confidence as the new system was being introduced.

The total amount of stock under the ownership and control of Texon was reduced from 29 days to 14 days. More importantly, the stock that remained was held at the ports of entry and hence close to the customer, thus enabling Texon to quickly respond to the variability in demand from the manufacturers. In consequence, service levels on T26 increased from 73% to 99% on-time-in-full.

The only forecasts used were medium-term forecasts of shoe sales obtained directly from Adidas HQ which were used as a basis for capacity planning at the factory.

The overall results of the introduction of lean improvements to the international supply chain are summarised in Table C4.1. Total pipeline time was reduced by approximately one-third from 95 days to 64 days. At the same time service levels to the South East Asian manufacturers were greatly increased from less than 90% to over 99% on-time-in-full.

(Continued)

(Continued)

Table C4.1 **Time summary**

	Original System	New System
Processing plus transport via Hong Kong	Not applicable	35 days
Processing plus transport via Singapore	52 days	36 days
Inventory owned by Texon	29 days	14 days
Inventory owned by shoe manufacturers	14 days	14 days
Total Pipeline Time	**95 days**	**64 days**

Conclusion

Internally, responsibility for the whole process was assigned to the Value Stream (i.e. supply chain) team and its leader, Peter Halliday. The Chief Executive of Texon issued a company-wide statement authorising the plan and explaining its logic and benefits. Externally, control of international transport operations was greatly simplified. The UK freight agent was given complete responsibility to organise product flow from the end of the factory production line to the collection of stock by manufacturers at the ports of entry.

As a result of this work, the delivery of the product T26 has increased to 99%. Texon had made savings in costs of production, transport and inventory.

Global supply chains are inherently costly and inefficient. Not only do they incur high direct costs, but they also tie up inventory in the transportation pipeline and require significant safety stocks to protect against the variability of international sea transport. From a lean supply chain point of view, the geographical separation of component manufacture, original equipment manufacture and markets should be questioned. It may be possible to relocate production facilities.

However, in practice many global chains do and will continue to exist either because no chain member is powerful enough to insist on relocation or because flow volumes between partners are insufficient to justify the establishment of local facilities.

Case questions

1. Why are international supply chains more complex than local supply chains?
2. List the organisations, and explain the parts they play, in a global supply chain.
3. What types of improvement can be made in international supply chains?
4. Under what conditions is supply from a distance likely to be economic?

REFERENCES

1 Van Hoek R, Chatman R and Wilding R (2002) 'Managers in supply chain management: the critical dimension', *Supply Chain Management: An International Journal*, 7(3&4): 119–25.
2 Ohmae K (2005) *The Next Global Stage*, Pearson Education, Upper Saddle River, NJ. Page 22. Copyright 2005 by Pearson Education, Inc. Publishing as Wharton School Publishing, Upper Saddle River, NJ 07458.

3   Taylor D (2000) 'The application of lean principles to the improvement of global supply chains', in H Katayama (ed.), *Global Logistics for the New Millennium*, Proceedings of the Fifth International Symposium on Logistics, Iwate, Japan, pp. 613–20.

4   Wikner J and Rudberg M (2005) 'Introducing a customer-order decoupling zone in logistics decision-making', *International Journal of Logistics: Research and Applications*, 8(3): 211–24.

5   Lirn T-C, Thanopoulou HA and Beresford AKC (2003) 'Transhipment port selection and decision-making behaviour: analysing the Taiwanese case', *International Journal of Logistics: Research and Applications*, 6(4): 229–44.

6   Simchi-Levi D, Kaminsky P and Simchi-Levi E (2004) *Managing the Supply Chain*, McGraw-Hill, New York.

7   Peck H (2002) 'Reconciling supply chain vulnerability, risk and supply chain management', *International Journal of Logistics: Research and Applications*, 9(2): 127–42.

8   Chopra S and Meindl P (2004) *Supply Chain Management* (2nd edn), Prentice-Hall, Englewood Cliffs NJ.

9   Bowersox DJ, Closs DJ and Cooper MB (2006) *Supply Chain Logistics Management*. McGraw-Hill, Boston, p. 295.

10 Luo WP, van Hoek RI and Roos HH (2001) 'Cross-cultural logistics research: a literature review and propositions', *International Journal of Logistics: Research and Applications*, 4(1): 57–78.

11 Huang Y, Rayner C and Zhueng L (2003) 'Does intercultural competence matter in intercultural business development?', *International Journal of Logistics: Research and Applications*, 6(4): 278–88.

12 Womack JP and Jones DT (1996) *Lean Thinking*, Simon and Schuster, New York.

13 Jones D and Womack J (2002) *Seeing the Whole: Mapping the Extended Value Stream*, Lean Enterprise Institute, Brookline, MA.

Information Communication

5

INTRODUCTION

A separate chapter is devoted to information because the current environment provides wide-ranging communications networks to transfer electronic information instantaneously with minimal effort. But this information is only as good as the overall system in which it is placed. Hence this chapter takes a systemic approach to all the information required to operate both a company and a supply chain. The underlying discipline is *information communication systems** (ICS). Rather than talk about technology, managers and operators *must* understand the system which is handling their information and speeding it around the world. A number of tools for analysing the information required to manage supply chains are introduced. Analyses suggested include a framework for information and many individual modules within planning and execution systems. All the analysis is qualitative, inviting the reader to compare systems in his or her supply chain with the components and outcomes delineated.

The first section explains the importance of effective information flow to the place where it is needed to make a decision. Three sections look at information for single links. Section 5.2 describes the basic information in one company. Section 5.3 examines the arrangement of all the electronic information relevant to logistics within the company's enterprise resource planning (ERP) system. The main logistics sub-systems in an ERP system are covered in section 5.4, separated into planning systems and execution systems. Section 5.5 examines the ways supply chains use electronic communications. The last section considers the means of implementing and developing these complex systems. The case at the end of the chapter examines how a company developed an information-supported supply chain. The part that information communication plays in the strategic planning of chains is covered in Chapter 8.

5.1 IMPORTANCE OF INFORMATION FLOW

At its simplest, information flow can be seen as the *driver for material flow*, starting with the end consumer and working up the supply chain. A variety of information systems and communication technologies are employed to move information along the chain.

But how is this logistics information arranged into a system? *A logistics information system** (LIS) is *the involvement of people, equipment and procedures to gather, sort, analyse, evaluate and then distribute information to the appropriate decision-makers in a timely and accurate manner so that they can make quality logistics decisions.* Note the involvement of *people* in the LIS definition. Information should be gathered by individuals and used by others for supervision and decision-making. Having the right information system does not remove the need for logistics managers to generate extra information to run the supply chain. For example, in the case 'Serving motorists'(see pages 90–7), Tony looks after the service station products and Combined Fuel's scheduling himself, in addition to using data available in the information systems.

Logistics managers need to manage information rather than to be steam-rolled by the most recent computer system. This frequently means the use of direct, immediate information, such as a *kanban* card or a phone call, rather than a complex computerised planning system. Managing information is important partly because it must be accurate. The more information communication is automated and the less the automated data is scrutinised by people, the greater the danger that inaccuracies will creep in and magnify. Operators and managers need to know that their information is accurate, or to know the limits to its accuracy. For example, it is very difficult to keep the stock levels correct in a distribution centre which contains 20,000 stock-keeping units (sku). Some warehouses have only 30% of computer records of products within acceptable tolerance of the actual stock in the bin.

We recognise three levels of information. The first level is *data*, a collection of facts about the company's orders or inventory. The second level is *information*, a valid summary of the data which can be used to make a judgement. Such summarised information is communicated to the place where it is needed for management action. The third level is *knowledge*, the ability of the companies in the chain to remember the ways of dealing with complex situations. Some managers take the view that knowledge can be distilled from information collected while running businesses of supply chains. Others consider that quite separate efforts are needed to collect strategic information, which must be known to make effective decisions on the future direction that supply chains should take.

The information system encompasses gathering, communicating and decision-making infrastructure. The *communications system** moves data and information up the supply chain, both within and between links, so that it is quickly available to operators, schedulers and managers. Thus there is a complex interplay between operations, generation of information and analysis of information that leads to physical action. Too much information can be as much of a burden as too little. However, managers must ensure that the LIS yields timely, accurate information that can be used to make effective decisions. This can be considered *active information**.

Decision-making is the purpose and outcome of information, particularly summarised information, in most information systems. Section 5.4 examines decisions to order materials, to schedule production and so on, which can be confidently made with the help of the information gathered together.

Functions of the logistics information system

Six main functions of the LIS are listed with examples:

1. Transactions accomplished: moving data around to identify the status of the physical system and customer orders. Transactions record individual elements of business processes carried out, such as allocating inventory to a particular customer order.
2. Product and order status information for customers: for example, a person is shipping a coffee table from York, in Britain, to Melbourne, Australia. During the shipment they want to know where the coffee table is located and when it is expected to reach its destination.
3. Status summaries for management control of the provision and movements of goods: for example, the supervisor at Bradley (case in Chapter 2, see pages 62–8) wants to know whether all the scheduled conversion of trimmings into sausage on this shift has been completed satisfactorily.
4. Summarised information for management decisions: a transport manager at Bradley uses summaries of transport usage this week and expected deliveries next week to decide how many refrigerated trucks he or she will need next week.
5. Providing data and summaries for other links in supply chains.
6. Information for performance measurement and for government requirements.

An example: the bull–whip effect

The bull-whip effect is an illuminating example of the great importance of information flow to supply chains. Small variations in the retail sales of products become larger variations of distributors' orders on the factory and enormous swings in manufacturer's orders on suppliers. This increase in variation in demand is known as the bull-whip effect, since it is similar to the increasing amplitude of cycles in a bull whip when it is moved at one end. This effect is widely observed in food supply chains. The term was coined by executives of Proctor and Gamble who observed that, even though the consumer demand of nappies was fairly stable, the retailers' orders were highly variable and production orders even more so.[1] Four causes of the bull-whip effect have been identified: links updating their forecasts independently, order batching, price fluctuations and inflated orders during periods of rationing.[2]

The simplest solution to this effect is to share the retail sales information with each link back up the supply chain. When partners further up the chain can see the steady

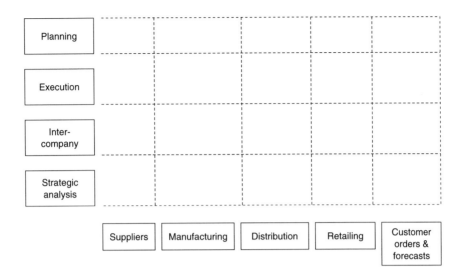

Figure 5.1   **A supply chain information framework**

demand by end consumers, the tendency to generate safety stock against feared future increases diminishes significantly.

Management and leadership of supply chain information

Building on the 'Double-Bell' model of a supply chain (see Figure 1.6, page 10), the information framework (see Figure 5.1) is proposed to analyse whether sufficient information is available across the whole supply chain. This information framework contains five basic supply chain stages and four decision phases. The five stages should be populated with the following information:

- *Supplier information.* The products available for purchase, their stock availability, lead-times and prices. Purchase order status and supplier performance analysis.
- *Manufacturing information.* The products available for manufacture, in what batch sizes and lead-times at what cost and what location?
- *Distribution information.* What is to be transported, to what distribution centre, by what mode, at what price?
- *Retail information.* Similar to distribution, but more local and detailed.
- *Demand information.* Who is buying what products, at what price, where and in what quantity? Forecasts of future orders and long-term trends.

The four decision phases are planning, execution, 'inter-company' and strategic analysis. The planning phase involves medium-term plans, say from a month to a year, for capacity, inventory and deliveries. The execution phase records transactions with short time frames. Strategic analysis is the use of information from other phases to model future situations and hence support strategic decisions. 'Inter-company' is the permission to move information between separate firms. It is considered a decision phase because it is a serious step even though it does not have the time parameters of the other three phases.

The information framework is a tool to investigate whether the information systems available are sufficient to support logistics decisions.[3] It is used by indicating where each of the available sets of information sits in the matrix. The resulting data pattern indicates areas which lack information and data sets that can be coordinated. Note that this information framework is used in Figure 4.4 (page 111) to investigate the adequacy of information for international supply chains.

How do we accomplish our task to manage and lead information communication in supply chains? There are four steps, which are described in turn:

- design,
- justification and trust,
- implementation, and
- management coordination and performance review.

Design is the act of preparing a system architecture which will provide the necessary vision of the whole supply chain for the decision-maker. The extent of supply chain vision depends upon the decision, its extent in time and effect on customers and chain partners. The vision comprises past information and future tracking signals informed by human experience and intuition. At its simplest, design is a statement of system capabilities and the hardware, software and people that will provide them. In practice design is a complex task in satisfying various conflicting needs because:

- software is outsourced,
- supply chains are many and dynamic,
- knowledge of the system in a company is ephemeral,
- architecture and documentation are not done or provided, and
- chain information systems must be capable of change to handle new customers and new business conditions.

Justification is the task of setting out the customer and economic benefits which will flow from the costs incurred in buying hardware, software and in installing and maintaining the information system. Justification is a normal task for capital expenditure in companies. *Trust*, so that sensitive commercial data is shared between chain partners, is a difficult relationship to foster. The logical approach requires information to be shared between all supply chain partners driven by the desire to serve customers effectively. This approach would increase the chain turnover and profit, which can then be shared between all partners. In practice it is not easy to create a climate of trust in a network of firms in a supply chain. Information will be shared to a greater extent in stable chains if it is past information. The hardest situation for sharing is in new chains, with partners jockeying for position and with future tracking knowledge. Information may be filtered in channels with low trust:

> Chain members may elect to use information filters that separate mission-critical information and pass along only that information considered essential to the transaction. The number and density of filters are a function of the level of trust that exists between chain partners.[4] (p. 49)

Implementation is the task of achieving system function in line with the design specification. Companies are used to major capital investments taking three to six months to commission. Modern ERP systems are said to take one to three years for the best companies to implement.[5] Such a long time is quite unacceptable in most business situations. Successful ERP system implementation, such as that achieved by Toyota Australia, would seem to require dedicated resources and a staged process. This topic is further addressed in section 5.6.

Management coordination and performance review refers to the pervasive job of managing information communication throughout the supply chain and each link within it. Management coordination is the task of running the chain's day-to-day operations with predominance of past information and existing policy. Performance review is the tactical task of checking whether planned performance is achieved and rectifying any failures found. These tasks are addressed in detail in sections 5.2 to 5.4.

In summary, information communication in supply chains is managed and led by all responsible employees providing accurate information and closely observing the extant system to ensure its information is correct and the inferences taken from it are well founded.

5.2 INFORMATION FLOW IN ONE LINK: THE ESSENTIALS

The five *essential information** elements in the link are: order-taking, purchasing, scheduling, inventory and delivery. Building on the discussion in the third section of Chapter 1, Table 5.1 sets out, for each of these elements, the documents used and their contents. This list does not cover wider aspects of information such as those required to develop new products or to cost and price them.

Order-processing

Imagine that the logistics manager of a company receives an order from a customer. This situation is used to develop the essential information into a list of the tasks that must be carried out to process the order and is explained by example. So order-processing means all the business processes (informational and physical) required from receipt of a customer order until the completed products/services are delivered to the customer.

Table 5.1   **Essential information in one link**

Element	Document	Content
Order-taking	Customer order	List of products, quantities and delivery location required by the customer
Purchasing	Purchase order	List of materials, components and delivery point required by manufacturing
Scheduling	Production schedule	Infrastructure to manufacture products in a particular sequence and quantity
Inventory	Inventory record	Quantity of each kind of material or product and bin location at a storage area
Delivery	Despatch advice or invoice	Confirmation to the customer of the quantity of each product delivered to its store

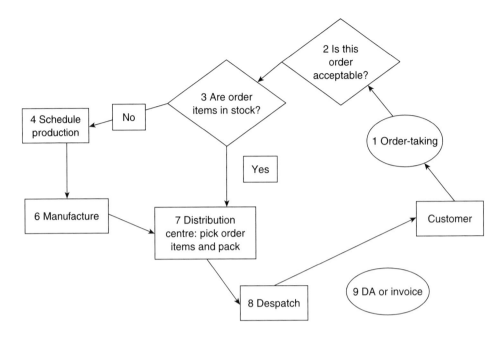

Figure 5.2   **The main areas in order-processing**
(Ovals = information; diamonds = decisions; boxes = physical processes)

See Figure 5.2 for the main areas required to process a customer order and Box 5.1 for an example in the biscuit trade.

List of tasks in order-processing:

1. Receipt of order and entry of each line item into the firm's database.
2. Check order for correctness: does it make sense and fit into the product range? And check whether the customer is capable of paying for the order.
3. Check whether items are in stock. If so, proceed to task 7.
4. If no, place order on manufacture/service operation.
5. Order materials and components from suppliers.
6. Schedule production, manufacture and pack product.
7. Order assignment: pick order-items, pack, and assemble load.
8. Ship to customer.
9. Raise despatch advice or invoice.

5.3 ENTERPRISE RESOURCE PLANNING IN ONE LINK

The essential information in the last section underpins the much more complex data structures that current computer systems use. Huge information systems, such as *enterprise resource planning* systems, are now pressured to:

- have all the information for a decision in one place,
- be 'fully relational' so that data entered at any one place will automatically update all other uses of the same data in other parts of the company database,

- integrate information from numerous divisions or subsidiaries of a company, irrespective of business compatibility,
- incorporate new versions of software, which are then forced on to original purchasers, whether or not the changes are useful to them.

Box 5.1   **Order-processing example**

Alpha Biscuits in Melbourne, Australia, collect orders by sales representatives visiting customer stores, checking what is needed on the shelves and entering the orders into a 'Telson' electronic storage. At the end of the day, the representative attaches the Telson to his/her telephone and sends the set of orders into the Alpha central computer in Sydney.

When the computer has received all the store orders for Victoria, it assembles truck loads by batching biscuit cartons as follows. Say one truckload comprises 20 types of biscuit in complete cartons going to five stores as ten pallets. For the first batch of picking, Alpha's computer adds the number of each type of biscuit (crackers, chocolates, cheese, etc.) for the first three stores. Stock of the 20 biscuits is held, among 110 biscuit varieties, in pallet slots in Alpha's distribution centre. Using paperless picking, the computer lights a number '8' beside the chocolate biscuit bin and the storeperson places eight barcoded cartons from the bin on to the moving belt behind him/her.

Further along the conveyor the barcode is read and the computer directs the correct number of chocolate biscuit cartons down an individual lane to an assembly area for pallets of biscuit cartons going to store 1. Another operator assembles the biscuit cartons into the required pallet loads for store 1 and then the other stores in this truck load. A forklift driver shrink-wraps each pallet by machine and drives the pallet into the correct pantechnicon for the delivery route which includes store 1. This procedure is followed for a sequence of batches until all the orders for all the stores have been picked, assembled and loaded into pantechnicon trucks, for delivery to the stores.

A description of an enterprise resource planning (ERP) system is beyond the scope of this book. It provides a brief overview of a particular, widely adopted ERP system, SAP,[6] followed by an in-depth review of the logistics modules in that system.

Architecture of current information systems

Figure 5.3 shows how ERP systems have evolved from materials requirements planning (mrp) and Manufacturing Resources Planning (MRP II) systems by capturing more and more of the firm's business computer systems. Mrp is a sequential system that is used to convert the master production schedule of the finished products into a detailed schedule for raw materials and components to be made in-house as well as purchased from vendors (see section 5.4). MRP II is a tool for planning the engineering, operational and financial resources of an organisation. The vital part of MRP II is the mrp system. Around this system other resources are planned and controlled.

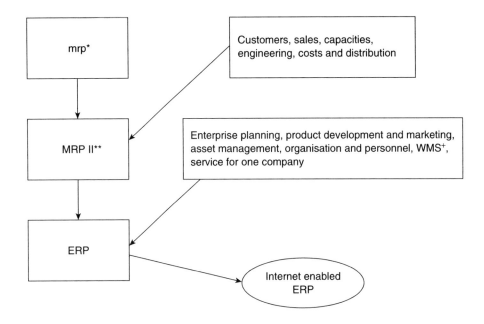

Figure 5.3 **The evolution of ERP**
(* materials requirements planning; ** manufacturing resources planning; + warehouse management systems)

MRP II deals with sales, production, inventory, schedules, and cash flows, which are the fundamentals of planning and controlling the manufacturing and distribution process.

MRP II systems are the predecessors of today's ERP systems and include fewer enterprise-wide functions than ERP systems. MRP II systems often run on proprietary mid-range computer platforms. The ERP system is an advanced information system that overcomes the limitations of MRP II. ERP systems are capable of integrating data across all functional units, thus being credited with improving business performance. An integrated system, such as ERP, is necessary given current market conditions because customers, having more choices, are becoming more demanding and product life cycles have become shorter. New technologies are changing the way organisations are organised and business processes are designed. A manufacturing planning and control system, such as MRP II, is becoming less relevant in today's context because of the following important changes.

'Mrp' systems focus only on the materials requirements using an infinite capacity-planning model, and these requirements are not in real time. In the current market environment, there is a need to plan and direct manufacturing processes in real time. MRP II systems overcame some of the drawbacks of the original mrp systems through applying finite capacity scheduling and manufacturing execution systems. ERP systems have now overcome the drawbacks of MRP II systems by providing organisation-wide integration. The ERP applications encompass the philosophy of execution systems, in addition to planning systems. They affect everything in an organisation from order-taking to accounting and from procurement to warehousing. Such systems are especially useful in discrete manufacturing environments.[7]

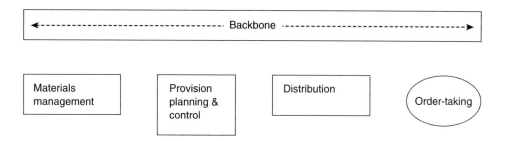

Figure 5.4   **The main logistics information systems for one link**

Electronic information communication systems have replaced manual forms of information for most transactions in the links of the supply chain. Orders are received electronically and systems are used to plan, procure and manufacture goods. The typical overall architecture for one link in the supply channel, ignoring non-logistics modules and external contacts, is shown in Figure 5.4.

Next, we consider the 'backbone' provided by the ERP system, in one partner company, in order to link the data and information in all the systems in the company and its subsidiaries. Section 5.4 examines 'Planning and coordination' systems, and 'execution' systems. The methods of communicating information *between* partners in a supply chain are addressed in section 5.5.

Backbone ERP

Enterprise resource planning systems provide a '*backbone*'* for all the data and information which a company possesses. Following this analogy, the essential information items, mentioned above, would be the critical ones in the backbone which link from it to the limbs. Figure 5.5 shows a typical example of the overall architecture of ERP for a company that is involved in both manufacture and distribution. The module interfaces are connecting programs which enable data and information recorded in one application module to be used in another. This enables the managers of one module to specify their information structure differently from the other. This can be important when a sales department wants to organise its customer data quite differently from the customer data in the despatch department.

The central data warehouse is the relational information repository for the entire ERP system. The data warehouse is described as relational because it links information between logistics activities in application programs with minimal duplication of information in the database. An important function of the data warehouse is to keep copies of past information status for management analysis. A fully relational database is able to keep all data in it completely accurate, in line with the human-entered and automatic data fed into it.

For example, if a customer address is contained in two different references, and the customer moves its address, it is likely that only one reference will be changed. If an inventory record for a particular product in a bin is contained in two computer database locations, when product is removed this may only be updated in one of the two references. These sorts of duplications are likely to lead to a gradual increase in errors, which are difficult to identify and correct.

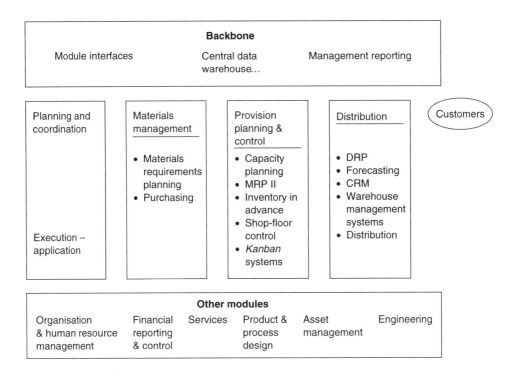

Figure 5.5   **Example of overall ERP architecture**

Preferably, the ERP system has an open database architecture which has been published. This is necessary for the data warehouse to be accessed by other systems which the company may wish to add on to the existing ERP platform.

A useful classification of ERP systems is by the side of the firm in which they specialise. 'Side' means the materials management, provision or distribution emphasis. Thus, in Figure 5.4, 'materials management' is on the left-hand side and 'distribution' is on the right-hand, or customer, side. In the Double-Bell model (Figure 5.6), the left side of the firm is looking upstream towards suppliers, while the right side concentrates on downstream towards customers. Using this classification, the ERP system 'SAP' concentrates on materials and provision, while Oracle is most effective in provision and distribution. SAP is the name of a widely adopted ERP system and the letters stand for systems, applications and processes. SAP is developed and marketed by SAP AG, a German company.[6]

Firms must carefully evaluate, select and implement the ERP system they purchase because the system will greatly affect their business, be very expensive to use and even more costly to change. Their evaluation should consider how well the system's module matches their particular business, its functions and features, its output capability, its support and its cost.

5.4 MAIN LOGISTICS INFORMATION COMMUNICATION SYSTEMS

This section describes the information communication systems required in the provision link of a supply chain and concentrates on *logistics-oriented* systems. The section first

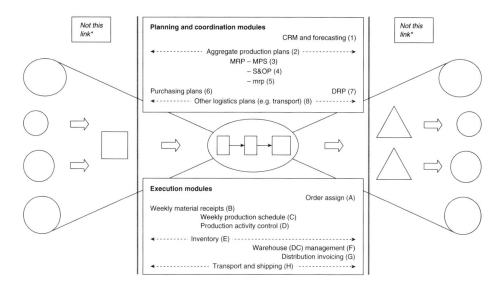

Figure 5.6   Information communication modules for one link* shown in relation to the Double-Bell model of the supply chain

This figure superimposes IC modules on Figure 1.6. Note that the IC modules for the one link *do not* cover the outer links in the supply chain. Refer to Figure 5.7 for the general arrangement of modules with respect to each other.

(*The IC modules for one link, or partner firm, are isolated between the two thick vertical lines)

addresses 'planning and coordination' modules, which prepare for activities weeks or months in the future. The second part contains 'execution' modules which, generally, carry out an activity or process a transaction (see Figure 5.6). The word *module* is used to connote a significant part of an entire information system. This section enables particular supply chain information systems to be analysed by comparison with the modules described.

The management information in these modules is driven by strategic and annual budget plans of their company or organisation. The clearest link is frequently from the budget sales and production volumes into an aggregate production plan, but many companies do not have such a plan. The development and implementation of systems are described in section 5.6.

Planning and coordination modules for logistics

This sub-section describes the management functions carried out by a number of computer modules which enable preparations to be made for the provision of products, commonly known as *production planning**. The sub-section refers to the modules in the upper part of Figure 5.6 or to Figure 5.7 for the links between the various modules. Figure 5.7 is a diagram, which applies generally to many discrete manufacturing systems, but its parts do not necessarily apply to any one system.

1. Customer relationship management and forecasting

Customer relationship management (CRM)* is a well-known term for an information system which helps companies change their relationship with customers from exploiting them to nurturing them. It is built on the management of sales and delivery transactions from the start to the end of the order-processing task (sec section 5.2). But a wider range of capabilities is required to achieve this friendly, sustaining relationship with the whole spectrum of customers. Typical functions within CRM, which clearly vary widely according to industry and market sector, are:

- sales tracking,
- sales history analysis,
- price setting,
- account management,

- promotion arrangement,
- product mix choice, and
- category management.

Category management refers to the practice of supermarkets and stores expecting suppliers to manage the inventory and mix of an entire range (= category) of products on their shelves.

Forecasting is described in section 2.3. Important points about forecasting in this context are:

- Many companies have large, expensive forecasting packages (such as 'Collaborative planning, forecasting and replenishment') which require a lot of data and servicing, yet lack emphasis on the errors and judgements required in using forecasts. Unless the package operators are qualified statisticians, there is a danger that the output is regarded as correct, without testing. Then managers, untrained in statistics, may accept the numbers, without allowing for the standard error in the forecast.
- Statistical forecasts *require* review by managers with practical knowledge of the business before they are acted upon.
- Accurate forecasts can only be made one period in advance (i.e. monthly data give a forecast one month ahead, while daily data forecast one day ahead). Maths can be used to forecast several periods ahead but, wherever there are changes (especially turning points), the forecast quickly gets a large error band.
- Lean thinking (see section 8.2) proposes few or no forecasts. While not often attainable in consumer goods supply, this is an excellent aim.
- Forecasting is part of considering the whole supply chain as subject to variability. However good your plans are, however stable you believe your orders to be, your company and its chain partners are subject to variations. You can estimate these deviations but you must still expect actual outcomes to surprise you, and so be prepared to flex your responses.

2. Aggregate production planning

Aggregate production planning (APP) for one company or link is a determination of the best monthly capacity to have available, given the budget or first year of the business plan. *Aggregate or capacity planning** looks at least a year ahead in monthly periods. A forecast or budget estimate of sales in a suitable unit of measure represents the anticipated demand. The APP, then, examines existing resources of machinery, operators, etc. to find out whether capacity is sufficient to meet demand. The planning task is then to manipulate available and contracted resources by the allocation or purchase of more machine capacity, or the hiring of more staff members to do this.[7]

Capacity flexibility depends upon the nature of the product and lead-time. For the long term (more than three months away, say) there is often substantial flexibility by

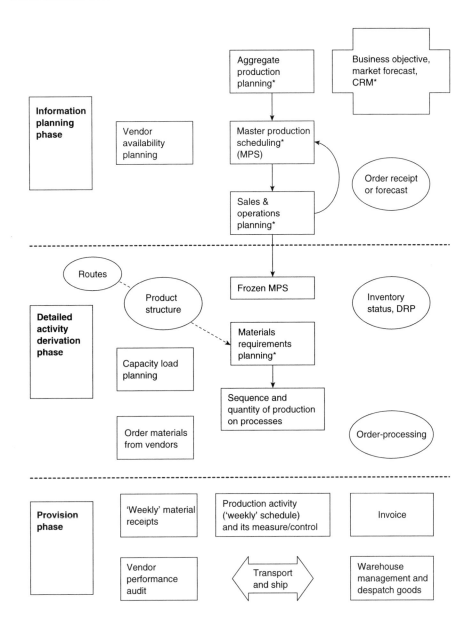

Figure 5.7 The main components of MRP systems in full

(after Vollmanmn et al.[8]) (* see text for meaning of abbreviations)

Source: *Supply Chain Logistics Management*, 2006, by Bowersox DJ, Goss DJ and Cooper MB, reproduced with permission of The McGraw-Hill Companies.

producing to inventory, buying from a supplier or contractor or acquiring more of the relevant resource. In the shorter term, flexibility is limited because resources are committed and operators will only go so far in overtime and cancelled holidays. However, operators are not often the governing factor in modern manufacture.

The aggregate production planning concept applies to a distribution centre as well as a factory. One would just vary the considerations for the different application.

APP is normally done for major pieces of equipment, such as rolling mills or assembly lines, which most products go through, rather than for every machine.

The process of APP or rough capacity planning requires the following (for a worked example for lawn mowers, see Box 5.2):

1. A forecast or budget estimate of intended/expected product sales is set down for each month for the next 12 months, starting in a few weeks time. This forecast is expressed in terms of one major product, all others being converted to the same unit of measure (see next step).
2. The unit of measure is often obvious (in Box 5.2 it is metres of linoleum) but may need some thought. Here are a few examples:

    - Airline industry – flight seats per route,
    - Brewery – thousands of litres,

    - Steel industry – tonnes of steel,

    - Distribution centre – pallet spaces or pallet movements,

    - Hospital – beds,
    - Electrical generation – megawatts of electricity,
    - Supermarket – area of shelving available for goods, or
    - Business school – number of full-time equivalent students.

3. The available monthly capacity of the mill, or other major equipment, is calculated from the daily normal time capacity multiplied by the number of planned working days for that month.
4. Where human operation affects production rates, the available monthly capacity of the mill operators is calculated from their daily normal time ability multiplied by the number of planned working days per person times the number of planned operators.
5. The capacities in steps 2 and 3 are compared with the forecast in step 1. Where the capacities are insufficient, an analysis is done to ascertain how they can best be matched. This could involve early production of inventory, overtime working, subcontracting some peak work, buying more machinery, running more shifts per week, hiring more operators or some combination of this list.

This APP process covers the central, typical items but it has many variations to cope with particular industry sectors which may have short-term responses, such as newspaper printing; short cycle times, such as electronic equipment; perishable outputs, such as fresh meat; inability to use inventory, such as bakery products; and so on. Important extra considerations are the capacity of key suppliers to provide materials and services, the ability of transport and logistics service companies to provide required capacity over the next year, etc.

Output from the APP goes to the master production schedule and, so, is a key precursor to materials requirements planning. APP is a precursor to capacity load planning, which can comprise rough-cut capacity planning and capacity resources planning. No connection is made here between APP and capacity load planning because the level of detail is so different.

Box 5.2   **Aggregate production planning for lawnmowers**

	Jan	Feb	Mar	Apr	May	June	Q3	Q4	Year
Forecast sales									
Product 18"	1430	2140	4870	5120	3210	1400	1320	2810	22,300
20"	2800	4390	9660	9980	6290	2820	3470	5290	44,700
22"	1120	1850	3210	3875	2650	800	2080	2015	17,600
Total	5350	8380	17740	18975	12150	5020	6870	10115	84,600
Capacity	8000	8000	16000	16000	16000	8000	24000	24000	
Production*	5400	8000	16000	16000	12150	5500	6900	10000	79,790
Planned overtime		400	1500	1500					3,400
Inventory	4,500								3,250
Inv. change	+50	+20	−240	−1475	0	+480	+30	−115	

*Normal time production, one shift per day, increasing to two shifts in March to May

(*Source*: amended from Vollmann et al.[8])

3. Master production scheduling (MPS)

Given some customer orders and an aggregate production plan, it is necessary to schedule the production of various families of products over a forward period of two to six months so that manufacturing, suppliers and other interested parties know what to prepare for. The master production schedule (MPS) is the most important planning schedule in a business and forms the main input to materials requirements planning (see Figure 5.7). In manufacturing, the MPS contains the volume and timing of end products to be made. It drives the purchase of materials, their transformation into components and the assembly of those components into products. It is the basis for arranging the utilisation of operators and equipment and the provision of cash to pay for these resources. In service organisations there is rarely anything equivalent to an MPS in terms of services provided or products retailed. Instead, a financial budget gives an approximate schedule of expected business.

*Manufacturing Resources Planning (MRP II)** is a widely-used name for the area of MPS, sales and operations planning, mrp, purchasing plans plus related provision functions: in short, MRP II comprises most of the functions shown in Figure 5.7. Many computer systems addressed the information area in MRP II from about 1988 to 1998. Now most software companies are using the term enterprise resource planning systems in an endeavour to supplant MRP II systems with later systems which have additional features, such as 'Year 2000' compatibility and e-business and Internet capability. MRP II is used to plan machine and human resources required to meet forecast orders by scheduling product requirements, converting them into component and material needs by working from the top to the bottom of the product structure, shop-floor control of the sequence of parts through each machine and scheduling the outsourcing of raw material and components from suppliers.

4. Sales and operations planning

*Sales and operations planning (S&OP)** is a recent development which bridges the divide between what the sales force hopes to do and what the provision or production operating system can achieve in the near future, say the next month. Essentially, S&OP is a monthly meeting of interested parties, headed by the sales, operations and logistics managers, or equivalent managers, with the General Manager of the business to see that the compromises made reflect the best interests of the whole business. Using available information about orders, forecasts, capacity and supplies, these executives *decide* on the amount of production, sales and inventory which will be made weekly for the next month, unless changes are made due to very exceptional circumstances. They aim to establish the best trade-offs, where conflicts exist, for the whole business between sales/marketing objectives, manufacturing schedule and cost objectives and the cost of having inventory.

S&OP is a very powerful tool; it ensures that all functions in the link work together to satisfy the customer. It is used by many companies such as Caterpillar Inc. and Toyota. S&OP largely precludes the prevalent ploy of changing things so frequently that no one knows what to do or whether they achieved what they should have.

5. Materials requirements planning (mrp)

Given the MPS and the S&OP, materials requirements planning time phases the purchase, production and assembly of materials into finished products. It does this using the product structure, which shows all the components required to make the product and the order in which they are assembled. Mrp works down the product structure from the end product requirement to the lowest level of manufactured or purchased material. At each level it 'nets' (reduces) requirements by the inventory of that component on hand or scheduled to be received. It does this day by day through a set of planning periods which typically cover four to ten weeks. When more of a component is required, a work order is released to make the required quantity, or some fixed minimum. Box 5.3 explains this mrp process in detail.

The whole idea of the mrp calculation is to examine likely future situations well before they occur to obtain economies of scale. Hence work orders many periods in the future are only 'planned' orders, which can be changed at will until a 'frozen' period of, say, the first two weeks is entered. Mrp also takes account of machine capacities that are available to carry out various manufacturing processes, using product routings, and consolidates the requirements in different parts of the product structures for all products for the same item, such as a screw or a tube.

The derivation of work orders is getting into the area of execution, which is dealt with below.

6. Purchasing plans (or vendor availability planning)

Purchasing plans covers a range of activities from discovering suppliers capable of providing materials, through negotiations to planned loads communicated to suppliers some months in advance of placement. Thus it comprises:

- discovering suppliers capable of providing materials,
- checking supplier capability,
- performance measurement on existing suppliers,
- negotiations of, generally, annual 'broad-brush' supply contracts, and
- communication of planned loads.

There is also a need to align purchasing plans with logistics schedules for finished goods inventories and distribution requirements.

7. Distribution requirements planning

A distribution requirements planning (DRP) system has the central task of planning the movement of quantities of finished goods and their holdings at all warehouses and distribution centres (DCs). This may involve up to three stages of inventory even before international movement of goods is considered. Essentially, the DRP system accomplishes this by the same multi-period planning system which mrp uses for materials. DRP links levels, or separate firms, of the supply chain by providing records that carry demand information from receiving points to supply points and that return supply information to the receiving points.

Distribution requirements planning is used to monitor available inventory at each level of warehousing for about 10 weeks ahead so that supply problems can be seen and prevented without holding excess stocks. Thus, the aim of planning ahead is to identify potential distribution problems in advance and correct product flows so that the problems are averted.

Box 5.3   **The process of materials requirements planning**

Data: Lead-time = 1 day; pieces per = 2; ordering method = at least 60; safety stock = 0									
Period (days)	0	1	2	3	4	5	6	7	8
Requirements (gross)		50	65	70	70	50	50	40	40
Scheduled receipts		40	–	–	–	–	–	–	–
On-hand inventory	65	55	50	40	30	40	50	10	30
Work order release		60	60	60	60	60	–	60	60

(Continued)

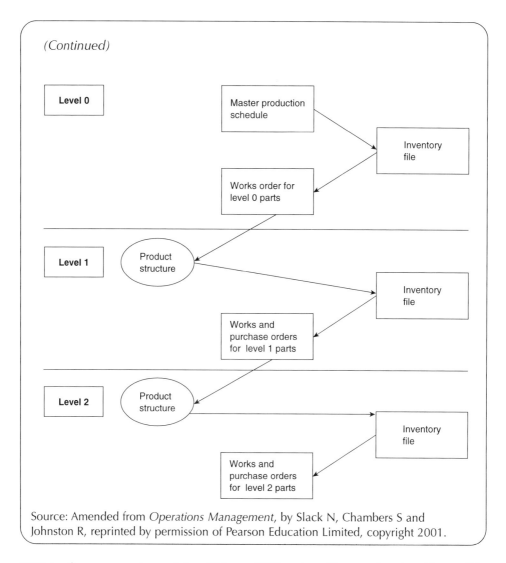

(Continued)

Source: Amended from *Operations Management*, by Slack N, Chambers S and Johnston R, reprinted by permission of Pearson Education Limited, copyright 2001.

DRP is often a separate module within an ERP system. It comprises (see Figure 5.2, page 130):

- order acquisition,
- order-processing,
- inventory status which communicates with the production control system,
- distribution centre (warehouse management system),
- transport,
- invoicing, and
- customer.

The DRP module provides planned quantities and timing for replenishing inventory to the master production schedule. The logic of DRP commences with a basic record which is similar to that shown in Box 5.3, but for a finished product. The first row is forecast requirements and the fourth row is planned shipments. Shipments are indicated for those periods which require a shipment to achieve an acceptable projected on-hand inventory. When all these records are calculated for each product at each location, the result is a plan for future distribution shipments to satisfy customer orders at the required service level. The use of forecast information as requirements and the mrp approach to develop planned shipments is known as the time-phased order point. Once DRP records are established for field warehouses, nearest the customer, this method is used to link records between distribution centres and regional DCs to the central manufacturing plant. Planners then use the DRP records to manage day-by-day variations from the plans and to ensure that sufficient safety stocks are held to achieve good customer service levels.

An important information system within the ambit of the DRP module is a warehouse management system (WMS) which is described in 'execution' modules (see below).

8. Transport plans

Transport planning is a separate task although the incidence of manufacturers or distributors providing their own transport is now unusual. Transport attached to one link in the chain is discussed in section 2.4. Transport across the whole supply chain is explained in section 3.8.

9. Extra information in ERP systems

Other areas in ERP systems which may contain information relevant to supply chains are:

- the human resource module,
- the financial accounting module,
- product development and marketing,
- asset management, and
- service, for example warranty.

To some extent ERP also communicates with customers and suppliers using electronic data interchange (EDI) and the Internet. A recent survey reveals that leading-edge manufacturers, dissatisfied with the traditional Manufacturing Resource Planning or ERP software solutions they have used so far to manage demand-driven just-in-time manufacturing, are adopting flow manufacturing techniques. ERP links are expected to bring the same efficiencies in purchasing, manufacturing and shipping that ERP systems are meant to bring to individual companies.

'Execution' modules in Logistics Information Systems

This sub-section describes eight important information modules which are used on a daily basis in carrying out the transactions of supply chains and their links. The modules are intended to cover the stages in the framework (see Figure 5.1). Their place in the Double-Bell model is shown in Figure 5.6 and their place in an MRP system of one link is shown in Figure 5.7.

A. Order assign

As part of the order-processing module (section 5.2), order assignment allocates available inventory to unfulfilled customer orders. Preferably, this allocation is done in real time as orders are received. For a variety of reasons, such as the hours when staff are available to supervise the process, many firms assign stock to orders in batch mode, such as once a day. A responsive, or lean, firm assigns inventory from planned production schedules. This is known as using *available-to-promise* stock.

Superior order assignment interacts with the whole order-processing function to generate an order that satisfies customer needs within ERP constraints. In this situation the salesperson talks to the customer to attain a combination of products, quantities and lead-time acceptable to both parties. Any conflict is resolved by delayed delivery, product change or shipment from another source. Delayed delivery may be acceptable in some situations, where customers are captive, but we believe it is generally bad for the business. Box 5.4 argues the case for acceding to customer demands at all times, whether they fit the ERP constraints or not. This is considered a more appropriate response to customer orders in the twenty-first century because customers are very demanding and may place fewer orders on a provider who does not accede to all their needs.

Box 5.4   The case for lean perfect delivery

The lean way, propounded by Jones and Womack,[10] requires providers and their supply chain partners to respond accurately to customer 'pull' by themselves pulling materials and products through value streams, as far as humanly possible. So a customer order should be met by accurate, entire delivery at the time and place requested.

An example of this is the delivery of plastic car components from a moulding company to Ford Australia (FA). The plastic moulder receives orders from FA every hour for exact numbers of bumper bars, consoles, dashboards and fuel tanks by quantity and type required for a car model-variant. These are assembled and sent from the moulder to the exact work station at FA in the required sequence 1–2 hours later. Mistakes are confined to a frequency of about one per week, or one in 11,000 products delivered.

Information involved in order assignment comprises the following:

- The customer file, which lists customer contact details, delivery location, contact and terms of sale.
- The order file, which contains all orders that have been received and not yet satisfied. It contains customer number and name, receipt date, and the list of products and quantities required. Most files now have to accept orders by EDI and the Internet as well as by internal sources.
- Product and price files, which state the product number, description, size, update, price and internal cost. These files can also list services available.

B. 'Weekly' material receipts

The receipt of materials and components is an important activity. The word 'weekly' is used to imply a short-term, regular activity which may need daily or even hourly review, depending on the factory or store involved. Information involved in material receipts comprises:

- a record of the order placed on the supplier so that incoming goods may be checked for correct type, quantity and quality,
- a confirmation that the materials were accurately received in perfect quality so that production can proceed and payment be made, and
- contribution to a summary so that performance of a particular supplier can be reviewed.

Advanced companies short-cut this process for their best suppliers, who have a track record of superior supply. Goods received from such firms are accepted without checking and sent immediately to production or to store. This procedure aligns with just-in-time supply, in which parts are called forward by a *kanban* card in exact quantities as they are used by the downstream process.

The main files used during materials receipts are:

- *Supplier file*, which contains the details of all companies which provide goods or services. Typical details comprise contacts, transport, price and payment arrangements.
- *Purchase order file*, which lists all orders placed on suppliers. Typical data include material items, date required, delivery point, quantity and price.

C. 'Weekly' production schedule

The production schedule aims to inform all operators of the products required during that period, such as a week. The schedule may comprise a list of products to be made or picked in the current shift. Such products could be components or modules which will be assembled into products later. Alternatively, the schedule may be a Gantt chart showing the required progress on a number of products in several work centres. In the service industry, a series of tasks would be used instead of products.

Implicit in the production schedule is the sequence in which manufacture is to take place. In many work places this is not important and is left to the preference of the operators. In most work places the time requirements of the customer, which may be the next process or the end product customer, strongly influence the order of production. In other places, the order of processing has a major impact on efficiency due to the need for cleaning or resetting between products, for example, in processing foods such as sausages. Then the sequence is controlled by policies or by using a computer program to determine the best sequence.[8]

The production schedule also sets out the amount of work which is to be carried out in one shift or day. This is controlled by the technique of 'finite loading' which calculates the time required by each job on the work centre and cuts off the allocation of more work when the planned time available has been reached.

Ten years ago, when MRP systems were used without just-in-time flow, the production schedule reflected the detailed lead-times for each component in making sub-assemblies and products. Now the use of small batch quantities and *kanban* pull systems greatly reduces the need to use information communication systems to control production.

D. Production activity control

Production control executes detailed material plans and measures the extent that the required production has been carried out. Such control is interested in the number, quality and cost of meeting the schedule. This may require control of individual jobs at factory work centres and vendor scheduling. Production activity control uses several techniques. Gantt charts are a form of detailed schedule which have time on one axis and the current jobs on the other axis. Planned production times are shown on the chart, which is then used to control the progress achieved. The theory of constraints is used to determine the work centres that cause a bottleneck and then schedule those bottlenecks with priority over non-bottleneck centres.

E. Inventory

Inventory is a very difficult topic to cover conceptually because it ranges from an essential asset, in a supermarket, to a form of waste in a queue between two work centres. In this information communication (IC) context, inventory is all the materials, parts and products that are flowing in and between all the link firms in the supply chain. The challenge for an information system is to maintain computer records which accurately reflect the physical status. In the past, computer inventory records of most companies were very different from what was in the bin. The advent of barcoded products and radio-frequency input to IC systems has improved the situation considerably. Cycle counting of part of the inventory each week is recommended to ensure that errors are quickly rectified.

Since inventory is frequently requisitioned in advance of orders, there are questions of ordering and replenishment for stocks that do not supply particular orders. These questions are addressed in section 2.5. They give rise to many computerised inventory management systems. A key factor in these systems is the extent of human interaction. The more automated systems are cheaper to run but they are likely to result in unnecessary stocks due to the absence of human judgement.

A typical inventory file contains product identification, exact location and quantity in stock for each product or component.

F. Warehouse (DC) management

A warehouse management system (WMS) is a 'real-time' inventory tracking, resource management and communication system which links the warehouse status with business-wide production, purchasing, scheduling and other logistics activities.[11] A WMS records the status of all stocks in a distribution centre and the movement of stock into the DC, between DC locations and out when despatched to a customer. It lists the product in each storage location. It keeps track of the location and activities of each piece of materials-handling equipment. It is so all encompassing, for the particular DC, that managers have to be careful to respect the privacy of employees! The essentials of warehouse management rest on the receipt, storage, picking and despatch of goods. Stand-alone systems are now available to account for all distribution centre activities in the same way that MRP systems look after all the activities in a factory. A list of the functions of warehouse management systems indicates the complexity:

- receiving,
- put away,
- pick,
- replenishment,
- pack,

- despatch,
- operator scheduling,
- inventory control,
- cycle count,
- cross-dock,

- reverse logistics,
- warehouse management, and
- services.

Cycle count is the physical regular checking of part of the storage bins. *Services* is the extra work done on products to make them more useful to the customer. They include labelling, setting up displays and repacking. *Cross-docking** is the transfer of incoming goods directly into despatch loads without putting them into stock.

G. Distribution invoicing

This module refers to the act of preparing and sending invoices to obtain payment for goods delivered to customers. These tasks are usually carried out in a sales or finance department. Clearly, they finish the business task for which all the other functions have aimed and complete the cash-to-cash cycle.

H. Transport and shipping

Transport usually involves three parties: the shipper, the carrier and the customer. Outsourcing the whole distribution function to transport companies has reduced the extent of transport information recorded by most supply chain companies. The main execution tasks are load consolidation, shipment notification to customers, preparing transport documents and managing which carrier takes which shipments. These tasks are developed further in section 3.8, freight transport services.

5.5 ELECTRONIC COMMUNICATION IN SUPPLY CHAINS

The full scope of the opportunity provided by electronic communication is still unclear. All partners in supply chains, especially in distribution, will be impacted because the ability to connect them is increased. Properly managed, real-time information makes all processes function better with less expense. Electronic communication, including the Internet, will not replace business functions but will serve to make them function more effectively.

Electronic communication (EC) has the potential to improve all business activity, including that in supply chains. There is a parallel with the total quality management (TQM) and lean thinking[10] movements which have increased our wealth through better quality and faster response. The impact of EC will be stunning if we harness its full power, rather than go for short-term, limited advances. EC is a tool that offers great opportunities to all firms but 'carries great peril to those that would use it incorrectly'[4] (p. xi).

The lack of superior electronic communication in supply chains can be seen as very similar to the lack of Internet utilisation in purchasing in 2000. According to a recent study,[12] the Internet failed to become a purchasing tool for these reasons:

- lack of data standardisation made setting up websites for selling product very expensive,
- access to the Internet was limited by bandwidth problems,
- business procedures used by many end users still required a written purchase order, and
- trust and security issues hampered the process.

The first three 'technical' problems should disappear over the next few years, leaving firms with two essential tasks: first, getting ready by matching traditional business processes with the new EC technology; and secondly, engendering trust between firms in the supply chain so that fluid movement of past information and future insight is obtained.

Researchers in the Netherlands have developed a framework of the characteristic elements of an e-business network[13] (see Figure 5.8). Vorst and colleagues state that e-business is used to improve the efficiency of established supply chains or for the creation of new chain networks with looser partnerships. Based on a review of electronic business-to-business initiatives in Dutch food supply chains, they propose the following characteristics:

- A value proposition conveying the underlying purpose of the network.
- Roles of the participants that are exchanging information via the e-business hub:
  - Demote context providers who deliver the intrinsic forms of value to satisfy customer needs,
  - commerce service providers, such as technical and logistics service providers, who enable the flow of transactions, and
  - customers who receive value from the network.
- Processes that are supported by the e-business initiative, such as sales, quality control and procurement.
- Functions, which support these processes, such as customer demand monitoring, benchmarking, catalogues and product tracking.
- Applications in the information communications infrastructure which enable these functions.
- Promote specific characteristics comprising:
  - type of cooperation in the operational process, such as horizontal or vertical,
  - the extent of value integration, and
  - cype of control: hierarchical under a leader or self-organising in response to the market.

To enable the implementation of good electronic communication in supply chains, the rest of this section surveys the methods that are available, examines some applications in the distribution field and then widens this to all parts of a supply chain.

Methods

Electronic data interchange (EDI) is the movement of data between two companies or between two different information systems. It enables data to retain precise, but different meanings in the two databases. EDI can be considered as a translator as well as a mover of data. The actual transmission is by telephone line. EDI is the oldest means of electronic data communication. It is quite expensive to install but provides a high-quality, secure link.

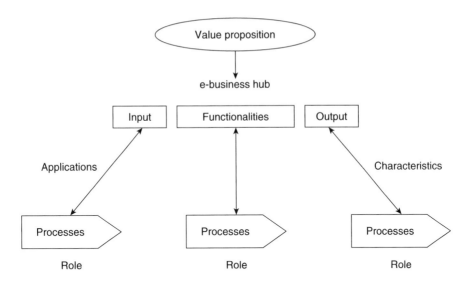

Figure 5.8 **Elements of an e-business model**[13]

Fax, or facsimile, is the transmission between two telephone numbers of an exact copy of a written page. It is a simple method, requiring no computer or knowledge of language. It connects between people at the two phones rather than between computer databases.

Phones are the most versatile means of communication between people or computers in different places. They combine the benefits of talking, sending faxes and various forms of automated electronic communication.

The Internet is world-wide connections between computers which can be used in several ways. At one end of the scale, email provides an electronic communication similar to a fax. In the middle point, customers can be permitted to look into distributor catalogues to identify the product they require and into stock records to place an order for goods available. At the complex end, a company computer can use the Internet to visit another company's website, access its computer database, and return with the information it requires in a similar manner to EDI.

Electronic point of sale (EPOS), known in some countries as EFTPOS, is the gathering of customer purchase data in real time. These data are used by the retailer or retail chain to assess current sales by product and to order replenishment stock. They are frequently communicated to parties back up the supply chain so that they can plan and manufacture goods. Optimally, this communication should go as far as the decoupling point, at which customer pull is replaced by forecasting and push production.

Radio frequency is the ability to obtain information about a package or a pallet of product by radio wave communication. There are now no bounds to the quantity or accuracy of information that can be obtained by radio contact. First applications were in stock placement in distribution centres and in goods replenishment in retail stores commonly known as 'RFID'-radio-frequency identity. Now it is possible for an architect to look at a design drawing in one country while he or she is using a mobile phone in another country.

Barcodes, such as GS1, provide a permanent form of identification which can be stuck on to a package or a load of goods. The identification can include as much information as desired, since the *barcode** can be used by an authorised person to access a database. The barcode can be used anywhere in the world to supply that encoded information. Perhaps the most common application is the use of a radio frequency reader, such as a barcode reader, to scan retail inventory for stock replenishment.

International electronic communication is used by global express freight companies, such as Fedex, to provide instant information about the status and location of packages entrusted to them. Such electronic communication (EC) is provided by major information communication systems fed by regular updates and radio frequency queries to the package.

Applications

Methods of electronic communication are only useful when they enable a supply chain application. Work by Lawrence and colleagues[4] provides three examples of EC applications supporting alternative channels of distribution.

'Manufacturer direct sale to end user' occurs when the manufacturer's website allows the end customer to choose and order the product that he or she requires. A transport company achieves product delivery with no other involvement in the product. This application is unusual in retail products, although Dell computers and Amazon.com are very successful. Manufacturer direct has not been used in industrial products.

'Manufacturer as information controller' occurs when a manufacturer-hosted website is used for ordering and routing demand by end customers. Demand is satisfied by the inventory holdings of distributors and retailers. The manufacturer gets all the point-of-sale information. The distributor carries out all the main distribution functions except order acceptance. Examples are motor companies such as Ford and Toyota. To purchase a Toyota vehicle, the customer must place an order on a Toyota manufacturing plant via a franchised dealer. The vehicle is manufactured by Toyota, conveyed to the dealer by contract transport and collected from the dealer by the customer.

'Distributor as information controller' is an application in which manufacturers, distributors and customers work together to develop an information centre controlled by the distributor. The distributor acts as a supply chain node using its information to optimise its operations and pass information to manufacturers for planning. Examples are Compaq, in computer assembly and William Adams, an Australian dealer for Caterpillar, Inc.

Mixed distribution channels are more common. Since most supply chains offer a range of products for different types of customer, the manufacturing companies will retain direct and 'intermediated' distribution channels. Companies and their supply chains more frequently use a mixture of distribution channels except in information channels such as airline reservations, music and films.

   Wider applications of electronic communication are as varied as businesses themselves in various parts of supply chains. These following examples illustrate some of the choices available.

In materials management a plastics supplier, Venture Australia, is instructed to supply a variety of bumper bars and dashboards for Ford car assembly every hour. Ford Australia broadcasts orders to Venture from its vehicle assembly system as an adjunct to telling its own work stations and operators what to make. By electronic communication, Venture is given both the exact number of each type of plastic product to deliver and the order in which the products are to be loaded into racks to suit precise assembly-line requirements.

In hospital goods supply, a small medical service company replenishes all the items required by the public hospital in Ballarat, Australia. This service, known as Vendor Managed Inventory, is driven by the medical goods distributor using electronic and visual inspection to determine the goods to be replenished. The distributor replenishes in accordance with hospital policy for a particular item and the goods are owned by the hospital once in its warehouse.

Toyota Australia (TA) has installed the enterprise resource planning system (SAP) to provide a 'backbone' for all its electronic communication needs. Previously TA[14] had a whole range of legacy systems covering production planning, materials management, order placement by dealers, reception of imported vehicles, etc. So TA did not need any of the execution modules of SAP. Rather, it wanted a central information communication system which was robust to handle data transfer for all existing modules. The legacy modules could then be replaced individually when TA chose to do so. An important feature of the ERP installation was the use of a considerable number of dedicated internal managers to complete the whole installation on schedule over 18 months.

A third-party logistics (3PL) transport contractor, such as Linfox or Pickford, uses electronic communications to cover all the distribution logistics for a manufacturer or distributor.

5.6 SYSTEM IMPLEMENTATION AND INTEGRATION OF SUPPLY CHAIN INFORMATION

This section describes the implementation of logistics information modules within ERP systems and a classification of stages of systems integration. Because the ERP systems are generic, or one flavour, and because companies have individual data and information needs, a long and complicated implementation process is required. This process usually requires external consulting assistance.

The development of logistics information systems (LIS) requirements within ERP systems is fraught with some dangers. Most purchased ERP systems are provided on a 'take it or leave it' basis: companies can only modify such a system if it has 'switches' which will achieve their needs without requiring program changes. Hence it behoves firms to clarify and simplify their information needs, perhaps towards the essential items described in section 5.2, before buying an ERP system. Firms also have to develop their LIS as their business changes after the purchase is made. There is a strong tendency for logistics mangers to see information systems as owned and specified by 'IT specialists'. Managers must take responsibility for their own data and information systems. We argue that information communication systems are *more* important to them than the physical movement of materials and goods.

ERP projects are typically evaluated in terms of timing, budget and objectives. Projects often fail in terms of these measures because the resources required are under-estimated.[8] LIS projects are seen as being largely a matter of information systems design, with too little attention given to the redesign of work processes. Moreover, information systems design can be sub-contracted to consultants, whereas the change to work processes must be largely done by internal people, often without any relief from their day-to-day responsibilities.

Projects must be tightly designed at the outset in terms of goals, definitions and deliverables. If key features are omitted from the initial project specification, large amounts of work and time may be subsequently added. When these additions are made informally it is extremely likely that the result will be missed deadlines and stressed employees. A good remedy is to place responsibility for project completion on one individual who is aware that the key to success is to be very tight on the project definition both at the start and also in terms of not allowing any increases in scope under any circumstances. This project leader must:

- know all facets of the project,
- have completion planned over a short time, such as three months,
- have the necessary resources available, and
- have a team committed to success.

The above ideas apply particularly when LIS projects span two or more companies. It is important to have systems spanning the supply chain. Projects to implement such systems should have changes in work practices, new business processes and system objectives clearly agreed before starting. Then the project, between say two companies, should not exceed six months in length.

The second key issue in project implementation is close control of critical activities in the project plan. Critical path techniques can be used to determine the bottleneck activities. Then these activities should be scheduled to start at the mean estimate of completion of the previous activity. Flexibility should allow subsequent activities to start immediately if an early finish permits.

The third issue in logistics systems implementation is the need to strive for perfect execution of the project. By auditing your own efforts and benchmarking other companies in the same industry, aim for perfect execution which implies minimal defects, routine achievement of schedule, supporting activities in other parts of the organisation, good software systems, and the means to recover from nasty surprises.[8]

A leading ERP vendor provides a classification of stages of system development which helps students evaluate the degree of integration achieved.[15] The four stages are:

1. *Disconnected systems.* Companies at this stage have many independent information systems, manual and ineffective communications and digitised internal data. They are organised functionally with little integration and low web capabilities.
2. *Internal and external interfaces.* Companies are organised functionally with a high degree of data integration and limited web capabilities. Organisations at this stage are transaction-focused in both purchasing and distribution activities.

3. *Internal integration and limited external integration.* Companies have integrated systems within the enterprise which link functions as required. Organisations have linked suppliers to their material systems and customers to their sales systems.
4. *Multi-enterprise integration.* Companies are cross-functionally organised and systems are extended to supply chain partners. Total visibility of the supply network is achieved by end-to-end integration.

The ultimate goal of information development is to standardise processes across the supply chain so companies can collaborate and cut cost.

Summary

Information is the supply chain driver that enables the other drivers, orders, inventory and transport, to work together to create an integrated supply chain. Information is crucial to supply chain performance because it provides the facts that supply chain managers use to make decisions. These decisions range from strategic through planning to operational. With information, companies have the view they need to make decisions that satisfy customers and improve company and overall supply chain performance. For information products and services, such as music and airline reservations, electronic communications can deliver the whole distribution channel.

A number of analysis tools are provided so that students can assess the extent of information available, the effectiveness of the various planning and execution systems and the degree of integration of information, both with companies and along the supply chain.

Managers must understand how information is gathered and analysed because information is critical to a supply chain's success. Data are summarised into information and analysed into knowledge to make the decisions required to respond to present requirements and plan for future needs of customers. Information must be carefully specified, so that it is understood correctly by all who use it. It must be communicated to the people and systems that require it. Such communication should transcend company boundaries so that all supply chain players are responding to the same 'drum-beat' from the customer.

The right systems with the right levels of complexity must be installed. CRM systems for distribution, MRP systems for manufacturing and ERP systems for entire enterprises are key examples. Automation should be used in supply chain information systems to the extent that it is effective in delivering customer value and enterprise profit. It should not be used lightly 'because the other firms have it', or ignored because it is too much trouble to map out the supply chain's precise requirements and obtain a system that provides them.

Questions

1. Describe the part that information communication plays in obtaining a view of a stated supply chain so that a function, such as order assignment, master production scheduling or product transport, operates effectively.
2. For a logistics area with which you are familiar, consider how electronic and person-to-person communication complement each other.
3. How should chain partners communicate transactions and plans? Compare the merits of EDI, the Internet, Internet-enabled ERP systems and facsimiles.
4. What should an enterprise resource planning system do? Choose one or two business processes and outline the functions that ERP should perform.

Case: Betta Struts develops an e-supply chain

Introduction

Betta Struts plc is a UK company which manufactures and distributes a wide range of metal framing, electrical and mechanical support systems nation-wide, with some export customers. The Betta Board was not satisfied with the earnings before interest and tax (EBIT) generated, and suspected there were problems with customer relations.

The Board appointed supply chain consultants KPMG to review the challenging business situation. The consultants' review revealed that Betta:

- lacks visibility with its customers,
- is not able to supply its products effectively,
- maintains its customers because of the excellence of its products, rather than customer ability to communicate easily with Betta, and
- has old information systems that do not incorporate real-time web access.

As a result of this review, Mike Potter, the Information Systems Manager, recognised the need to upgrade Betta's information systems and to develop an e-supply chain.

Betta supply chain

Betta Struts has a turnover of £55 million and employs 650 people. Betta provides fasteners and framing for nearly every industrial building site in Britain: office blocks, schools, factories and hospitals. Betta purchases components from 80 suppliers, both local and overseas, and manufactures and assembles them in a factory in Milton Keynes. Completed products are distributed by 14 transport companies to distributors and building sites throughout Britain and overseas.

Supply chain vision

The consultants' review was discussed by Betta Struts' senior management at length in a half-day meeting. They adopted the vision to become:

(Continued)

'A total framing solution provider with one face to the customer.'

Management's aim is to address the changing business environment in which:

- customers are demanding more from fewer suppliers – service is just as important as the physical product delivery.
- B2B (business-to-business) commerce is becoming a requirement, rather than an extra.
- acquisition of other businesses by Betta will continue to complicate the provision of customer access to the range of building products.

A review

Consultants KPMG held strategic workshops with senior management and functional workshops with operations and information systems management. The seven main issues that they identified are given in Table C5.1.

Table C5.1   Issues identified

1	ad-hoc customer relationships
2	'old mindset' business culture
3	14 transport companies
4	poor costing and financial visibility
5	no materials requirements planning or sales and operations planning processes
6	poor inventory control
7	poor visibility of components purchased

The consultants considered the consequences of these issues to be:

- safety stock duplication,
- inconsistent delivery times,
- manufacturing pushing stock to customers,
- large number of back-orders,
- customer dissatisfaction, and
- increasing pressure on prices.

The effect of all these problems was an unacceptable EBIT (earnings before interest and tax), currently running at 5.5% per annum.

The consultants recommended the following four strategies which would improve customer service (the first) and reduce supply chain costs (the other three):

- Align the service model to what the market requires.
- Plan product movement along the supply chain.
- Introduce common data and processes.
- Improve in-bound logistics.

The poor attitude of Betta's people towards its business was an important issue reported by the consultants. Senior managers agreed with the criticism and considered that a restructure

(Continued)

(Continued)

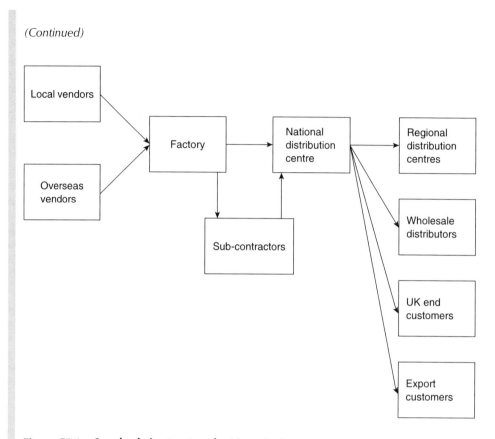

Figure C5.1   **Supply chain structure for Monostrut**

of management was essential. The aim of the restructure was to move away from department 'silos', with their own internal aims, to an integrated company. In this integrated organisation all managers' efforts would propel the business towards their common goals of customer service. Betta Struts would appear connected from the point of view of the customer. But how to achieve this?

In one productive workshop, Mike Potter, the Information Systems Manager, was in a group with Fred Beale, the Logistics Manager and Tessa Florey, the National Sales Manager. Picking up on three of the issues found by the consultants, the group realised that they must define a supply chain model to achieve the common goal. That model would provide the common thread around which the unified management structure could be developed. The model they chose for the pilot product, Monostrut, is shown in Figure C5.1.

Realignment

Mike Potter and his colleagues considered the evidence from the review and its recommendations. They consulted widely with their colleagues and they spoke to industry contacts and software providers. From this analysis they constructed a realignment programme which they believed would tackle all Betta Struts' problems, achieve the four strategies and

(Continued)

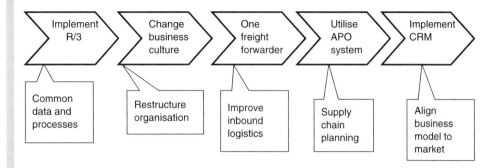

Figure C5.2   **Planned realignment**
CR/3 = Version of SAP ERP; APO = Advanced Planning Optimiser; CRM = Customer Response
Management)

improve the company's EBIT to the figure which the Board required, that is 14%. This
programme is given in Figure C5.2.

Software adopted

The first step carried out by Mike and his team was to implement five key modules of the
SAP enterprise resource planning system. Sales and Distribution (SD) allowed customers'
orders to be tracked from entry of the original order through the whole order processing
until the required products were delivered. Production Planning (PP) enabled weekly
schedules of the 750 finished products to be planned to enable the expected sales. The PP
module also kept track of the amount of each fastener available to promise to customers
so that delivery dates could be accurately achieved. Materials Management (MM) tracked
all the materials required to assemble the products required by the production plan.
Costing (CO) and Financial Investment (FI) systems translated the inventories and operating costs into the profitability expected for each future period. These modules gave good
product costs, to support *ad hoc* product prices and an excellent set of financial reports.
The Advanced Planning Optimiser (APO) system was also installed at this time, but it was
only partially implemented.

This software, along with the corresponding changes in management responsibility,
effectively automated the Betta Strut supply chain. It delivered a solution which spanned
the whole enterprise. The information was loaded only at one point and it became very
accurate. It easily surpassed the Class A targets of inventory 95% accurate and bill of materials 98% correct because of the faster flow of information achieved. This information
accuracy helped the sales, customer service, manufacturing and distribution departments.
After the initial implementation, fewer people were needed to administer the whole information system, even though the functions available had increased markedly. The cost of
managing purchase orders decreased by 70%.

(Continued)

(Continued)

Industrial customers were provided with web-based access to Betta's catalogue, prices and product descriptions. Qualified customers could also access stocks available of individual lines of fasteners and framing and indicative delivery times. Then, if they wished, customers could place an order for the products they wanted. Betta would respond with order and delivery confirmation by email.

Restructure

The management restructure required many employees to move from functional departments, such as Purchasing, Operations and Marketing, into process teams. Process teams were established for new product introduction and order fulfilment. These teams were given performance measures of customer delivery, response times and cost containment. The functional departments retained staff specialists who had authority in their specialisation, but only an advisory role in customer transactions. Training was provided for all staff to understand their new roles and the support provided by the new IT systems. Managers explained the new responsibilities to all their staff and counselled them as necessary.

Other changes

An important change was the move, in 2002, from 14 transport companies to one. The use of 14 hauliers had come about because each distribution centre appointed local companies which covered part of its area. Now that national hauliers were available, such as Pickfords, Betta could obtain better prices and service from one firm. Moreover, it was much simpler to deal with one firm, which could be trained in Betta's precise requirements and with only one external information system to deal with.

Demand planning

The first part of APO, the SAP Advanced Planning Optimiser, to be implemented was demand planning. Tessa Florey, the National Sales Manager, developed a forecasting process which used 24 months of history on stock-keeping units (sku) and regional level for the 1,200 make-to-stock products. Each forecast gave both the best estimate and its accuracy. Branch sales managers combined the statistical forecast with their experience of past and present market conditions, to predict sales for product groups over the next three months. Tessa then met with the Demand Coordinator to agree on the final forecast which would be submitted to the monthly sales and operations planning (S&OP) meeting. The S&OP meeting was chaired by the General Manager. Held in the third week of the month, representatives of all areas involved met to decide a production plan for the following six months, of which two months were 'firm'. That is, they would not be altered unless a major upset occurred.

The new role of Demand Coordinator was introduced, responsible to the National Sales Manager for product sales information and to the Information Systems Manager for technical functions. The Demand Coordinator managed the whole sales and operations planning process each month, including:

* forecast preparation and revision,
* review of forecast by brand managers,

(Continued)

- update of changes to forecast,
- sending out pre-S&OP reports,
- attending S&OP meeting, and
- update of forecast in ERP system.

Advantages of e-supply chain

After all these changes had been bedded-in, Mike Potter jotted down a list of the advantages that were accruing to Betta as a result of the automated supply chain:

- Enterprise-wide information solution with accurate and timely information.
- B2B collaboration between systems removes data processing.
- Information is more reliable for sales, customer service, manufacturing and distribution departments.
- Streamlining of departments allows resources to be used in other areas.
- Faster information flow provides better inventory control.
- Cost of purchase orders is decreased.

Results achieved

Two years later, Mike, Fred and Tessa met to evaluate the success of the supply chain realignment in preparation for a Board presentation. They agreed that the key results obtained over that period were:

- the implementation of SAP R/3 and, partially, APO,
- that the improved procurement of parts had led to a 22% delivered cost reduction,
- that better production planning, given the forecast and the S&OP process, had reduced the costs of inventory by 30%, without injuring customer service levels,
- that a marked shift in the business culture gave Betta a market-driven, customer focus, and
- that progress had been made towards the higher EBIT return required.

Case questions

1. What are the recommendations of Betta Struts' supply chain vision and why is each important?
2. What status had Betta Struts achieved for each major information system at the end of the case?
3. How did Betta Struts ensure that its people and their culture supported the e-supply chain?

REFERENCES

1   Holland W and Sodhi MS (2004) 'Quantifying the effect of batch size and order errors on the bull–whip effect using simulation', *International Journal of Logistics: Research and Applications,* 7(3): 251–61.

2   Lee HL, Padmanabhan V and Whang SJ (1997) 'Information distortion in a supply chain: the bull–whip effect', *Management Science*, 43: 546–58.

3   Closs DJ and Xu K (2000) 'Logistics information technology practice in manufacturing and merchandising firms', *International Journal of Physical Distribution and Logistics Management*, 30(10): 869–96.

4   Lawrence FB, Jennings DF and Reynolds BE (2003) *eDistribution*, Thomson South-Western, Mason, OH.

5   Koch C (2003) *The ABCs of ERP*, ERP Research Centre, at www.cio. com/research/erp/edit/erpbasics.htlm (accessed 21/2/06).

6   Perez M, Hildenbrand A, Matzke B and Zenke P (1999) *SAP R/3 on the Internet*. Addison-Wesley, Reading, MA.

7   Ashayeri J and Selen WJ (2003) 'A production planning model and a case study for the pharmaceutical industry in the Netherlands', *International Journal of Logistics: Research and Applications*, 6(1–2): 37–49.

8   Vollmann TE, Berry WL, Whybark DC and Jacobs FR (2005) *Manufacturing Planning and Control Systems for Supply Chain Management (5th edn)*, McGraw-Hill, New York.

9   Slack N, Chambers S and Johnson R (2001) *Operations Management* (3rd edn), Prentice Hall, Harlow, Essex.

10   Jones D and Womack J (2002) *Seeing the Whole: Mapping the Extended Value Stream*, Lean Enterprise Institute Brookline, MA.

11   Min H (2006) 'The applications of warehouse management systems: an exploratory study', *International Journal of Logistics: Research and Applications*, 9(2): 111–26.

12   Papazoglu MP and Tsalgatidou A (2000) 'Business to business electronic commerce issues and solutions', *Decision Support Systems*, 29(4): 301–4.

13   Van der Vorst JAG, van Dongen S, Nouguier S and Hilhorst R (2002) 'E-business initiatives in food supply chains: definition and typology of electronic business models', *Internatinal Journal of Logistics: Research and Applications*, 5(2): 119–38.

14   Toyota Best Practice Bulletin (2003) 'How Toyota Australia saved $20 million annually through Sales and Manufacturing teamwork', Toyota Motor Corporation Australia Limited, *Cutting Costs in Customer Supply Chain*, Volome 12, December (unpublished).

15   See www.sap.com/scm/

Integration of the Supply Chain

6

Work collaboratively with customers, suppliers, trading partners, and third parties to change the way operations are viewed, performed, and measured. Manage across the business on behalf of the customer. Think in terms of the *extended supply chain*.[1]

Objectives

- To stimulate the design and operation of supply chains for customers and to use tools to make chains more effective
- To understand a framework for managing and directing supply chains in the long run
- To allow for the impacts of inter-company lack of unity (trust, communication) and dynamic effects
- To investigate the challenges of using various types of partnership between companies in supply chains

INTRODUCTION

After covering the parts, it is now time to bring the whole supply chain together. The business logistics of each link have been studied in detail and assembled in the 'Double-Bell' model. The processes in the supply chain have been examined from individual functions to leadership of the whole chain. Information communication has been seen to provide orders for the goods that customers want and to enable plans to respond to future needs. The scene is set to integrate all the links, direct their value-adding towards customers' needs and provide a return for the chain partners. Several tools are provided to assist this integration, including setting chain boundaries, flow-creating criteria, choices of chain relationships and how to set logistics priorities in the supply network.

The overall aim is to move from the task-focused strategies, used conventionally by European companies, to a process focus. As shown in Figure 6.1, the *task* focus is only able to produce the sum of a series of individual tasks. By adopting a *process* focus, the supply chain solution is delivered by a single team for each key process.

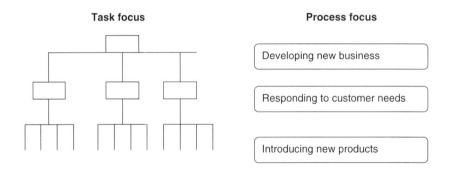

Figure 6.1   Compare task and process-focused strategies

There is no single recipe for supply chain integration. Recent research suggests that emphasis should be directed to focused efforts rather than overall integration.[2] So this chapter provides advice, which can be tempered to the situation, rather than a recipe. It aims to enable practitioners and scholars to modify and operate chains so that customers get their products and services while value is added to the companies involved. Complicating issues in particular situations, such as chain leadership, power and supply chain creation, and the extent of outsourcing, are covered in Chapter 7. This chapter addresses immediate central issues. It is rarely possible to start with a 'green field site' to eradicate past errors. The chain operators must make day-to-day running decisions as well as attain the right strategic direction.

There is no section in this chapter on information. Rather, each section considers product flow and the information which is required to achieve the flow. To a certain extent this is true of management. The chapter addresses the management of parts, products and services so that customers may be supplied, but glosses over strategic change to all organisations in a supply chain, which is covered in Chapter 8.

6.1 KEY CONCEPTS FOR CHAIN INTEGRATION

A number of key concepts influence the successful or unsuccessful operation of all supply chains. These concepts are flow of products, the decoupling point, the supply chain boundary and the variability of the chain system.

Product flow examines the movement of products and services through the supply chain to the customer. Irrespective of the type of goods, the key aim of a chain is to provide and deliver the correct products to customers. Recall the water channel analogy used in Chapter 1. We must change the emphasis from orders and inventory, static measures, to turnover per month, deliveries per week, proportion of items right first time – dynamic measures of flow. In our experience flow is not being recorded along the whole supply chain. Rate of flow must be planned and executed and measured for the whole chain. For example, in the case 'Shoes go global' in Chapter 4, Texon produces lining material for shoe manufacturers. Texon should consider the delivery of finished shoes to Nike's world-wide customers, rather than its own sales of shoe lining. Texon should stop focusing on the production of rolls of shoe lining and highlight the delivery of finished shoes which contain its lining.

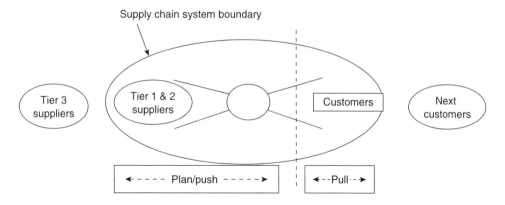

Figure 6.2   **Decoupling point and system boundary in a supply chain**

The flow in supply chain operations is crucially affected by the decoupling point, the point which separates unassigned materials and products from those allocated to particular customers. The decoupling point separates planned provision of materials from goods being *pulled** by customer orders.[3] Figure 6.2 depicts a generalised view of the 'Double-Bell' model of a supply chain. The ellipse surrounds chain partners which are deemed important enough to be part of the chain. The vertical dotted line represents an example decoupling point. On the customer side of this point, goods are provided and delivered according to known customer orders. This side, comparable to the major change when a weir separates the tidal part of a river from the non-tidal part upstream, can be accurately served with just-in-time selection and delivery of goods to customers. On the upstream, or provision, side of the decoupling point, products and services are planned and pushed. Planned means that capacity is provided, materials are purchased and people are put in place. *Push** means that the whole philosophy is to use experience and forecasts to carry out all the preparation for an expected order. Push is done with good intentions but it may not result in deliveries and turnover. Push leads to MRP systems where plans start a year in advance, materials are purchased and manufacturing is completed: all against an estimate, a forward reflection of the past. In these times, when the customer is king and competitors are promoting new products every day, such estimates are likely to lead to enormous supply chain waste.

To determine the correct decoupling point, two times, which dictate supply chain behaviour, must be known. Production time ('P' time) is the total logistics lead-time that it takes a product or a service to go through the pipeline from procurement until it reaches the customer. Demand time ('D' time) is the time a customer is prepared to wait to have their demand fulfilled. 'P' and 'D' times should be individually measured for different product groups and different market segments, respectively. If production time is greater than the demand time, the focal firm is not able to make-to-order. It may still be possible to assemble-to-order, as seen when Dell responds quickly to an Internet order.

How does one put a boundary around a supply chain system? We must decide which firms and which stages are important enough to influence the flow of goods to customers, rather than those that serve or do not affect the system. This is an individual decision which is made by reviewing the stages in the Double-Bell model, the information flows and other drivers. Box 6.1 provides an example. The decision requires managers to consider which firms and service contractors have a primary effect on goods flow. An important part of the boundary is the number of links or steps that are included. It is possible to go upstream forever. For example, Texon is the ultimate supplier of linings for your shoes but it also buys chemicals. Also consider how far downstream to go: does the chain conclude with the retailer, the consumer or outputs downstream of the consumer? Such outputs include those engendered by employers or another company. This deciding where to put a boundary is similar to 'big picture' mapping advocated by Jones and Womack.[4]

Box 6.1   Example of supply chain boundary

This diagram uses the example of Shavers Inc. from the case study in Chapter 1 (see pages 20–9) to illustrate the idea of putting a boundary around the links in the supply chain, to separate the major influences from secondary factors. Suppliers are left outside the boundary because they are, mainly, located outside Europe and therefore have limited influence on the main chain which requires shavers to be assembled and supplied to stores throughout Europe. The customers who buy the shavers are also left outside, because they choose from the range available in the stores. Shavers are not customised for end customers.

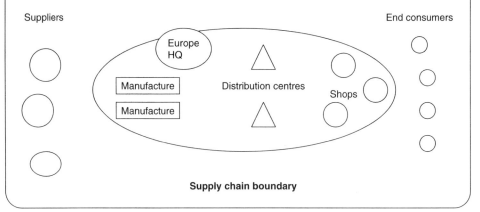

Once the boundary is established, the important functions and partners can be placed inside it. The choice of these functions and partners depends upon the order-winning criteria in the next section. With manufactured products it is fairly easy: how are the products provided and distributed? What materials and components are needed? Using the Pareto principle, put in the functions and partners which account for the majority of flows. For services it is harder: is this service important in the chain? Some transport services go in because they are particularly important. Others stay out because they do not affect the flow or they can easily be replaced. The touchstone in these is effect on the flow of the whole chain system. The local effects are of secondary importance.

In integrating supply chain flow, consider the inherent variability of the system. Conventionally, people think in point values, means. But systems contain distributions of order rates, variable quality performance and distributions of customer outcomes. Hence, we need to determine the range of performance of functions and think about how this affects the workings of the chain system. Here are some examples:

- An average consumption of beer is no use for predicting flow of beer on a summer day.
- Normal purchases of blue shirts in Italy are no guide to sales of shirts in a suburb of Birmingham, Sydney or Singapore.
- The average sales of windscreen wipers confuse those assembled on new cars and those used to replace worn-out ones.
- Tomatoes are not available for preserving at the annual rate of consumption.
- Ships do not often sail from Europe to Singapore in the average time.
- An inventory system which is 99% right will not protect a distributor from a stock-out if the product wanted is in the 1% in error.
- Variability in the time to develop a new product.

Building on these mechanistic concepts, consider the *relationships** between organisations in the supply chain. Such relationships between supply chain partners have a major influence on how the chain functions, how it flows goods or services to customers. To do supply chain relationships justice, they are covered in a separate section, 6.3.

We have now set out the main concepts of chain integration. Next integration is guided by examining the *flow-creating criteria** and the supply chain drivers.

6.2 FLOW-CREATING CRITERIA

This section first examines the main parameters that affect the form of supply chains. Secondly, it considers how the needs of end customers lead to a number of criteria which will win orders. These criteria are chain performances which are critical to win customers, to obtain orders and to retain both. Thirdly, the section examines how these criteria flow from the stages of the chain, such as supply and distribution, and its drivers, such as inventory and transport.

Product parameters

Types of supply chain (see section 1.2) are mainly predicated by the kinds of goods and services that they provide. Among goods are they custom-made or commodity? The chain for a custom-made product, such as a wedding dress, will be quite different from that for a commodity product, such as socks or shirts. Where is the product on its life cycle? A product needs a very flexible supply chain in its early stages to take advantage of early buyers and product changes. When the product reaches maturity, the higher volumes and steadier product features will probably require a broader, steadier channel to the customer. Consumer products have very different supply chain characteristics from industrial products. The essence of fast-moving consumer goods is convenient supply of cheap commodity items. The majority of products bought by businesses are more quality and delivery-date sensitive with less emphasis on price and variants.

A range of product supply chains depends on the manufacturing complexity of the end product. Simple products may comprise a single plastic moulding, such as a bucket or a paper clip. A medium-level product may require assembly of 10–20 components, such as a model toy or a meal. An elaborately-transformed product will require hundreds of parts. This may need several tiers of suppliers to produce components and modules. A separate company at a separate site may assemble these modules into the finished product. Those examples were all 'assembled' products. There is a further division into process goods which come from a continuous processing line. Process goods include fuels, glass, foods and chemicals. The main differences from assembled products are:

- an inability to maintain exact specification,
- the need to carry out long runs of one product, and
- a greater capital cost of equipment.

A third division is between stable goods and perishable ones. In some ways supply chains for perishable goods are exemplars of what chains *should* be like for stable goods without an expiry date. Milk and meat and newspapers have short lives so the flow from supply of materials through provision to delivery has to match them. Fortunately for the companies in those chains, many of the goods are commodities. Hence lack of actual orders can often be substituted by last week's sales. The fast flow prevents a lot of the problems that occur in longer supply chains for stable goods. For example, books go through long writing, publishing, selling and remaindering stages, whereas a newspaper spends only half a day over the same stages.

Service supply chains comprise a radically different division. The emphasis on intangible benefits, in which products are only secondary, is one cause. The inability to store service products, such as an airline seat, improves the flow time of the service considerably. The direct involvement of people in many service processes also impels them towards rapid flow and good performance. In effect, most service chains are customised compared to commodity products. Mass services, such as air travel or retail shops, have less interaction with the customer. The retail supply chain is very similar to a product chain. Airlines have large set-up costs, in purchase of aircraft and terminals, and then limited supplies in the areas of meals and cleaning. Service shops, such as a garage or a hairdresser, have a highly customised service which may require a continual supply of spare parts, with a garage, or supplies limited to consumable creams and soaps, in the case of a hairdresser.

In information flow, service chains and product chains have similar needs for fast, accurate information. With a product chain it may be possible to flow the goods to the customer after the order is placed. With a service chain, it is necessary to set up the chain according to prior experience and then use the capability provided to the best effect as customers present themselves. With hotels and restaurants, it may be possible to get the customer to pre-book her needs, but the facility has to be flexible since the customer may change her requirements at short notice.

In short, classify your product or service into the best categories and be careful not to use insights from other categories in deciding the features of your supply chain.

Order-winning criteria

With these main chain parameters in mind, now consider how you may determine the order-flow criteria which will lead to well-integrated supply chains. The aim is to find a

Table 6.1 **Derivation of major flow criteria (* by consumers; values in table mean contribution to customer satisfaction)**

	CHAIN-WIDE		STAGES				
CRITERION	As is	Aim	Suppliers	Manufacturing	Distribution	Retailing	Customer orders
Quality							
Features							
Delivery speed							
Delivery reliability							
No. of varieties							
Rate of change*							
Other							
INFORMATION							
Transaction data							
Availability							
Scheduling							
Accuracy							
Vision							
System development							
TOTAL							

small number of qualifying criteria, which your chain must attain, and a number of order-winning criteria,[5] which your chain will pursue to satisfy customers, and gain orders at the expense of competitors. The qualifying and order-winning criteria should then be related to the chain stages and partners which provide them. This assessment should be done for the current situation and for the future anticipated state.

The method of deriving the criteria in Table 6.1 should be along the following lines. Hill[5] suggests using a 'Q' for qualifiers and having 100 points which each respondent can allocate to the criteria on the left-hand side. The emphasis is on giving large amounts to the most important criteria rather than putting some numbers against every one. The importance of the 'aim' column will vary from one supply chain to another. The faster the rate of change in customers and hence chains, the more important it is.

Table 6.1 is a worksheet to assist in deriving flow criteria. The left-hand side lists a number of criteria for the product and service flow plus information criteria to plan and execute product flow. The first two columns are used for chain-wide assessment of the importance of various criteria. The following five columns are used to identify which stages in the chain contribute to that decision.

Stages in the chain

Finally, we examine the mapping of competitive criteria on to stages, drivers and partners. This chain integration will only work if responsibility for the important flow criteria is sheeted home to the processes and people responsible. It is not sufficient to map criteria on to existing partners, as their position and its extent may require change. Therefore, although the net result is to go from criteria to the partners that will attain them, it is essential to go via the stages and drivers of the supply chain. The matter of how chain partners provide these stage criteria is discussed in Chapter 7.

Box 6.2 provides an example of supply chain integration for Shavers Inc. (see case in Chapter 1, pages 20–9). For simplicity, chain-wide criteria have been restricted to the current situation and most qualifiers have not been shown.

Box 6.2   **Example of supply chain integration at Shavers**

Q means qualifying criterion

The reader is recommended to read the Shavers case at the end of Chapter 1.[6]

Flow-creating criteria

CHAINWIDE			STAGES			
CRITERION	As is	Suppliers	Manufacturing	Distribution	Retailing	Customer orders
Quality	Q	.				
Features						
Delivery speed						
Delivery reliability	30	✓		✓		✓
No. of varieties	10	✓		✓		
Rate of change						
Other						
INFORMATION						
Transaction data						
Availability	10			✓ (promotion)		
Scheduling	10		✓	✓		
Accuracy						
Vision	20		✓	✓		✓
System development	20		✓	✓		✓
TOTAL	100					

Planned direction

Supply chain strategy to align with global marketing strategy.
Coordination of European product flow by a central planning function.

Current achievement

Order fill rate only 78%.
Order delivery time varied from five days to 20.

(Continued)

Policies

Comparing Figures C1.2 and C1.3 in the Shavers case, reveals a major change in the location of decisions. Most functions, except order-processing, have moved from national into European headquarters. Decisions on factory operations moved from two European locations to the European HQ. Changes have been made in computer design and information processing support.

Systems development included central forecasting at European HQ and a new distribution requirements planning system.

Relocation and reduction in distribution centres from 13 to eight.

Outsourcing distribution centre management to contractors.

Results

Order fill rates improved from 78% to 98%.

Logistics costs reduced to a smaller percentage of sales turnover. Includes reduced number of people.

Steady inventory levels in spite of 50% increase in products.

Faster cycle times achieved by fast information communication rather than reduced manufacturing and distribution times.

Change from mainframe computers to client-server computers.

Improved international data transmission networks.

6.3 RELATIONSHIPS

The rationale for supplier partnerships is that, without them, no customer can ever know enough about a supplier, and vice versa, to take full advantage of both partners' combined resources and expertise.[7] (p. 11)

Partnering, the basis of chain integration

Cooperation between firms belonging to the same supply chain is now recognised as a powerful source of competitive advantage. Such companies do not transfer costs along the supply chain. They cooperate to increase overall sales and reduce total cost rather than competing for a bigger share of a fixed profit.

Companies are unlikely to achieve significant supply chain integration unless they develop close relationships with key partners up and down the supply chain. Let's define business partnership in general and in three specific types:

Partnering is a defined business relationship based on mutual trust, openness, shared risk and shared rewards that yield a competitive advantage (and provide value and build resources for stockholders), resulting in greater business performance than the companies could achieve individually.[8] (p. 231)

In some recent work in India, three types of *partnership** are recognised from the least to the most advanced:[8]

1. *Transactional partnering** implies that transactions between the two firms are carried out in a seamless way without the companies being committed to a long-term relationship.
2. *Strategic partnering** exists because the customer, or buying partner, wishes to create new value by moving some operational parameter in the provision of goods and services to the supplier in exchange for the customer obtaining a higher profit or reference sales. Examples of operational improvement are quality or delivery improvement and cost reduction.
3. *Exclusive partnering** demands that the customer will have exclusive rights over some supplier capabilities, such as capacities, products or product lines, in return for committed growth for the vendor.

An important part of supply chain design is to decide which type of partnership is most appropriate for a particular relationship.

Box 6.3 gives an example of the benefits a partnering can give when a major incident prevents a supplier from making the parts required. Next, investigate a number of parameters, which partnerships should have, working mainly at the strategic partnering level. Research carried out into logistics partnerships between shippers and logistics service providers (LSPs) questions the proportion of LSPs which are strategic partners with the shippers they serve.[9] Makukha and Gray used the Delphi approach to investigate the experience of 12 shippers and nine LSPs from five European countries. Taking 'strategic' as implying sharing of commercial intention, rewards and culture, the experts took the view that functions can be outsourced but strategic control elements should be kept in-house.

Box 6.3   Partnership prevents business dislocation

In February 1997 a fire destroyed the factory of Aisin, one of Toyota's largest suppliers and the sole source for a P-valve. The valve was an essential brake part used in all of Toyota's vehicles throughout the world. Because of Toyota's renowned just-in-time system, it had only two days supply in stock, after which the plant would have to shut down. Sixty-three suppliers worked together around the clock to replace the dies and machine tools. They managed to get P-valve production restarted in two days at different plants. Their highly responsible and responsive action allowed Toyota to continue production almost without a hitch. The power of ingenuity and collaboration was never felt so highly in the supply chain before. When Aisin had rebuilt its plant, it took back manufacture of the brake part.[10]

Partnership development

There are three main steps to set up a mutually rewarding partnership.[7] The first step is to achieve internal readiness. Each partner must be led by its CEO and must treat its own

Table 6.2   **An example of supplier metrics**[7]

Measure	Current performance	One-year target performance	Three-year target performance
Average lead-time	8.2 weeks	7 weeks	5 weeks
Average stock turns	3.6 per year	4.5 per year	6 per year
Forecast accuracy	38%	40%	45%
Delivery on time	74%	85%	95%
Customer returns	61,000 ppm	30,000 ppm	10,000 ppm

(ppm = parts per million)

employees as family members. The prime example is Toyota, where employees helped the company build a very strong relationship to suppliers. The partner company has to have a uniform culture across its organisation to achieve internal readiness. It also helps to have as small a number of suppliers as is feasible.

The second step is to set up the partnership. It is important to identify the right partner, just as in marriage! Companies need to compare value systems and their emphasis on short-term gains versus long-term development. The right partnership model must be chosen, from the three already described. The more critical the item being supplied, the more likely the partners will choose an exclusive partnership. It is important to establish mutual expectations for the partnership: set measurable targets and the means to attain them. It is also necessary to integrate business processes and technology. Without necessarily sharing databases, the two partners must have a common definition of items supplied or confusion will result.

The third step is to maintain the partnership. Regular feedback between the two partners enables urgent matters to be addressed and prevents dislocations. Periodically a review should be jointly conducted by the manufacturer (or service company) and its supplier to examine all the parameters in the supply partnership agreement. Any failures should be immediately addressed to recover the partnership aims. Key people from the supplier community should be recognised for their contribution. Part of partnership maintenance, coming from the periodic review, is a recognition that the original goals are unrealistic or the business situation has changed. In this case, the expectations from the partnership may need to be redrawn.[7]

Partners within a supply chain

This section gives an example of partnerships in a supply chain and addresses some other facets for companies in chain partnerships.

An example of an organised supply chain is the provision of wiper assemblies to a car manufacturer. In the new car development cycle, the automobile manufacturer specifies the position in the car and the task of the window-cleaning module. The wiper manufacturer sets up partnership agreements with the car manufacturer and with its suppliers of steel, rubber and motors. This requires forward forecasts, communication of the expected mix of wiper types required and a supply contract of at least a year. As a result, second-tier suppliers are providing materials and parts to the first-tier supplier. The latter is quickly, effectively and cheaply delivering modules to suit the manufacturer's exact needs.

Control corrections are required to ensure that supply partnerships work according to plan for the benefit of all partners. Table 6.2 shows the improvement in supply parameters agreed between Ampere Components and its key suppliers. The metrics in the table were agreed between all parties to the supplier association. The partners also put in place actions to achieve the better outcomes. Without these measures having the legal status of a contract, they represent a basis for the supply of electrical components. The measures will be reviewed each quarter by Ampere's supply chain purchasing officers. Failure to achieve any of the parameters can be investigated and rectified.

Close collaboration is the basis of successful relationships between companies. For supply chains to work well, it is necessary for each link company to be prepared to share the exigencies of business life as they happen with upstream suppliers and downstream customers to become one supply enterprise. This encompasses everything from receipt of orders and costs to business plans, the flow of information up the chain and of goods down the chain to customers. This includes knowledge sharing.

Successful partnering in supply chains is at odds with some of the new tenets of corporate governance. The trend to self-protection in governance of individual companies needs to be set aside. Link companies are proceeding down a path of close collaboration which will satisfy customers so well that there is no need for concern that the minimum standards of business behaviour will be met. Successful movement to a coherent supply enterprise should amply satisfy all stakeholders, including shareholders.

6.4 PLANNED DIRECTIONS

Given the criteria that are needed in various stages of the supply chain to serve customers effectively, we must set our goals. The starting point of goals is usually the corporate goals of each partner in the supply chain. Select the ones which have the most application to the supply chain task. Resolve conflicting goals as far as possible. For example, one partner may have a goal to increase turnover by 6% per year while another aims to increase their margin by 4% per year. The supply chain goal may be increased throughput of 5% per year accompanied by cost control so that the margin is correspondingly increased.

In some cases, supply chain integration will be aimed at part of the chain, rather than the whole. Recent research questions the notion that full integration should be the aim of all supply chains. Developments in the areas of strategy, processes, relationships, organisation and performance measurement suggest that selectively integrated chains may be a better goal with prevailing shorter product life cycles.[2] Without questioning the benefits of cooperation, this research advocates that integration is also about trade-offs and a tolerance of disharmony. On a spectrum from vertical integration to discrete market exchanges, planners should consider what type and level of integration applies to each link of the supply chain.

The direction the supply chain partners should take to achieve the agreed goals is most likely to be found through a democratic planning process. Managers of the partners have time to sit down, learn about other parts of the chain system, and invent the innovative actions most likely to succeed. In a recent supply chain mapping exercise, a factory operations manager talking to a farm director said: 'We would never spend an afternoon thinking about the process of harvesting vegetables, if it were not for the lean management project.'

Permanent capacity must be put in place to handle the flow of goods agreed in the chain goal. Capacity may be in several forms:

- capital equipment to provide processing ability,
- people appointment and training, and
- outsourcing service functions.

The planned direction should state the value that the chain expects to generate for its partners through superior flow of products to customers. Value includes the ability to remain in business, the value of the working lifestyle of the people involved and the profits that partners anticipate.

   An example of planned direction is given in Box 6.2 for the Shavers supply chain. The most important criterion to achieve to win business is 'delivery reliability'. The table shows that this criterion is driven by effective receipt of customer orders and achieved by the actions of suppliers and distribution. An important information criterion is 'vision', the ability of chain managers to have an accurate view of supply chain status. The table shows that this vision will primarily be achieved by the efforts of order entry, manufacturing and distribution.

6.5 CURRENT ACHIEVEMENT

Current achievement asks 'How good is the performance of the existing supply chain?' Chain managers need to assess how well they are performing against the flow-creating criteria set in section 6.2 in achieving the goals discussed in section 6.4. They measure their performance in the areas discussed below with the overall aim of attaining delivery to customers profitably. The managers consider whether information and contacts are giving them a proper view of the supply chain. Also they review management of the processes required for success.[7] Students can use the achievement in these areas of key performance to analyse the health of a supply chain.

Demand management

Typically, a supply chain uses forecasts, on the upstream side of the decoupling point, as well as actual orders to configure its resources to excel at this task. So demand management comprises:

- choice of the market areas to supply,
- production planning to set up long-term resources for each link,
- sales and operations planning to get agreement between sales, logistics, production and commercial elements across all links in the chain for a medium term (1–3 month) forward period,
- order forecasts, converted into implications for each upstream link,
- distribution requirements planning which comprises detailed plans for the movement of finished products along the chain, to complement existing inventory, for a number of time periods, typically weekly for 15 weeks, and
- receipt of actual orders.

A method of responding to customers' demand more effectively is the concept of an 'agile' supply chain in which logistics capabilities focus on individual end-consumer demand.[11] The essential difference in an *agile** supply chain is the development of the ability to respond to a range of possible customer needs in advance and hence increasing the value that logistics processes create for customers.

Scheduling and inventory

Each company in the chain has provided a capability to process certain levels and mixes of materials and products. Each company is also driven by a master production schedule of the finished items, from that partner's point of view, that should be produced each week. Then a review of scheduling comprises a measurement over a few weeks of the extent that the company achieves its plan.

Linked to the schedule is the inventory that chain partners are holding either as part of the pipeline through the chain to the end customer, or as safety stock in case of some emergency situation.

The inventory should be reviewed against the companies' targets and, possibly, against a leaner set of guidelines for stocks really required. This review should take account of:

*   the purpose for which inventory is held (see section 2.6),
*   the method by which inventory is managed (see Figure 2.9),
*   whether the stock is managed by vendors or comprises goods on consignment, and
*   the extra inventory complications imposed by global sourcing or global distribution.

Inbound logistics

The overall purpose of inbound logistics is to develop effective alliances with suppliers and transport companies for current and novel situations. The case at the end of this chapter is an example of improving inbound logistics by means of supplier associations. These areas should be examined to ensure inbound logistics are effective:

*   Evaluation and cooperation with suppliers. Working with second-tier suppliers.
*   Supply of all the numerous components needed to meet the production schedule as generated by material requirements planning (mrp).
*   The establishment of just-in-time purchasing for day-to-day supply to improve on mrp-driven flow of materials. This technique should improve inventory levels and reduce cycle times.
*   Transport of materials and components from suppliers to a warehouse or production line at the manufacturer.

Provision

Provision is the wider term which includes the transformation of manufactured goods, the replenishment of distribution centres and the assembly of materials required by a service operation. The overall aim of provision is to make the conversion of materials into products, or the stocking of service operations, highly effective through scheduling and coordination of departments and services while achieving sufficient flexibility. This list gives the main areas to be examined:

*   capability to transform materials into a variety of products, meaning availability of machinery, people and materials-handling,
*   receiving materials from suppliers,

- actual manufacture of the required products to daily and longer-term schedules,
- quality assurance, meaning that yield losses and error rates will be very low in output products that conform to customers' specifications,
- packing and assembly into product orders,
- equipment maintenance by engineers,
- information flows to facilitate all of the above, and
- disposal of unwanted materials and products.

Distribution

The overall aim of distribution is to deliver products to customers using distribution centres (DCs) as staging posts where the distance warrants this. The key measure of distribution is the proportion of orders delivered in full on time to the customer's premises. Effective distribution requires good bulk transport from manufacturers to DCs and capable delivery transport. Within the DC, the main tasks are storage of receipts, maintenance of the inventory, picking items to customer order and efficient despatch of consolidated orders.

Organisation and management of the supply chain

These areas are intangible. Consequently, they are much more difficult to audit. The primary evidence of good or bad management comes from symptoms rather than the methods and actions of managers. The audit should separate the effectiveness of management in each individual link company from the coordination between companies. Areas to consider:

- Are decisions made effectively and on time?
- Are staff motivated to give their best efforts?
- Are employees informed about the current business situation and the companies' aims?
- Are staff encouraged to speak out to improve the *status quo?*
- Do discipline areas support overall company and supply chain processes or do they form barriers?
- Are meetings provided with coherent information and is this used to resolve substantive problems, not who gets the best parking space?
- Does the organisation structure support flow of products through companies along the supply chain, or does it hinder such flow?
- What management forum considers the health of the whole supply chain?

Financial control of the supply chain

Cash flows in the opposite direction to goods and materials. An important aim is to shorten the time between cash being spent and returned through sales. Clearly, reductions in inventories and the cycle time to supply goods contribute to this aim. A fairer allocation of cash between supply chain partners is an increasingly important part of logistics. Although it is the ultimate aim, few companies are currently examining the financial control of the whole supply chain. Therefore this analysis will confine itself to the narrower area of cost control. Cost is one of the major measures of logistics performance and this applies all the way along the supply chain for both product and service chains. It is common to monitor and report cost data for specific logistics functions such as purchasing, warehousing, transport, distribution and order-processing as well as broader functions such as manufacturing and information technology. So a natural audit method is to compare actual with planned costs in each of these functional areas.

How can logistics costs be best represented? The older forms of costing, such as direct and indirect costs and standard costing, are not effective in sheeting home costs to the activities that should bear them in an age when the amount of direct labour contributing to products is shrinking. A better alternative is activity-based costing (ABC) which recognises that overhead costs are caused by activities, such as moving product through a distribution centre.[12] ABC breaks down the business into major processes, such as purchasing, manufacture and distribution, and then breaks each process into activities. For example, the distribution activity would include goods receiving, picking, consolidation and despatch. Then the ABC process establishes the item that drives the cost of each activity, known as the cost driver. For example, the cost driver for picking the goods for an order in a warehouse would be the number of locations that the picker has to visit to pick the required cartons. Activity-based costing can become quite complicated in practice since there may be more than one cost driver for a given activity.[13]

There is a danger in just looking at logistics as a cost-expending process. The other side of the equation is all the revenue earned, which would not be gained without the part played by logistics in each stage of the supply chain.

New product introduction

The introduction of new products brings into contention the whole design of the supply chain, as described in section 1.2. In the current achievement of the chain, we only address the ability of the firms involved in the chain to introduce new products to existing customers without causing problems in logistics. When a new product is provided it is necessary to follow the following rules:

1. Is the introduction controlled so that it is achieved on time and within budget?
2. Is information made clearly available to customers and throughout the chain?
3. Is time compressed, so that the order cycle time is minimised?
4. Are steps eliminated, so that the product passes through a minimum number of hands?

The introduction of a new product can be a major opportunity for improvements to be made to the chain, more easily than for existing products.

6.6 STEPS TO INTEGRATE SUPPLY CHAINS

Having investigated how well the supply chain is performing, there will probably be some areas which require improvement. Figure 6.3 suggests a preferred order in which

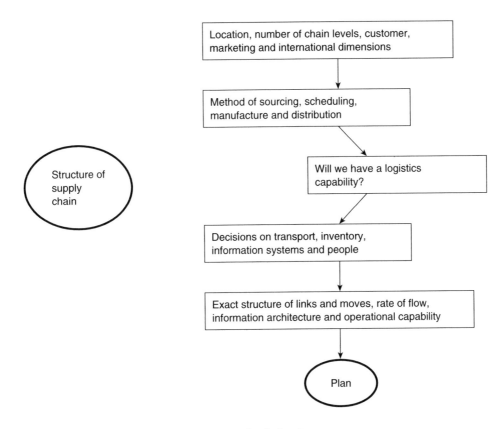

Figure 6.3   **Steps to create a strategic supply chain plan**

supply chain integration decisions are taken. The question 'Will we have a logistics capability?' refers to the decision to outsource some or all of the logistics tasks to a logistics service provider. While the figure is written for a manufacturing supply chain, it can be applied to service chains with some modification. A retail service chain would require all the steps in the figure. Other service businesses, such as insurance, banking, hairdressing and public transport, would use the steps which apply and omit those that are not appropriate. Applicable steps include the outsourcing decision, scheduling and information systems. Inappropriate steps include the number of chain levels and inventory.

Figure 6.3 suggests that there is a set of decisions which should be taken first, that is those concerning customers and market areas. Next decide fixed facilities, and so on until, lastly, the specific operating conditions are chosen.

The extent of outsourcing of logistics services is a secondary decision after the main shape of the supply chain or network has emerged. In general, services will be outsourced if a contractor can do them better than any partner can. The impetus will be lower if the service is seen as a core responsibility and higher if it is peripheral. A consideration is the company's ability to manage the service effectively while it is externally provided.

Another important policy is the use of clusters to achieve supply chain advantages. This can be seen as the encouragement of suppliers within a small driving distance of the production plant. It can also represent transport providers, or other contractors, who are local to respond quickly to changed needs for flow of products.

Complementing the cluster of suppliers is the international dimensions of supply chains. Many supply chains include components sourced in far corners of the world. Many manufactured products end up in the hands of customers all over the globe. Key situations include the greater response time required by a global supply chain. Where customer demand changes and requires up-to-date input, such as in a newspaper, policy is impelled towards local service. Where customer demand of product type is static, such as in petrol, global sourcing is quite effective. An important factor is the ability to move information quickly to anywhere in the world so that order receipt and scheduling *need not* add to the time required to move materials or finished products long distances.

Recent research proposes three elements to consider in organising international supply chains: layering and tiering, the evolving role of plants and reconfiguration processes. First, managers are recommended to lay out the flow of information and coordination differently from the physical flow to obtain global coordination and local operation.

Secondly, Van Hoek[14] suggests that the division of operations between factories and distribution centres will evolve to suit international supply chains. For example, the factory could despatch product modules to local centres for assembly into the (postponed) format required by local customers. Practical examples already adopted are the use of CKD (completely knocked down) packs for local vehicle assembly and flat packs of furniture sold by IKEA for delivery and assembly by the retail customer.

The third element, the reconfiguration process, exhorts supply chain owners to consider carefully which logistics structure best suits their needs. Traditionally, companies manufactured in one factory and performed distribution locally in each country. This can be replaced by distribution centralisation with supply from one DC to several countries. The Shavers case (Chapter 1) provides an example of this structure. Alternatively, under postponed manufacture, only primary manufacture is done in the source factory, with final manufacture and distribution being carried out at a DC serving several companies.

Important in this hierarchy of decisions and the international implications is the management of the supply chain. Management includes both strategic coordination and local supervision. It also includes the development and retention of knowledge to drive specific decisions. This area is developed in Chapter 7.

A further slant on policies depends on the relative influence of manufacturers and distributors in the supply chain. Where a manufacturer retains the ability to command the chain, because of the regard in which it is held by consumers (e.g. in the insistence of PC buyers that they have 'Intel inside'), this leads to very different chain results from when the retail distributor has a more powerful influence. The ability of supermarket chains throughout the western world to dictate terms and conditions of supply to captive vendors is well known. For example, the capture of the majority of meat and dairy product markets by supermarkets in the UK and Australia has meant that the supermarkets largely dictate to farmers and processors. Producers try to use branding and separate delivery channels, such as restaurants and butchers, to preserve their product variety and margin, with limited success.

Chains designed for products for customers

Supply chains operate most effectively if they have been designed with specific products in mind. Superhuman efforts are no substitute for advance preparation. About 80% of the effectiveness of chains devolves from the way in which they are set up, incorporating the following ideas:

1. *Pulling the chain together.* Conventional wisdom requires managers to operate with their own company's interests predominantly in mind. But returns for the chain depend substantially on all links pulling together. In Goldratt's 'Optimised Production Technology',[15] a manufacturer is told to preferentially schedule the workstation with the least capacity to improve output through the whole factory. In the same way, supply chains only earn money from the products that reach the end consumers. There is no point, except in the shortest term, for one link to 'outshine' all the others. Supply chain operation is an exercise for team players.
2. *Chain performance measures* (using the Balanced Scorecard and the SCOR Model). Following from (1) performance must be measured along the whole supply chain. Local performance is less important than overall achievement. It is necessary to use individual measures developed for the particular chain. These measures should span the areas covered in the Balanced Scorecard: order satisfaction, innovation and external impacts as well as financial measures. A very useful model, which provides components for measuring and comparing supply chains, is the SCOR model. All links are constructed from a combination of supply, make, deliver and service components.
3. *Trade-offs.* The supply chain should be designed and operated with suitable trade-offs between processes, movements and stocks along the chain.

The 'Steps to create a strategic supply chain plan' and the above design ideas aim to help you set logistics priorities to ensure the quality of service required by customers is achieved. First, identify the criteria which will cause customers to order from the supply chain, that is for one group of products. Then identify the gaps in providing such criteria. According to the particular gap, such as response time, one can identify the service item, such as order status or order shortage, which needs to be improved to fill that gap.

Tasks

Given all this preparatory work, you should now be in a position to specify the tasks required to improve your supply chain. Looking at Shavers in Box 6.2, the tasks were new information systems, centralised management decisions on forecasts, production scheduling and inventory, and a halving of the number of distribution centres.

If you do not have the agreement of supply chain management and leadership to make the required changes, you may have to latch on to a new product and ensure that its chain embodies the logistics improvements that you require. Then, by progressive product replacement, you may attain your chain improvements. This topic is addressed in Chapter 8.

Summary

This chapter recommends how a current supply chain can be designed and operated in an integrated manner so that customers and companies both benefit. This requires an examination of the boundaries of the chain and the effect of product parameters. Secondly, derive the criteria which the chain must attain to satisfy its particular customers: the specific items which will cause customers to place their business with our chain, rather than a competitor. Thirdly, map those criteria on to the stages of the chain. Fourthly, consider the best form of relationships between supply chain partners. Fifthly, assess the current situation of the supply chain across the stages and functions of the chain. Within this area, look at the management of demand and the response in terms of in-bound logistics; the transformation process, which provides the goods and services, and the internal services which enable the whole chain to function; the distribution of finished goods to customers throughout the marketplace. The current situation must also address the organisation of people to run supply chains and their financial performance. Taking these five facets together enables the derivation of the steps which will integrate the chain and the tasks required to achieve those steps.

The facets examined in this chapter provide a number of qualitative tools to assist supply chain integration. These tools include deriving chain boundaries, establishing criteria that cause goods to flow along the chain, choices of inter-company relationships, performance measurement and setting logistics priorities.

This chapter deals with normal issues which affect all supply chains. The more complicating issues, which tend to affect particular chains, are covered in Chapter 7. Both these chapters examine improvements (*kaizen*) which can be achieved without revolutionary change. The latter is covered in Chapter 8.

Questions

1. What conditions are required to obtain flow along a supply chain?
2. Suggest the best types of partnership for a company in an industry with which you are familiar.
3. Explain the main factors to consider when auditing a supply chain to find out how effective it is.
4. When you want to integrate a supply chain, how do you set the objectives and determine the actions that would achieve them?

Case: Preparing for a seamless supply chain[7]

Ampere Components is part of Electro-Components plc, one of Europe's leading distributors of electronic, electrical and mechanical components and instruments. Ampere sells its 70,000 products primarily through a state-of-the-art distribution system as well as a

(Continued)

network of regional trade counters. It dispatches more than 15,000 orders per day from 100,000 square metres of warehouse space and employs 3,000 staff in the United Kingdom, France, Germany, Italy, Austria, Denmark, Ireland and Spain.

Ampere is structured around a well-knit, 'three-tier' culture comprising senior management team, process teams and action teams. This culture encourages cross-functional involvement as well as a very high level of customer service. This is borne out in the use of supply chain groups to control the internal and external logistics processes. This style of management allows the elimination of separate purchasing, inventory control and marketing departments. In their place, cross-organisational teams manage along product areas, known as value streams (or supply chains). Seventeen product areas are supported by small dedicated competence centres in purchasing and inventory control.

Ampere Components is regarded by its industry as the 'best of the best'. The staff have a strong continuous improvement motivation and an openness to learn and try out new ideas. It was no surprise, therefore, that they saw value in joining a research and networking forum called the Supply Chain Development Programme, which is facilitated by the Lean Enterprise Research Centre (LERC) at Cardiff University.

The starting point for a supplier integration programme at Ampere Components was a strategic review of the organisation carried out by a company cross-functional team, including the supply chain director, Keith Pacey. Hines and Rich, from LERC, acted as facilitators in this process. The review included the use of value stream mapping tools designed to highlight areas of opportunity within companies. The tools, which are drawn from several domains, such as logistics, industrial engineering and systems dynamics, can be applied by cross-organisational teams both within and between organisations.

The reason for the strategic review was not that the company was in trouble. Quite the reverse, it was easily outperforming its rivals. However, Keith Pacey and his staff realised that, although the company was world-class in its distribution arrangements, other parts of the business needed improvement, such as the level of inventory held and lead-times from suppliers, which averaged ten weeks. The value stream mapping was performed over one month at the end of the year with these findings:

- internal value-adding was low,
- there were many delay points in the flow of goods inwards,
- product quality was excellent,
- high urgency in the internal supply chain was not reflected in the external supply chain,
- long supplier lead-times were a problem because of short internal lead-times,
- very high levels of available stock were common,
- there was lack of 'pull' from market needs,
- dislocations were occurring between purchasing and customer demand,
- there was a need for improved supplier on-time performance, and
- there was a need to link customer 'pull' with supplier demand.

The carefully executed mapping did several things for Ampere Components. First, although it confirmed a number of hunches that staff had, it also gave the lie to a number of other gut feelings. Secondly, it created a shared understanding of what the real situation was, allowing the opportunity to manage according to real evidence, not theory. Thirdly, it created a new and crucial desire by senior management to create a supplier integration programme.

(Continued)

(Continued)

Work on the supplier integration programme began early the next year and incorporated a three-tier system of management and a cascading series of teams, as shown in Table C6.1. The cascading system was put in place with as many members of the original mapping team as possible. For instance, Keith, Pacey was brought into the steering group, made up of senior managers and directors of the company from all the relevant functions. The purpose of the steering group, led by the head of the purchasing competency centre, David Noble, was to ensure that a critical target was set for the programme. This target was simply and unambiguously set at doubling the stock turns within three years. This group also scheduled bimonthly meetings to measure the progress of the work, to ensure that adequate resources were being employed, and to make sure that nothing interrupted the supplier integration process. The steering group made no attempt to tell the process facilitation or project teams how to achieve the target set but provided the support to help them.

Table C6.1   **Three-tier system of management for supplier integration**

Team	Roles and responsibilities
Steering Group (Tier 1: senior team)	• Set outline targets • Review progress of programme • Ensure resources available • Unblock functional barriers
Process Facilitation Team (Tier 2: process team)	• Learn and disseminate supplier integration process • Facilitate supplier integration process across project teams • Develop generic, motivational metrics • Measure performance of groups • Provide technical resources to project teams
Project Teams (Tier 3: action teams)	• Implement integration programme with key suppliers • Monitor day-to day development of supplier integration

Then the process facilitation team, led by Ian Kellie of the purchasing competency centre, was formed from middle managers from the various competency centres in the business. These included representatives from the central inventory support group, the strategic purchasing group and two of the managers responsible for a number of product group teams. Hines and Rich also supported this process facilitation. A key responsibility was to develop a set of metrics and performance gaps to motivate and guide action teams in planning and executing their day-to-day work. These are shown in Table C6.2. Around these goals the team designed the broad guidelines of an optimal supplier integration process and disseminated the guidelines to the individual project and action teams. The process team also established ties between different project teams and ensured that knowledge was shared between them.

These key metrics do not seek simply to measure the performance of suppliers, but also to gauge the degree of supplier integration obtained. Some of them, like forecast variability, are more a measure of Ampere's performance. Others, such as delivery on time, are more a reflection of the supplier's performance. A third group, including average stock turn at

(Continued)

Table C6.2   **Metrics and performance gaps**

Measure	Current performance	Three-year target performance	Gap
Average lead-time	8.2 weeks	5 weeks	3.2 weeks
Average stock turns	3.6 per year	6 per year	2.4
Forecast accuracy	38.2%	45%	6.8%
Forecast variability ratio	1:2	1:3.1	–
Delivery on time	74%	95%	21%
Deliver correct quantity	62%	95%	33%
Rejections	5,314 ppm	1,000 ppm	4,314
Customer returns	60,815 ppm	10,000 ppm	50,815

(ppm = parts per million)

Ampere Components, reflect how effectively the downstream customers and upstream suppliers work together.

Individual action teams are made accountable for attaining these targets a step at a time. Meantime, the process-owning team provides technical resources and support when required. The first action team was created early in the second year, with members representing the value stream: a buyer, an inventory controller, and a product manager. They are supported by staff from quality assurance, goods inwards and accounting. The team is led by the champion, who happens to be the buyer.

The role of this team is to implement the supplier integration process with key suppliers. Seven of the 32 suppliers in this product area were chosen based on level of expenditure on their products as well as their previously proactive stance towards Ampere Components. These seven represented around half of the external expenditures by the product group and they were targeted for a 25% increase in business in the second year. The companies are a mixture of European manufacturers and distributors of non-European products. At the start of the process they had a wide span of abilities and divergent attitudes towards supplier integration.

Creating a supplier association

The operating mechanism chosen to integrate suppliers was the 'supplier association'. Such an association is a mutually benefiting group of a company's most important suppliers brought together on a regular basis to coordinate, cooperate and share best practice. Hines's methods were used by Ampere to:

- raise awareness by the customer and key suppliers of the need to change and what to do,
- educate the different companies on how to make the change, and
- serve as a vehicle for successful implementation.

As mentioned, seven companies were invited by the project team to join Ampere's supplier association, which held its first meeting in February at a local hotel. Prior to this, the team had undertaken a careful analysis of what they wanted to get out of the supplier association and how this might be achieved. Value stream analysis tools (VALSATs)[16] were used

(Continued)

(Continued)

Table C6.3　**Ranking improvement methods**

Rank	Ampere's improvement methods
1	Self-certification
2	Due-date performance
3	Vendor rating
4	Stabilise schedules
5	'Milk' rounds for delivery
6	Co-managed inventory
7	Electronic data interchange
8	Replenishment modules
9	Hotline to suppliers
10	Safety stock at suppliers

Table C6.4　**Top-rated improvement methods and the inputs required**

	Improvement method	Inputs required
1	Co-managed inventory	Mostly supplier initiative
2	Due-date performance	Mostly supplier; better information from Ampere needed
3	Milk round	Mostly supplier; Ampere to coordinate
4	Self-certification	Shared work
5	Stabilise schedules	Ampere initiative
6	Electronic data interchange	Shared work

to brainstorm the outputs that Ampere wanted from the programme, with importance weightings developed for each. Members of the project team considered different approaches to achieve the desired outputs. They scored each analysis tool according to how much improvement it was expected to give on each performance measure. They found the overall usefulness of each method (see below) by adding the scores for each tool across the performance measures.

The result was a ranking of the top ten supplier integration methods to achieve the needs of customers. This was presented to supplier association members at the first meeting together with a briefing on the goals of the association and how it could be used in the supplier integration programme. During this event individual suppliers were asked to undertake a similar VALSAT exercise on what they wanted to achieve from the programme. This allowed the company to take their views into account before deciding what work to undertake. The result of the Ampere exercise is shown in the Table C6.3.

The suppliers came up with different ranking of improvement methods but with a similar content. Seven methods were common to both top-ten lists. Six of these were feasible in the short- to medium-term horizon as shown in Table C6.4. Some would require joint work and some input from the customer or supplier alone.

Once the awareness-raising stage was complete, it was then necessary to educate and share knowledge about how to effect these improvements and craft an action plan to meet the targets. The company undertook this with a series of workshops early in the second year. Participants drew up detailed plans permitting both Ampere and the suppliers to implement the improvements either together or on their own, depending upon the particular circumstances.

(Continued)

After the early success of this work, Ampere launched a second project team working in the connector's project area with a similar-sized group of suppliers. The same process facilitation team facilitates this work. Over time such project teams will be used within the supplier association mechanism to integrate key suppliers in each of the product groups.

Acknowledgment

This case study is adapted from material in Dimancescu D, Hines P and Rich N (1997) *The Lean Enterprise: Designing and Managing Strategic Processes for Customer-winning Performance*, AMACOM, New York.[7]

Questions

1. What are the advantages of Ampere Components' three-tier management structure? Does this structure help Ampere relate to suppliers?
2. Name the three most important improvement methods adopted by Ampere Components and its key suppliers. Explain how each improvement will benefit the supply chain.
3. Use the methods of analysis proposed in Chapter 6 (product typing, flow creation, etc.) to criticise Ampere's work. Will Ampere obtain a seamless supply chain?

REFERENCES

1   Tyndall G, Gopal C, Partsch W, Wolfgang P and Kamauff J (1998) *Supercharging Supply Chains*, Wiley, New York. Page 10, original emphasis.
2   Bask AH and Juga J (2001) 'Semi-integrated supply chains: towards the new era of supply chain management', *International Journal of Logistics: Research and Applications*, 4(2): 137–52.
3   Auramo J, Tanskanen K and Smaros J (2004) 'Increasing operational efficiency through improved customer service: process maintenance case', *International Journal of Logistics: Research and Applications*, 7(3): 167–80.
4   Jones D and Womack J (2002) *Seeing the Whole: Mapping the Extended Value Stream*, Lean Enterprise Institute, Brookline, MA.
5   Hill T (2000) *Manufacturing Strategy: Text and Cases*, Palgrave, Basingstoke.
6   Christopher M (1997) 'Creating a European logistics strategy', in DH Taylor (ed.), *Global Cases in Logistics and Supply Chain Management*, International Thomson, London, pp. 38–46.
7   Dimancescu D, Hines P and Rich N (1997) *The Lean Enterprise: Designing and Managing Strategic Processes for Customer-winning Performance*, AMACOM, New York.
8   Upadhye AV and Battacharya S (2004) 'Successful partnerships in supply chain – an approach paper', in *Logistics and Global Outsourcing*, in KS Pawar, CS Lalwani and J Shah (eds). Proceedings of Ninth International Symposium of Logistics, Bangalore, India, pp. 230–6.
9   Makukha K and Gray R (2004) 'Logistics partnerships between shippers and logistics service providers: the relevance of strategy', *International Journal of Logistics: Research and Applications*, 7(4): 361–77.

10   Mason-Jones R, Naylor B and Towill DR (1999) 'Agile, or leagile: matching your supply chain to the marketplace', *Proceedings of the 15th International Conference of Production Research*, Limerick, pp. 593–6.

11   Liker, JK (2004) The Toyota Way, McGraw-Hill Education Europe.

12   Van Damme DA and van der Zon FL (1999) 'Activity-based costing and decision support', *International Journal of Logistics Management*, 10(1): 71–82.

13   Fearny J, Freathy P and Tan E-L (2001) 'Logistics costing techniques and their application to a Singaporean wholesaler', *International Journal of Logistics: Research and Applications*, 4(1): 117–31.

14   Van Hoek R (1998) 'Reconfiguring the supply chain to implement postponed manufacturing', *International Journal of Logistics Management*, 9(1): 95–110.

15   Goldratt EM and Cox J (1992) *The Goal: Process of Ongoing Improvement* (2nd revised edn), North River Press, New York.

16   Hines P, Lamming R, Jones D, Cousins P and Rich N (2000) *Value Stream Management*, Prentice Hall, Harlow, Chapter 5.

Applied Integration Issues

7

Wherever there is a product for a customer, there is a value stream. The challenge lies in seeing it.[1]

Relationships between provider and customer are increasingly to be conceived as ones in which the provider helps the customer create value – at the extreme taking responsibility for the customer's bottom line. Customers, in turn, are to be conceived not as passive consumers of offerings* but as active contributors to value creation.[2] (*offerings provide some products or relieve the customer of some tasks)

Objectives

- To consider how a supply chain can be analysed, designed and operated in an integrated manner, allowing for applied issues in that chain
- To investigate the leadership of supply chains by executives from companies in the chains
- To use supply chain analysis to understand the 'constellation of value' that is created for customers and hence to choose the most effective means of resource allocation and operation
- To consider which supply chain functions are carried out by strategic partners, who source, transform and distribute products, and which functions should be outsourced
- To organise reverse logistics so that faulty and unwanted products, packaging and used products are returned to their source for reworking or recycling

INTRODUCTION

Building on the integration issues essential to most supply chains covered in Chapter 6, this chapter addresses other issues which help to integrate existing supply chains and networks, in the first four sections. Students are encouraged to visualise improved forms for particular supply chains and their constituent parts. Since a supply chain is serving a dynamic set of customers, it needs to get into the right form rapidly. This correct form must then be maintained and improved to cater for ongoing movements in customer requirements.

Two separate complicating issues, decisions to outsource logistics and reverse logistics, are investigated.

7.1 APPLIED INTEGRATION: THE ISSUES

We live in an age of 'short-term values': 'I want it now!' People want fast food, mobile phones, global news, quarterly company reports and online share market prices. Supply chain integration is the opposite of a short-term fix. Cooperation between firms belonging to the same supply chain is now recognised as a powerful source of competitive advantage.[3] This chapter examines leadership of the chain and the leaders are challenged to envisage a 'perfect' chain for the particular customer requirements. The aim in moving towards an optimum is to carry out only those actions that add value for the customer and for the partners. The aim is not to transfer costs along the supply chain, rather to remove costs without value. Firms in such a chain cooperate to increase overall sales and reduce overall costs rather than compete for a bigger share of a fixed profit.[4]

What method of chain change and improvement is used to move towards perfection? Since a supply chain is chasing a dynamic set of customers, it needs to get into the right form rapidly and then maintain that form and amend it to cater for ongoing significant movement in customer requirements.

Stevens[5] suggests that effective supply chain management requires a restructuring process leading in steps from market relations to supply chain integration. He advocates that companies flatten their organisations, increase the emphasis on internal flow of goods and an orientation towards process (such as order-processing) instead of functional departments (such as manufacturing), and then extend the scope of integration to include suppliers and customers.

At what rate is the industry changing to supply ephemeral customer needs? That is 'clockspeed',[6] in which certain industries have shorter product life cycles and faster product development times than others. Industries with fast clockspeeds are mobile phones, electronics, computers and software. Innovation and competition may increase the 'clockspeed' of the supply chain so that it will never catch up to customer needs unless it is very simple and well managed.

Given a desire to integrate a supply chain properly, how might we go about it? This chapter addresses that desire in conceptual terms, while Chapter 8 suggests methods to carry out the changes.

First, we examine the size and shape of our supply chain: what product and service groups does the supply chain represent? Secondly, consider the executives who provide, or should provide, leadership of the supply chain. Thirdly, how can innovative supply chains be created?

7.2 CHAIN INTERACTION AND ANALYSIS

Interaction

The first issue is to examine the size and shape of the supply chain to represent particular product and service groups. To what extent can it be separated from all the other supply chains going through the focal company and through other chain partners, and can it be dissected from the supply network (see Figure 7.1)? Strictly, each product group required by a set of customers forms its own supply chain, needs its own system, functions and boundary. In practice this is rarely possible due to shared distribution, capital processing equipment and shared information and transport services. So the task is to decide which organisations and processes form the main interactions required to perfect the supply chain, which processes must be considered as part of the supply network, because they have first-order interactions with this chain, and which organisations and processes can be left outside the chain/network boundary because they have a lesser interaction.

Figure 7.1 is an attempt to provide the major components which must be considered for a supply network. For partners which have a significant effect on the supply of goods and services, the chain extends upstream to, say, two tiers of supply companies. Processes are then followed from the suppliers through the factory, or distribution centre, and downstream through wholesalers and retailers until the end consumer is reached. The wide bells represent many-to-one relationships in both inbound supply and outbound distribution areas. Each process in the chain must be considered from the four dimensions of product flow, information communication, local management and chain-wide leadership. The supply chain can then be envisaged as one thin slice running horizontally across the Double-Bell from left to right, involving a limited number of suppliers, conversion processes and a single distribution channel. This analogy must not be pushed too far.

For some focal companies, such as mass retailers (e.g. supermarkets), one or two suppliers provide the products which go through a particular shop section to supply consumers with a product group, such as canned soup. However, a car assembler requires parts from most of its suppliers to make one family of cars, such as saloons, whereas a meat processor disassembles one cow through all its operating stages into a whole range of food products from steak to chops and liver.

The other extension of the 'Double-Bell' model in Figure 7.1 is the annotation of process links with four key parameters: chain leadership, information communication (Chapter 5), product flow (Chapter 2) and management (Chapter 6). The implications of chain leadership are addressed in section 7.3.

The point about 'interaction' occurs because we are not interested in the outcomes of individual processes in the supply chain. Our interest is in the outcome of the whole chain and on individual processes only to the extent that they contribute to the whole system. This point is heavily stressed because it reverses the normal relationships in companies in which an employee's loyalty is seen as being due first to the company he or she works for.

Analysis

This examination includes a chain analysis sufficient for strategic supply chain integration. What are the components of the chain? How well do they function? How well do they satisfy customer needs? Ohmae[7] suggests that we should split a business situation into its parts, think very carefully about what parts are needed and how they relate to each other, and then put the chain together in an improved form. This new form should deploy policies[8] in concert with corporate objectives, to achieve the aims of customers while creating value for partners.

An important method consideration is the use of bottom-up thoughts on required strategy as well as top-down ones. Mintsberg's[9] work demonstrates the need to include or utilise emergent strategies as well as those from directing managers. Emergent

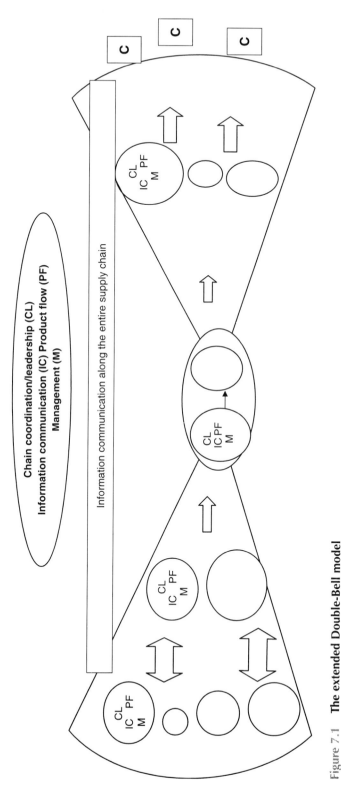

Chain coordination/leadership (CL)
Information communication (IC) Product flow (PF)
Management (M)

Information communication along the entire supply chain

CL
IC PF
M

CL
IC PF
M

CL
IC PF
M

CL
IC PF
M

C

C

C

Figure 7.1   **The extended Double-Bell model**

The left-hand bell shows many suppliers sending materials and components into the factory (central ellipse) by transport (arrows). The factory contains several processes producing finished goods. The right-hand bell represents the movement of products through distribution centres to many end customers (C) by transport. Each symbol, or process, is regarded as comprising product flow (PF), information communication (IC), management (M) and chain leadership (CL), so that the model represents an integrated supply network. This composition also applies to the whole network. Information communication is shown along the top of the network to indicate its ubiquitous nature as a chain driver.

strategies comprise those that just happen, as a result of industry, company or market forces and they include strategies devised by operators and lower-level managers.

The boundary of the synthesised supply chain is wide enough to encompass all organisations and processes which have significant, or first-order, effect on the aim of providing goods for customers and value for the chain 'owners' (operators). Organisations and processes, which have only a second-order effect, are then omitted from the supply chain, for planning purposes.

For example, consider the supply network for smallgoods products (Figure C2.2, page 64). This network comprises three supply chains, of which one is the production of sausages for sale through supermarkets. This chain starts with the piggery, the supplier of grown pigs to the abattoir, the primary manufacturer. The piggery must be included since the choice of pig genetics and feeding regimes has an important influence on the pig meats in the sausage. The supply of materials, such as grain and medicines, to the piggery is considered to be insignificant, or a second-order effect. Should the supplier of packaging to wrap the finished sausages be included? With the current development of more sophisticated packaging, to protect and identify the type of sausage, it is likely that the packaging firm should be included, unless it can be provided in advance at low cost, so that the firm has no practical effect on the retail sausage supply chain.

In this way, we argue that supply chains should be individually built up to suit the particular business aims and circumstances. We believe there are no 'rules' for specifying supply chains.

Since this examination is limited to *strategic* chain analysis, the main parameters to be considered are cycle times, product variety and rate of introduction, capacity and loading. Not all these parameters will apply with equal importance in any given supply chain; you must decide which is critical to your product chain. Cost is omitted because, although it is obviously very important, future cost, and especially future variable cost, is rarely known with any certainty. This fact is not often recognised; huge amounts of time and energy are frequently expended on future cost estimates for particular products and routes and these are not worthwhile. Cycle time refers to the time that a customer will wait to get his or her product and the time that it takes to make the product. Product variety is the number of different stock-keeping units that are required, while introduction rate refers to the number of truly new products brought into the chain per year. 'Truly new' means products which are more than changes in packaging, style or appearance, and hence are likely to affect chain flow or configuration. Chain capacity refers to the volume of materials and products that can be handled, while the loading is the extent that capacity is being used now, or is forecast to be used according to a production or distribution schedule.

Restructuring

Stevens[5] argues that the successful achievement of an integrated supply chain requires 'bottom-up' implementation going through four stages:

- A 'baseline' company vests responsibility for different logistics activities in separate departments. Such a company has staged inventories, independent control systems for sales, manufacturing and purchasing, and organisational boundaries preventing seamless control of materials and products.

- In the second stage functional integration is achieved, focusing principally on the inward flow of goods. This stage is characterised by emphasis on cost reduction, discrete business functions buffered by inventory, internal trade-offs such as between purchase discounts and the level of inventory investment, and reactive customer service. Companies in this stage typically have time-phased MRP II planning and control systems.
- Third-stage companies integrate those aspects of the supply chain directly controlled by the company. They embrace outward goods management, integrating supply and demand along the company's own part of the chain. Typically, they use distribution requirements planning (DRP) systems, integrated via a master production schedule to an MRP II system. Stage three supply chains are characterised by full systems visibility from distribution to purchasing, a focus on tactical issues, and an emphasis on efficiency and reacting to customer demand rather than trying to manage the customer.
- Only in the fourth stage is full supply chain integration achieved by extending the scope of integration to include suppliers and customers. This development involves a change of focus from being product-oriented to being customer-oriented. By deep consideration of the customer's products, culture, market and organisation, the company becomes attuned to the customer's requirements. Integration proceeds back along the supply chain to include suppliers in an attitude of mutual support. Then cooperation starts at the early stages of product development. Cooperation includes the supply of high-quality products shipped direct to the production line on-time, shared change information about product and process, and long-term commitment, including the end to multiple sourcing.

The aim of this chain restructuring is to consider the supply chain during strategy formation, manage it as a single entity and ensure the appropriate use of tools and techniques to meet the needs of the market.

7.3 SUPPLY CHAIN LEADERSHIP, POWER AND TRUST

Consider the executives who provide, or should provide, leadership of the supply chain. How is the chain led? Is there a predominant manufacturer or distributor? Do all the major chain constituents (i.e. chain partners) pull together to achieve agreed operating parameters and flow rates? How are decisions taken quickly while input is obtained from consumers, from all partners, from all appropriate levels of employees? This section considers these questions in real supply chains.

Until recently, powerful companies would build, or buy, a vertically integrated chain so that they could order each link in the chain to operate in concert to ensure that their customers get all the goods they want and the integrator makes good, sustained profits. There are many examples that demonstrate that this assumption is wrong! The previous Steel Division of BHP Billiton, an Australian miner and steelmaker, owned all the links* from iron ore and coal mines to manufacture of end products, such as buckets, roofs and car panels. BHP Steel is currently being broken up and sold. Marks & Spencer, a British clothing retailer, contracted material suppliers and garment manufacturers and abolished wholesalers to revolutionise the provision and sale of a wide range of clothing to the public. Marks & Spencer made major gains for a long time but, in the 1990s, was in the doldrums because competitors had caught up. There are underlying problems in vertical integration: it conceals the performance of each process/player and relies on *transfer prices** and power for decisions.

Leadership and power

Think about the supply chain in Figure 7.1 which, generally, comprises three to six significant companies. Who will lead this chain? Conventional *corporate governance** practice in most western and Asian countries holds that each firm is a separate entity, only beholden to its chain partners according to specific contracts and second to responsibility to its own shareholders and financiers. Moving from that corporatist view to a supply chain view, opinion holds that 'marketing' companies or supermarket chains are the practical leaders of supply chains. Thirty years ago, manufacturing would have more frequently held the power. There are some signs that the emphasis is moving back towards manufacturing to provide more product features and provision flexibility.

We take the view that there must be a focal company to lead the supply chain and that this company must have a dedicated interest in the product and concomitant services. We believe that many broad retailers and supermarkets are predominantly interested in dollar turnover in a given selling face. They cannot be trusted to lead supply chains. They are too likely to take a short-term, adversarial, selfish stance. Box 7.1 gives an example of adversarial partner relations in Britain.

Box 7.1   Leadership in a UK retail meat supply chain

Bestco (disguised name) is a UK supermarket chain which buys some of its lamb supplies from Wales Abattoir which kills and processes lambs from many Welsh farms. Recently, lean supply chain consultants brought together farmers, abattoir managers, meat processors and retail executives. When one of the farmers saw the Bestco category manager, he said: 'You are the enemy'.

This lamb supply chain contrasts with production of beef for the British food-service market. The packing plant, where beef is cut into portions and packed, is served by two meat suppliers. The first supplier is UK Beef farms supplying abattoirs which deliver to the packing plant. The second is Argentine farms which send cattle to Argentine abattoirs, from which the meat is shipped to the packing plant not far from Southampton. The packed beef portions are distributed through distribution centres to the food service customers, mainly a chain of steak houses. Because the restaurants have menus with fixed contents and prices, for a period of six months, this creates a commercial climate in which partners consult with each other, share information and forward plan supply chain flow.

(Source: Based on value chains studied by members of Cardiff Business School[10])

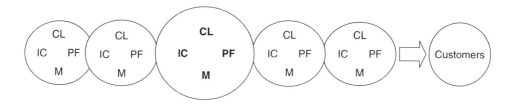

Figure 7.2 **Supply chain management as a series of company links**

(CL = chain leadership, IC = information communication;
PF = product flow; and M = management)

However, we also assert that no good supply chain leader would command other chain partners. Rather the approach should be collaborative, coaching and jointly-made decisions, especially where strategic decisions are involved.[11]

Secondly, consider the management of all the main organisations in the supply chain for a particular product group, as depicted in Figure 7.2 (a copy of Figure 1.5 from page 9). Note that the owners and head offices of these organisations are excluded. Integration is to be achieved for a particular product group. However, the solution derived must be relatively consistent with the aims of those owners and be vetted by them before it can be implemented. Figure 7.2 suggests that there are two central factors, information communication and product flow, which feature in each organisation; then there is management of the local, or within-link, processes; and, finally, there is 'chain leadership' which is a goal-setting and coordination of all the managements in all the chain organisations. Recall that the management of each organisation actually comprises numerous processes, such as order entry and product development.

The importance of *power* in supply chains is examined in the following quote. Cox[3] defines a supply chain entrepreneur as a company which positions itself in the chain with ownership, or close partnership, relations to those resources (companies) which provide distinctive competencies, while outsourcing highly contested areas:

> Essentially business is about appropriating value for oneself; it is not about passing value to customers unless this is the only option available to a company. From an entrepreneurial perspective, the business ideal is to attain a position where you have leverage [i.e. power] over customers, employees, competitors and suppliers whilst they have no leverage over you. Such a position would put us in a situation of power over all others in our supply chain relationships.[3] (p. 171)

The decision

Given all that preparatory discussion, how should supply chains be led? We recommend that top logistics management of the focal company should call a meeting of general management representatives of all the primary organisations. This meeting should then plan the future strategic direction of the chain, and all its components. Such planning requires:

1. A recognised process (such as 'SOLP', see section 8.4) to allow democratic but effective decisions to be made.
2. A level of trust between representatives.
3. An external facilitator to level the influence of all company representatives.

4. A series of working assumptions to delineate the business area of the chain.
5. A forward horizon of at least two years in which the partners intend to proceed with the chosen strategy.
6. An output of action plans for the whole chain and for each link organisation in it, comprising tasks, projects and performance measures.
7. An agreement on how gains and 'pains' (losses) will be shared between companies.
8. A formal method of approval of the action plans by the chief executives of all the organisations and, where relevant, the group owners of the organisations.
9. A set of tactical and information systems plans to sit under the strategic action plans to deploy the consequent tasks.

Personal trust

The last section talked about leaders and management without mentioning relations between individual people. Yet, the extent to which leaders and individual managers trust each other is a key enabler for supply chain integration. Consider the influence of powerful partners, such as supermarket chains, on a supply chain. Do partners trust each other? If not, how can trust be restored? Many people take the view that business is a 'rat race' in which you must push others out of the way to succeed. We take the view that, just as cooperation in supply chains can create more value and less conflict, so trust and mutual help by managers (where their top management and owners permit) can provide vision, value and effective product flow to customers.[12] This may not be possible in all chains.

Trust is confidence in the loyalty, strength and truthfulness of a person. An important area, which may reduce cooperation and trust, is the existence of restrictive practices.

Restrictive practices

A restrictive practice is an arrangement in an industry or trade aimed at restricting or controlling competition or output. Such practices can form a major barrier to supply chain integration. The following points list a number of forms of restrictive practice which can affect supply chains:

*   *Unions.* Often union or cultural allegiances can prevent necessary changes in job location or work practices from being made. For example, in Australia, warehouse operators may be represented by either of two unions, the Transport Workers' Union of Australia or the National Union of Workers. Union delegates and officials appear to be more interested in the short-term monetary benefits and historical working conditions of storemen and order pickers rather than the companies for whom they work.
*   *Companies and managers.* Companies such as retailers have restrictions on what information they will pass up the supply chain and what strategies they will share with upstream partners.
*   *Professions.* In many western countries, professional people such as lawyers, consultants and chartered accountants frequently work for themselves rather than for the companies they advise. In Australia these professions are not covered by the Trade Practices Commission so that anti-competitive practices occur. For example,

company lawyers push privacy, insurance and corporate governance issues when directors and managers are concerned to keep the business operating in the future. The last thing the other executives need is to sue, or to insure for non-risk situations (such as people and profit). By non-risk we mean situations which are not inherently variable and should be managed rather than insured against. Executives are also loathe to take contractual penalties when dealing with partnership, governance and warranty issues.

• *Governments.* Governments in many countries tend to prevent supply chain integration by taxes, regulation and slowness of decision.

7.4 INNOVATIVE SUPPLY CHAIN CREATION

A key aim of a manufacturing or service provider is to create an innovative supply chain which will deliver something different to the customer, thereby both capturing the customer's interest and developing an advantage over its competitors. This section addresses several routes to innovation:

• relationship marketing, one of the building blocks of supply chains,
• flexible supply chains to cater for unknown customer needs and volumes, and
• the value constellation concept, which addresses the foundations of supply networks.

Relationship-building in the supply chain

Figure 7.3 shows the various markets which should be considered when making innovative changes to supply chains.[13] The customer markets domain comprises three broad groups: buyers (representing the direct customers of the manufacturer), intermediaries (the retailers to whom the wholesaler sells goods) and end consumers (the individuals who purchase from the retailer). This terminology varies in different industries as, for example, in the insurance industry where the provider is the underwriter, the buyers are known as 'brokers', and the broker sells to the final customer, who is known as a 'client'.

There is a wide range of distribution options by which a company may serve the end consumer. The choice within that range depends upon the value proposition relevant to the end customer. The use of new instead of existing distribution channels is driven by the desire to build channel relationships that will maximise the lifetime value of the desired customers. It may be necessary to use different channels for different market segments. New distribution opportunities, such as the Internet and electronic commerce, should be used if they provide a superior value delivery network.

While in some industries intermediaries may be valuable channel members, in others the value of intermediaries is being challenged. Unless the intermediary is adding value to the customer relationship, it may be bypassed, thus saving unnecessary cost.

Flexible supply chains

Some recent research suggests that a future challenge is to make the supply chain flexible so that companies can work together to achieve a level of agility which customers will find attractive. In the wider literature four dimensions of agility are defined:[14]

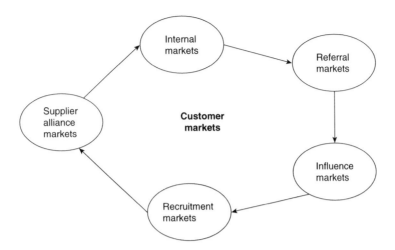

Figure 7.3   **Relationship marketing with respect to supply chains**
(amended from Peck et al.[13])

- enriching the customer,
- cooperating to enhance competitiveness,
- organising to master change and uncertainty, and
- leveraging the impact of people and information.

Van Hoek and colleagues[15] argue that customer responsiveness is the key to success in today's markets. Agility is about creating that responsiveness and mastering the uncertainty of forward customer order levels. They advocate manufacturing schedules that are not 'frozen' (unable to be changed, however customer needs change); production that is driven by sales at the till; and precision engineering investment before work from the customer eventuates.

   This flexible response is only necessary with products and services which lack a stable demand. The aim is to separate unpredictable items and use early market signals and a flexible response to satisfy the customer.

Value constellation in practice

A supply chain (see section 1.1) has to be seen as part of a *value constellation**.[2] Norman and Ramirez consider a value constellation to be the extra value created by a number of stars in a galaxy of businesses in a market and industry situation. To understand we must start with the customer '*offering*'* shown in Table 7.1. This table provides a 'picture' of the 'whole' business of a firm's customers. Once the firm has this picture, it can proceed to consider the shape of its (and its partner stars' [firms']) offering.

   The idea is that each firm feeds off 'all' the other firms to create value for the customers. For example, music on television requires:

- a composer,
- a musician,
- a signal network,
- an antenna,

- sheet music,
- recording,
- electronic parts,
- a publisher,

- an instrument,
- a studio,
- a TV set, and
- a producer.

Table 7.1   An offering comprises all the elements in this picture[2]

Product	Before purchase	During purchase	After purchase
Manifested physically			
Manifested in people			
Manifested in systems			
Manifested in the client			

This idea is a good way of understanding how partners in a supply network can create and operate a supply chain, within the network, for the benefit of customers and themselves. Figure 7.4 attempts to put down a value constellation diagram for third-generation mobile phones.

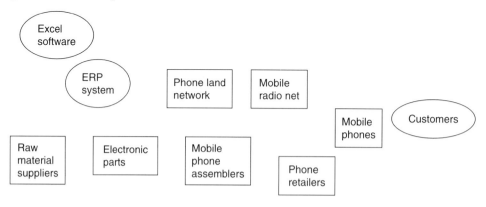

Figure 7.4   Value constellation for third-generation mobile phones

There are multiple interactions, forwards and backwards between all the parts in this figure.

When you use a third-generation phone to look at a production schedule on an ERP system 150 kilometres away, what supply chain players are you using and paying for?

Although they could be relevant, this section does not address iteration, learning curves, or supply chain optimisation. These areas of supply chain investigation are part of a full analysis which is covered in Chapter 8.

The foregoing three sections discuss a number of complicating issues that need to be addressed to integrate existing supply chains and networks. The next two sections examine two particular issues, outsourcing logistics and reverse logistics.

7.5 OUTSOURCING LOGISTICS

This section first examines *outsourcing** in relation to the most frequent application: outsourcing part or all of the distribution function. Within this, consider the strategic implications and potential risks caused by giving some tasks to third parties. Secondly, it looks more widely at all the 'make or buy' decisions faced by organisations at various parts of the supply chain. Thirdly, third-party logistics companies are examined.

Outsourcing means using a contract with outside parties for services such as transport, warehousing and other distribution functions, often including concomitant information services.[16] It appeals to companies that view logistics as a necessary business

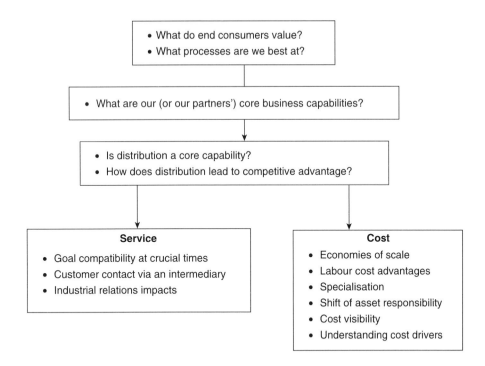

Figure 7.5   **The strategic dimension of outsourcing (adapted from Dapiran[17])**

expense rather than as a competitive weapon. However, outsourcing distribution can be much more than a money-saving option. Outside service vendors, such as transport companies and public warehouses (uncommon outside the USA), can often provide a better, more cost-effective, logistics service than a manufacturer or a chain retailer.

Consider the strategic and risk dimensions in outsourcing before a decision process is suggested and an example is provided. This discussion is primarily drawn from work by Dapiran.[17]

The strategic dimension

Strategic outsourcing decisions are made by answering a series of questions before making a choice based on service levels and cost (see Figure 7.5). The questions should apply to supply chain partners as well as to the focal company. So, the question: 'What processes are we best at?', applied to product inventory control, must be directed to the receiving company chain (perhaps a supermarket chain) as well to our own company (a manufacturer).

When all these questions are answered and the correct balance of service and cost is established, then the company is in a position to decide what functions should be out-sourced and what should be retained.

The risk dimension

There are many possible risks incurred when outsourcing a function to a third party. Some of the main categories are:

- loss of in-house expertise,
- dependence on/dominance by a third party,
- deteriorating performance of a third party,
- cost of switching between in-house and a third-party operation,
- legal legitimate power versus traditional legitimate power, and
- cancellation of competitive advantage.

Contract logistics – the decision process

We recommend the following steps should be taken in the decision to place an outsourcing contract with a third party:

- evaluate the strategic dimension,
- benchmark in-house versus contractor, and
- evaluate risk.

Key issues that should be considered in the contract are:

- the volumes to be handled and services provided,
- the basis for cost calculations and cost fluctuations,
- who is responsible for loss, damage and stock discrepancies,
- what performance criteria and regular reporting are required,
- whether any special storage, handling, security or fire protection is needed, and
- the length of contract and termination arrangements.

A contract is the fall-back document to mould business dealings. Be careful not to *assume* anything important will be done. You should also talk, rather than argue or sue, when the relationship is not working.

Make-or-buy decisions

An important decision faced by a company or a supply chain is the *make-or-buy decision**. Which components should be manufactured in-house and which should be outsourced? A framework developed by Fine and Whitney[18] provides advice on this decision, depending upon the class into which the component falls (see Table 7.2). A firm which has the knowledge and skills to produce the component, but lacks the resources, is dependent upon capacity. A company which lacks the skills and knowledge to produce the component is dependent on knowledge. Companies fall into one of the columns according to whether they are independent or dependent on either of these factors. Table 7.2 also distinguishes between:

- modular products, which are made by combining different components which are independent of each other and interchangeable, and
- integral products which are made from tightly related, non-commodity components.

For example, Toyota outsources two-thirds of its transmissions; it has the knowledge to make the products but lacks the capacity to do so. Since the transmission is an

Table 7.2   **A framework for make-or-buy decisions[18]**

Product type	Dependent on knowledge and capacity	Independent for knowledge, dependent for capacity	Independent for knowledge and capacity
Modular	Outsourcing is risky	Outsourcing is an opportunity	Opportunity to reduce cost through outsourcing
Integral	Outsourcing is very risky	Outsourcing is an option	Keep production internal

integral component within the drive train of Toyota cars, Table 7.2 suggests that outsourcing is an option for Toyota.

Third-party logistics

Third-party logistics (3PL) is the use of a transport company to carry out a variety of transport and distribution tasks along the supply chain (see section 2.5). 3PL is a particular application of the general concepts already enunciated. If transport has no particular importance to a business, and it is just a commodity to be purchased as required, then there is a strong case for using a third party to carry the goods. The 3PL operator specialises in this area and can achieve economies of scale beyond those available to most small or medium-sized companies. A 3PL is also indicated if a company's in-house skills are deficient in this area.

When transport is a key performance objective for a company, then there is a strong argument for keeping it in-house. If the company still desires to outsource, then it must be careful in its choice of a capable 3PL operator and ensure that the contract covers the particular facets which are important to its business.

7.6 REVERSE LOGISTICS

*Reverse logistics** is the movement of products or goods up the supply chain in the opposite direction to the normal flow of products. It can be caused by a number of factors, considered in this section, such as faulty goods, recycling containers when the active ingredient has been used, or disposal of products which are no longer required by the customer or retailer.

A great deal of physical work related to logistics is performed at distribution centres and warehouses. Reverse logistics supports:

1. Returns of unwanted or faulty goods, e.g. unsold books and magazines.
2. Remanufacturing to add an active ingredient, such as computer printer ink, to a container.
3. Recycling and disposal to remove goods, which have ceased to work, from the consumer. Recycling returns product following its useful life with the aim of breaking it down into constituent materials which can be re-used. Metals, plastics and precious metals are frequently recycled.

Reverse logistics also results from the increasing recycling of drink containers and packaging materials. The operational requirements for reverse logistics include achieving lowest total cost, such as returning bottles for recycling, and maximum control when products are found to be defective. Firms that design efficient reverse logistics are able to reclaim value by reducing the quantity of products that might otherwise be scrapped. Reverse logistics is a major service to the customer, who gets rid of goods, which are possibly bulky, with little personal effort.

Summary

This chapter, together with Chapter 6, suggests how a current supply chain can be operated in an integrated manner. It looks at the issues of supply chain restructuring and the effect of the speed at which customers and industries are changing. Chain restructuring must focus on the partners with whom our company has the most important interactions. For the resultant set of supply chain partners, an analysis should be carried out of cycle times, product variety, production and distribution capacity and the loadings provided by current and expected customer demands. Further tools for analysis are provided by methods of envisaging innovative supply chains and considerations of which goods and services should be outsourced while others are provided in-house.

Supply chain leadership introduces the idea that coordination of supply chain partners is essential to achieve an effective supply chain. Tyndall and colleagues[19] foresee the evolution of supply chain operations into 'co-options' between 'grand alliance' supply chains: supplier/provider, manufacturer, channel partner, one-to-many, and many-to-many. We examine stages on the way to co-option and their implications and contents leading to decisive strategic plans for the supply chain. This building of relations gives the best climate for innovative logistics solutions to customers' requirements.

The chapter also addresses the topic of outsourcing, what are the strategic implications of giving tasks to third parties and how should an outsourcing decision be made? Finally, reverse logistics examines movement of products up the supply chain as a result of faulty goods, recycling containers or disposal of products at the end of their life.

Questions

1. For a known supply network, draw a diagram which shows the major partners whose informational and product flow links provide the main interactions for a chosen product group.
2. Explain the major complexities in a known supply network and suggest how you would tackle them if you had a leadership role in the network.
3. What evidence of supply chain coordination exists? How do you think it may be further developed?
4. Working with the supply chain defined in questions 1 and 2, estimate which activities are likely to be outsourced and which will be retained in the partners' full control. What are the reasons behind this?

Case: Lucent Technologies Company

Introduction

The Lucent Technologies Company designs and delivers networks for the world's largest communications service providers. The products it offers range from high-bandwidth core optical and multi-service data networks to new metropolitan and broadband access networks. More than half the world's phone calls are made over Lucent's remote access equipment – 30 million calls per day. A strong research and development background provided by the support of Bell Laboratories enables Lucent to present many products and services to their customers. However, Lucent's communication system is relatively weak. It is difficult to link data between regions of the world because each has individual software to operate their logistics system.

This case presents Lucent's problems and then provides three upgrades which could be provided. In order to be the world's leading supply chain network provider, Lucent needs to improve its information technology infrastructure. It requires applications systems using a protocol, transport to move the data and an effective interface for the users to access the service. Lucent's choices involve:

- the network – will it be private satellite or public Internet?
- the application layer – will it be XML from machine to machine or a web portal using a human interface?
- will the solution be prepared in Lucent or outsourced, that is EDI (electronic data interchange)?

The first upgrade being considered is based on electronic data interchange, using a dedicated satellite network to link Lucent's distribution centres, customers and suppliers because they are geographically dispersed. The second upgrade would use XML as the communication format between Lucent and their partners. Customers could order on the Lucent website or transfer their order with XML format to the website using the public Internet as carrier. The third possible upgrade is a business-to-business (B2B) solution providing a portal on which customers can look up technical information on products and download a software upgrade. Lucent would use networking technology to link customer, partners, suppliers, distributors and employees tightly and enable all the parties to look and act as if they are one company.

The upgrades focus on information system infrastructure. The whole logistics plan to redesign Lucent's supply chain would also require other strategies, such as refocusing on core businesses and intensifying the use of contract manufacturers.

Current situation

Lucent Technologies designs and delivers networks for the world's largest communications service providers. The company leads the world in Internet infrastructure for service providers, optical networking, wireless networks and communications networking support and services. The company's systems, services and software are designed to help customers quickly deploy and better manage their networks and create new, revenue-generating

(Continued)

(Continued)

services that assist businesses and consumers.[1] Lucent Company currently employs 30,200 people worldwide with revenue of US$9.4 billion in the year 2005. Its major markets are in North America, China, Japan and Europe. Lucent has headquarters in New Jersey, USA and it is supported by Bell Laboratories research and development.

Lucent's Mission is: 'To be the partner of choice for the world's leading service providers by helping them create, build and maintain the most innovative, reliable and cost-effective communications networks and meet their customers' growing needs through the rapid deployment of new communication services.' Lucent Technologies is facing heightened domestic and global competition.

Supply chain

Figure C7.1 shows the Lucent Technologies' supply chain in diagrammatic form. Lucent has close relationships with suppliers to provide the materials and services, so that they can deliver the products and services customers need at a price they can afford. Lucent focuses on a relationship with their suppliers, which are critical to their strategy for success. Being a Lucent supplier is much more than being a reliable source for quality materials and services at a competitive price. In January 2001, Supply Chain Networks (SCN) was formed to knit all supply chain functions throughout Lucent into a single organisation. One of the most significant achievements to come out of SCN to date is the supplier relationship programme. The goal of the programme is to bring Lucent and their suppliers much closer for the mutual benefit of all of the participants. Lucent's partners include Accenture, Hewlett-Packard, IBM and Microsoft. Currently, Lucent's enterprise resource planning (ERP) system maintains all logistics information.

Audit of Lucent's strengths and weaknesses

A major strength of Lucent is the investment by Bell Laboratories, which spends the industry's largest amount of research and development resources focused solely on the communications

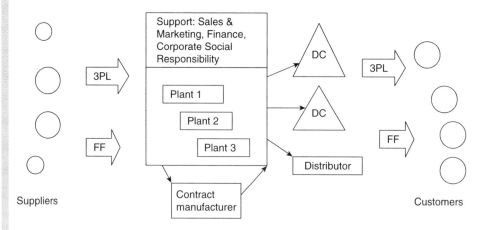

Figure C7.1   **The whole supply chain of Lucent Technologies**

(3PL = third-party logistics provider; FF = freight forwarder; DC = distribution centre)

(Continued)

of service providers. Lucent has restructured its global supply chain network by launching Lucent Worldwide Services which has 20,000 professionals to provide network design, engineering, installing, managing, monitoring and repairing some of the most sophisticated networks in the world.

Lucent's Network Solutions Group focuses on the world's leading wire line service providers, which include long-distance carriers, incumbent local service providers, public telecommunications providers, emerging service providers and backbone builders throughout the world.

Lucent's first weakness is the lack of a global communications and transport system which would allow it to go direct to customers when problems occur and when Lucent wants to return products and services to the customers. A logistics third-party provider called Citadel developed the current system. But it requires different districts to be served by different logistics systems under the same policy from the USA. Further, Lucent has a limited time to deliver products and services. They have been trying to reduce the delivery time from six weeks to 15 days. Therefore, Lucent crucially needs a good information system to support their logistics channel and distribution to provide products/services. Such a reduction would save at least US$150 million per year.

In fact, Lucent has spent a lot of time redesigning its supply chain. The biggest change is bringing this company from a vertically-integrated enterprise to a virtually integrated one. Lucent had to make changes because it is relying on supply chain management as a tool to restore growth and profitability. According to Jose Mejia, Vice President of Lucent's Supply Chain Network: 'Because of our crisis, we have moved faster than any other company. The supply chain needs to continuously adapt to its surroundings. Anyone who does not see that will fail.'

Lucent's logistics network involves a large number of organisations: corporate headquarters, subsidiary companies, wholesalers, distribution centres (DCs), suppliers, manufacturers, distributors and carriers. Their logistics activities involve many steps from sea to air and from trucking to warehousing. With so many partners involved and so many steps of their logistics activity, visibility becomes crucial to Lucent's supply chain.

However, some of Lucent's partners and customers are still relying on telephone/fax-based communication. A recent survey showed that one-third of all faxed orders contained errors that delayed processing. Finding out the required information via telephone from these partners and customers wastes a great deal of time. In addition, the partners were using different information technology systems, standards and protocols. Linking them is a far more complex task than integrating systems within a single organisation.

To achieve logistics strategy, Lucent has launched a restructuring programme.[2] This programme was instigated to accelerate and deepen efforts to refocus the company, streamline operations and drive out more costs in order to ensure that the company will be well positioned when market conditions improve.

To facilitate better communication with their partners and to allow their clients to view the supply chain, Lucent needs to rebuild their information technology infrastructure to enable greater collaboration, synchronisation and optimisation across the broader supply chain.

Strategic logistics plan

Lucent's goal is transforming itself into a virtual original equipment manufacturer. Most of its manufacturing and logistics activities will be outsourced. The telecom equipment maker

(Continued)

(Continued)

has reduced its direct component suppliers to approximately 60 from 1,200 two years ago, and plans to cut its enterprise management systems (EMS) providers from nine to about three. The company is also preparing to sign an EMS provider to handle its optical manufacturing activities, increasing from 10% to about 90% the amount of production it outsources.

As a giant with US$9 billion revenue, the company is now focusing solely on the biggest telecom carriers, instead of trying to satisfy dozens of customers. Its smaller customers will be serviced through specially appointed global business partners. Lucent will use networking technology to link customers, partners, suppliers, distributors and employees tightly and enable all the parties to look and act as if they are one company. Lucent itself will concentrate on new products development, looking after customer needs and brand management.

System upgrades

The Supply Chain Vice President has identified three possible upgrades to address Lucent's information communication inadequacies.

Upgrade 1: Electronic data interchange solution

One possible change is to implement an EDI network involving Lucent, customers, suppliers and other business partners (see Figure C7.2). Under this plan, EDI provides direct transfer of information between the computers of trading partners. The documents that the partners send each other, such as purchase orders, bills of lading and invoices, are formatted and converted to standard messages during the transaction process. The standard messages can be interpreted, processed and transmitted directly to the destination very quickly, using the same data communication protocols via a communications network. EDI is an outsourced solution in which communications are by a direct link or by a third-party network.

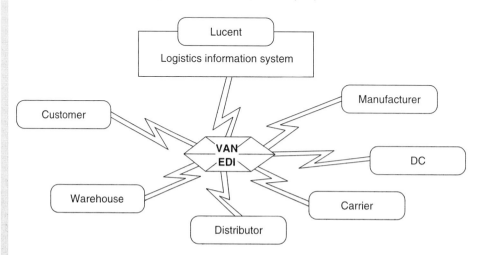

Figure C7.2 Network diagram for the EDI solution

(Van = value-added network)

(Continued)

Because Lucent's DCs, customers and suppliers are geographically dispersed, a dedicated satellite network would improve the links between them. Satellite communication provides a fast and high-volume channel for information movement. Customers use EDI and the satellite network to transmit orders or other logistics information to Lucent's regional logistics information centre which would be linked to Lucent's ERP system. Purchase orders are transmitted directly and accurately from the ERP system to the computers of the vendors.

Upgrade 2: XML-based solution

The second change uses the language XML and the Internet to enable the customer to interact with Lucent's logistics information system via a web browser. XML is used as the communication format between Lucent and their partners. Customers can order on the website or transfer their order in XML format to the Lucent website. Lucent's ERP database has an interface to receive XML input. These orders are processed on the back-end. Then Lucent transfers the purchase order or delivery order to their partners by XML.

The related logistics information in Lucent's enterprise resource planning database is posted on the web page regularly. Customers and business partners have access to key information on order status, invoices, deliveries and inventory levels.

XML is a more advanced language than the Hypertext mark-up language, which is currently used to exchange data on the Internet. XML offers a more flexible standard for the direct transfer of information, routing and manipulation of data, tailored to common and predefined business processes. With it, data can be stripped out of one form and automatically entered into another for easier collaboration with partners.

For an extended enterprise engaged in supply chain management, XML tags could be placed on such common messages as the purchase order or the advance shipment notice. A web browser capable of decoding XML then would be able to ascertain quickly the nature of the messages from a supply chain partner. Furthermore, it would become possible for one member's computer system to respond automatically to information requests from another member's system. XML thus could provide an alternative to electronic data interchange, which has been limited so far to big companies willing to make the investment in the requisite computer services and hardware.

In this option, XML and the Internet replace the use of EDI and a satellite-network in Upgrade 1. However, the information flow and processing between Lucent and their customers and business partners is similar.

Upgrade 3: B2B portal solution

The third possible change is to build a business-to-business portal called Lucent.net. It will use the Internet and e-commerce technology to re-engineer Lucent's organisation and transform its supply chain from the inside out. This solution is based on a new generation of web-based, enterprise logistics applications that enable collaboration and optimisation. They are built upon a central logistics information backbone that provides visibility across the enterprise and the extended supply chain.

Lucent.net requires two portals: a Customer Portal and a Business Partner Portal.

(Continued)

The Customer Portal has three key components:

- Marketplace is an online product catalogue to be used by more than 10,000 authorised representatives of direct customers and partners to supply Lucent products and services online. It contains a suite of applications for order-processing that enables customers to configure, price, route, and submit orders.
- Online Tracking enables Lucent's sales force, direct customers and partners immediate access to information on the status of orders.
- Customer Support provides technical assistance, software and drivers to download and supply other information.

The Business Partner Portal is a supply chain 'extranet' portal which would link Lucent's contract manufacturers, assemblers, distributors and logistics partners. It enables Lucent and its business partners to access real-time manufacturing information, including data on demand forecast, inventory and purchase orders. Under this option, Lucent would open up its internal information system to suppliers and other supply chain partners, giving their employees the same access rights to information as Lucent employees.

This e-supply chain strategy involves the following initiatives:

- A single enterprise system embracing contract manufacturers, distributors, logistics partners, sales force and customers in a single information system. This enables business partners to manage much of Lucent's supply chain.
- Information sharing in real-time: the entire supply chain operates from the same demand signal. This means that any change in one node, or link, of the network is immediately transmitted throughout the network.
- Direct fulfilment whereby most of Lucent's contract manufacturing partners ship directly to customers.

This upgrade would seamlessly link customers and business partners to Lucent and it would enable all the parties involved to present a unified face to the outside world. Separate decisions could be made about the type of network and the language used for the data transport.

Analysis of the upgrades

This section addresses the advantages and disadvantages to Lucent of the three alternatives canvassed.

The EDI solution

The first upgrade, the EDI solution, provides a mature technology to support the supply chain with these advantages:

- quick access to information,
- better customer service,
- reduced paperwork,
- better communications,
- increased productivity,

(Continued)

- improved tracing and expediting,
- accuracy, and
- improved billing.

Although EDI has a significant technological platform for supply chain organisations, it is expensive to adopt and implement because it is outsourced. There is also a lack of standard formats. EDI formats differ not only from industry to industry, but also among firms in the same industry.

The XML solution

The second upgrade, an XML-based solution, gains the advantages of EDI and has some additional important advantages. First, using the Internet to transmit the messages will allow a reduction in the use of value-added networks, which are expensive per character. XML only requires a free web browser, a $500 computer, and $15 per month for Internet access. One source suggests that EDI systems are seven to ten times more expensive than Internet-based options. The IT manager will also value XML because the programming effort for this kind of document is much lower. XML is a key technology for integrating various corporate systems. Most of the ERP systems have interfaces programmed to accept XML inputs. Unfortunately, XML is still fraught with problems because there is no single XML standard. XML has yet to be proved in a large-scale environment and there are still some security concerns. The Uniform Code Council, which acts as the maintenance organisation for EDI, is working to define a uniform XML standard but the solution will take some time.

The next advantage of the XML solution flows from the practice of companies in batching the delivery of outbound and inbound EDI messages periodically during a day. As supply chain flexibility and integration grows, even these delays, measured in hours, will be unsatisfactory. More flexible timing and more immediate response will be available via the use of XML.

XML will appeal to logistics managers because the production and modification of logistics documents can be managed directly by general logistics staff. Imagine XML documentation for an international shipment. If the bill of lading were not complete, this XML file could be sent to an export manager's email inbox. He or she could add the correct carrier, cite the proper international documents, save the file, email a copy to the recipient, and then forward the document to the warehouse management system for addition to a picking list. This same email-like document flexibility would also apply to carriers, third parties, customers and the accounting department.

The B2B upgrade

There are many benefits of developing supply chain efficiencies using B2B portals. Using the Customer Portal, customers can easily look up technical information on products and download them. This will save Lucent a lot of money by eliminating the delivery of product manuals and software CDs. Customers can report problems and submit queries on the

(Continued)

(Continued)

web. The Customer Portal will automate order-processing. Once the product is configured, customers can obtain its price from the pricing agent. Order placement allows customers to drop their selections into a shopping area in a virtual marketplace. An invoice agent allows the customer's accounts payable staff to trace invoices online. This application also connects directly to the freight forwarder's tracking service so that customers can immediately find out where their orders are in the shipping process.

The Business Partner Portal enables Lucent and its partners both to conduct business and to access real-time logistics information, including data on demand forecast, inventory and purchase orders. This portal consolidates the access points of numerous modules of Lucent's ERP system to simplify and strengthen its processes. For example, direct fulfilment enables a supply chain partner to monitor customer orders and ship product without Lucent touching the order. The system prompts Lucent to pay for the parts used. Also, working with suppliers in an integrated portal, Lucent can streamline procurement, cut delivery time, errors and inventory.

There is a cost to these B2B benefits. Each participant must be willing to cooperate. Otherwise the businesses have the problem that, if one link fails, the entire chain is defunct. Other problems, such as lack of e-skills, immaturity of the B2B model, and an unsupportive company culture, could hinder the attainment of the B2B solution.

Conclusion

It is questionable whether the current information technology infrastructure available is suitable for Lucent in redesigning its supply chain. However, the more extensive use of Internet and e-commerce technology is an inevitable trend. The result will be higher velocity logistics flows, with greater execution precision, faster response to problems, improved customer service, and lower costs and inventories throughout the supply chain. The savings are estimated to be US$150 million per year.

The alternative options given in this case focus on the information system infrastructure. The whole logistics plan to redesign Lucent's supply chain includes other plans, such as refocusing on core businesses, selling or shutting less profitable units, greater standardisation of production and intensifying the use of contract manufacturers.

Lucent is in the vanguard of telecom equipment companies overhauling its supply chains. However, Lucent is not travelling alone. Other major telecom equipment companies, such as Cisco, Nokia, Ericsson and Nortel, are preparing similar reforms. As Mejia, the Vice-President of Lucent's Supply Chain Network, said: 'We have reduced the expense associated with managing the supply chain. I'm not as worried about the tough times we're dealing with now as I am about assuring that we're ready as the market comes back.'

Acknowledgement

We thank C Duan and T Kanjanakajit for providing the material on which this case is based.

Case references

1. Lucent Company (2006) 'Company Information' [Online]. Available at: http://www.lucent.com/corpinfo/ins.html (accessed 28/9/2006).

(Continued)

2. Lucent Company (2002) 'Company Restructuring' [Online]. Available at: http://www.lucent.com/corpinfo/restruct.html (accessed 26/9/2002).

Case questions

1. What service is Lucent providing to the communications companies?
2. What are the current weaknesses of Lucent's supply chain, especially in information systems?
3. What combination of the three possible upgrades presented would you choose now? Why?

REFERENCES

1   Rother M and Shook J (1999) *Learning to See*, The Lean Enterprise Institute, Brooklyn, MA, p. iii.
2   Normann R and Ramirez R (1994) *Designing Interactive Strategy: From Value Chain to Value Constellation*, Wiley, Chichester, pp. ix–x.
3   Cox A (1999) 'Power, value and supply chain management', *Supply Chain Management: An International Journal*, 4(4): 167–75.
4   Cigolini R, Cozzi M and Perona M (2004) 'A new framework for supply chain management: conceptual model and empirical test', *International Journal of Operations and Production Management*, 24(1): 7–41.
5   Stevens GC (1989) 'Integrating the supply chain', *International Journal of Physical Distribution and Materials Management*, 19(8): 3–8.
6   Fine CH (1998) *Clockspeed*, Perseus Books, Reading, MA.
7   Ohmae K (1989) *The Mind of the Strategist*, Penguin, Harmondsworth.
8   Akao Y (1991) *Hoshin Kanri: Policy Deployment for Successful TQM*, Productivity Press, Cambridge, MA.
9   Mintzberg H and Quinn JB (1991) *The Strategy Process: Concepts, Contexts and Cases*, Prentice-Hall, Englewood Cliffs, NJ.
10 Francis M (2004), 'Application of the food value chain analysis method in the UK red meat industry', in *Logistics and Global Outsourcing*, KS Pawar, CS Lalwani and J Shah (eds). Proceedings of the Ninth International Symposium on Logistics, Bangalore, India, pp. 104–9.
11 Arnulf JK, Dreyer HC and Grenness CE (2005), 'Trust and knowledge creation: how the dynamics of trust and absorptive capacity may affect supply chain management development projects', *International Journal of Logistics: Research and Applications*, 8(3): 225–36.
12 Kidd J, Richter F-J and Stumm M (2003) 'Learning and trust in supply chain management: disintermediation, ethics and cultural pressures in brief dynamic alliances', *International Journal of Logistics: Research and Applications*, 6(4): 259–75.
13 Peck H, Payne A, Christopher M and Clark M (1999) *Relationship Marketing*, Butterworth Heinemann, Oxford.
14 Goldman SL, Nagel RN and Preiss K (1995) *Agile Competitors and Virtual Organisations*, Van Nostrand Reinhold, New York.
15 Van Hoek R, Harrison A and Christopher M (2001) 'Measuring agile capabilities in the supply chain', *International Journal of Operations and Production Management*, 21(1–2): 126–47.

16 Gattorna J (ed.) (1990) *Handbook of Logistics and Distribution Management* (4th edn), Gower, Aldershot, p. 38.

17 Dapiran GP (2004) Lecture notes on Warehousing Decisions, Monash University, Department of Marketing, Australia.

18 Fine CH and Whitney DE (1996) 'Is the make–buy decision process a core competency?', Working paper, Massachusetts Institute of Technology, Boston.

19 Tyndall G, Gopal C, Partsch W, Wolfgang P and Kamauff J (1998) *Supercharging Supply Chains*, Wiley, New York, p. 24.

Implementing Change in the Supply Chain

8

In strategic thinking one first seeks a clear understanding of the particular character of each element of a situation and then makes the fullest possible use of human brain power to restructure the elements in the most advantageous way.[1]

Objectives

- To check whether a supply chain is performing for customers and its companies
- To find out which supply chain activities add value quickly and which processes need to be simplified to perform better
- To carry out strategic change throughout all the partners in a supply chain to achieve major long-term improvements

INTRODUCTION

Previous chapters have examined logistics in various types of companies, described several important topics such as 'Information Communication' and provided a method to integrate logistic activities through supply chains. This chapter investigates means of engendering revolutionary change in chains. It starts by investigating how well the supply chain is performing. Secondly it examines an important technique to generate quick improvements, lean value stream mapping. Thirdly it describes one method of achieving major change in supply chains by joint strategic planning involving several key partners. Finally, the chapter takes stock of present knowledge and suggests the goal of supply chain strategy.

8.1 MEASURE CURRENT PERFORMANCE

Before change can be implemented in a supply chain, we need to know how well it is performing. Existing company measures are unlikely to cover the whole supply chain. They are probably focused on the one company. So a new set of metrics for the wider task will probably be required.

Table 8.1   **Typical performance measures**

Customer service	Cost management	Quality	Productivity	Asset management
Fill rate	Cost per unit	Picking accuracy	Units shipped per employee	Inventory turns
On-time delivery	Cost/sales %	Document accuracy	Warehouse labour productivity	Return on net assets
Cycle time	Order-processing	Damage, customer returns	Productivity index	Inventory in ABC classes

Harrison and van Hoek[2] suggest that there are three key questions to answer in measuring supply chain performance, all focused on time:

- Do we meet the customer's target?
- How good are we compared to the competition?
- Is our performance getting better or worse?

The first question implies knowledge of the customer's need for timely delivery in response to his or her order. We can never know too much about the end customer. It may be more difficult to gather information about customers if they are several stages removed from our company. This underlines the need for close cooperation with downstream partners who are in a better position to gather such information.

The second question compares the time that we take to supply customers with that commonly offered by our competitor chains. The third question requires regular measurement to determine whether chain delivery performance is getting better.

Table 8.1 provides examples of typical performance measures adopted to monitor five important performance areas. These measures need to be adapted to measure the performance of the whole supply chain in the particular instance.

Another method that can be used to measure supply chain performance is the Supply Chain Operations Reference (SCOR) model.[3] This model requires each link in the supply chain to be represented by five management processes: plan, source, make, deliver and return, as illustrated in Figure 8.1. The three operational processes work under the existence of an overall plan for the chain. These management processes are defined as follows:

- *Plan* – contains demand and supply planning and management of many elements of supply chain rules and data.
- *Source* – sourcing stock and make-to-order products, including selecting suppliers, scheduling deliveries and managing inventory.
- *Make* – the execution of make-to-stock and make-to-order production. This involves scheduling production, managing work-in-progress and release of finished products for delivery.

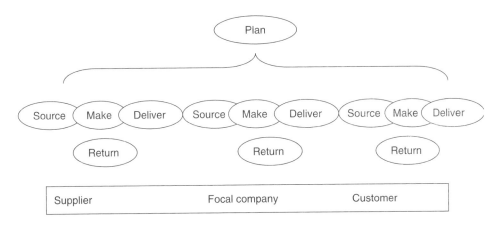

Figure 8.1   **SCOR management processes**

- *Deliver* – contains the order, warehouse, transport and installation for all types of product and includes all the steps of order-processing, warehouse management, carrier selection, product shipment and invoicing.
- *Return* – the return of raw materials to supplier and finished goods from customer. It includes all steps necessary to return and dispose of defective products.

SCOR is said to integrate the concepts of business process engineering, benchmarking and process measurement into a cross-functional framework. The process reference model used by practitioners for their own supply chains contains standard descriptions of management processes and metrics to measure their performance. It has a framework of relationships among the standard processes and standard alignment to features and functions. The model is said to suggest management practices which lead to best-in-class performance.

The SCOR model contains the following three levels of process detail which then drive a fourth (implementation) level carried out by the user:

1. The Top Level delineates process types which define the scope and content of the model and provide the basis for performance targets relative to the competition.
2. The Configuration Level uses 24 process categories to configure the model to the desired supply chain.
3. The Process Element level deconstructs processes into requirements, resources, balancing of production resources with supply chain requirements and linkage to the chain plan.

Wider supply chain analysis

Each of the preceding Chapters 2 to 7 has provided a number of (mainly) qualitative tools to investigate facets of supply chain performance. Table 8.2 summarises the tools which relate to the topic covered by each chapter.

Table 8.2   **Summary of analysis tools**

Chapter	Topic covered	Tools provided
2	Logistics in manufacturing	Operations functions, forecasting demand, inventory management and supply development
3	Logistics in service organisations,	Customer service levels, supplier relationships, freight
	Customer service and transport	transport types and distribution centre strategies
4	International logistics	Appropriate functions, organisation and information, international sourcing and risk readiness
5	Information communication	Information framework, planning and execution information systems, electronic communication and information integration
6	Supply chain integration	Chain boundaries, flow-creating criteria, choice of relationships, extent of current achievement and management framework
7	Applied integration issues	Chain interaction, innovative supply chain creation and outsourcing decisions

This chapter provides methods of analysing the changes needed to make entire supply chains more effective. The SCOR model enables the achievement in each part of the chain to be compared with the best practice achieved by other comparable companies. Then *lean value stream mapping** is cited as a method to achieve immediate, wide-ranging improvements in the supply chain. Finally, a process of strategic planning, *Strategic Operations and Logistics Planning(SOLP)**, is chosen to enable the reader to create a complete strategic plan for a supply chain.

8.2 IMMEDIATE IMPROVEMENT

Having measured performance, there are a number of ways in which immediate improvement of supply chains can be achieved. We choose lean value stream mapping[4] (LVSM) for students to understand because it has had wide success in the UK, USA and Australia over the last ten years in a wide range of manufacturing industries and some service situations. 'Value stream' is an equivalent term to supply chain. A brief description of the principles of lean thinking[5] is given, followed by an explanation of the steps necessary to carry out LVSM.

It is worth emphasising that 'lean' is only one approach to making supply chain improvements. There are many others, such as total quality management and agile. Each of these has its own benefits. Lean is chosen because of its success and because the author has more experience of this technique.

The authors of *Lean Thinking*, Womack and Jones,[5] suggest that the management of supply chains should be taken one step further with the formation of a 'lean enterprise', which they define as 'a group of legally separated but operationally synchronised companies' (p. 276). They envisage such an enterprise achieving an enormous increase in the performance of the supply chain:

If individual breakthroughs can be linked up and down the supply chain that creates, sells and services a family of products, the performance of the whole can be raised to a dramatically higher level.[5] (p. 267)

Principles of lean thinking

Womack and Jones state five principles of lean thinking:

1. Specify what the customer sees as value.
2. Identify all the steps in the supply chain.
3. Create product flow.
4. Supply only what the customer pulls.
5. Make improvements towards perfection.

The first principle requires supply chain owners to define 'value' as what the customer sees in the whole product. Value can only be defined from the ultimate customer's point of view. It must be defined in terms of a specific product, incorporating goods and service, which meets the customer's needs at a specific price at a specific time. The concept of value must not be distorted by the financial mind-set of senior managers, the existence of novel features specified by engineers or the kind of product preferred in home markets, intended for export destinations. Frequently, a target cost of the product is derived at this stage.

Secondly, chain owners must identify the steps in the entire supply chain for each product. This identification must include:

- taking the product from concept to detailed design and product launch,
- managing the information from order-taking through scheduling to delivery, and
- the physical transformation task from raw materials to a finished product in the hands of the end customer.

Each of the steps thus isolated is classified as value-adding (in terms of the value specified in principle 1), non-value-adding but necessary with current technologies and assets, or not value-adding. The aim will be to remove these wasteful non-value-adding steps as soon as feasible.

Thirdly, supply chain owners arse required to make the remaining value-adding steps flow. This principle means moving from batches, which queue as they move from one department to another, to specific products for which the supply chain flows, without organisational barriers and with the right-sized tools. 'Flow' requires focus on the specific order, ignoring the traditional boundaries of jobs and functions, and changing work practices to eliminate backflows, scrap and stoppages of all sorts so that the design, order and production of the specific product can proceed continuously.

The fourth principle, 'pull', in simplest terms means that no one upstream should produce a good or service until the customer downstream has asked for it. The first visible effect of converting from departments and batches to product teams and flow is that the times from concept to launch, sale to delivery and raw material to customer fall dramatically. This is a revolutionary achievement because it means you can throw away the sales forecast and simply make what the customers actually tell you they need. That is, let the customer pull the product from you as needed rather than pushing products on to the customer.

The final principle requires a regimen of continuous radical and incremental improvement. The four initial principles interact in a virtuous circle. When you add in transparency, so that all supply chain owners can see everything along the chain, then it is easy to discover better ways to create value. The picture of perfection is envisaged during the mapping process and inertia is overcome by a change agent to get the improvements started.[5]

Value stream mapping

The principles of lean thinking can now be applied by mapping and managing supply chains. Value stream mapping is a record of all the actions required to bring a product from raw materials to the end customer in a supply chain. It includes both value-creating and wasteful actions, exactly as currently exist.

> Value stream mapping is the simple process of directly observing the flows of informa-
> tion and materials as they now occur, summarising them visually, and then envisioning a
> future state with much better performance.[4] (p. 1)

Start by selecting a single product at the closest point to the customer to be mapped. The product should be one which has sufficiently large sales to be significant to the chain and which commands interest either because it is under some threat or it is considered to be inefficient. Then determine a manageable field of view. This should be at least one or two supply chain links upstream from wherever you start. As your mapping experience grows, so you can include larger numbers of levels. The team that is going to map the value stream (i.e. supply chain) should include at least one member from each constituent firm. It is very useful to have a facilitator, who is knowledgeable about the mapping process, to guide the team.

You are now ready to take a walk along the supply chain. The best procedure is to put down on a large sheet of paper each of the current steps in the stream, using Post-it notes for easy redrawing. Team members then take a walk together along the supply chain, correcting and developing the current state map. The resultant current state map shows every physical action. Actions must be classified into value-adding and non-value adding according to whether the end customer would be prepared to pay for a step to be carried out or not. There are also some data to be added below each step. We want to know the cycle time, the number of people involved and the quality loss, if any.

Two more items must be added to complete the current state map. First, add the transport links between each step, showing their frequency and duration. Secondly, add the information flows which drive the physical flow in the chain. Start at the right-hand side of the map, where orders are received from end customers and follow the flow of information from department to department and from downstream firms to upstream firms. From the point of view of the customer, all information is waste: the customer does not care whether information is used or not. So managers ought to be minimising the need for information rather than collecting as much as possible.

A dangerous effect, which arises from too many managers revising the order information, is known as demand amplification. Often, proceeding up the supply chain, away from the customer, buyers and purchasing managers will add extra amounts, just to be on the safe side. This can happen several times until the variation in demand is several times higher than that coming from the customer and the total demand is quite unlikely to eventuate.

When this information is assembled into a whole value stream map, many activities and lots of data, which create no value for the customer, become apparent. So we now proceed to get rid of as many of those non-value-adding steps as possible.

A lean value stream

A lean value stream, or supply chain, is one from which all unnecessary actions and wasted information, and their concomitant costs, have been removed. Team members are next invited to imagine the ideal future state. What would the supply chain look like if all unnecessary activities were removed, quality was perfect every time and flow was just what the customer needed at the time when he wanted it? The concept of an ideal state is very useful because it prevents team members from arguing that a particular improvement is less useful or less likely. Criticism is temporarily circumvented.The ideal state is drawn out on a sheet of paper, in a similar way to the current state but with far fewer activities in it, less inventory and less complicated data flows.

Future state

The next step requires team members to agree on the improvements that will be made towards the ideal state over the next year. Many of the changes identified in the ideal state can be achieved quickly. Others will require capital investment or restructure of information systems. These changes are likely to affect each partner in the supply chain. Some of them will be internal to one partner; others will require joint efforts by two adjacent partners in the chain. A useful tool in achieving these improvements is an action list, setting down:

- each change,
- the action required,
- the savings anticipated,
- the person responsible for leading the change, and
- the time when the change will be effective.

In this way, lean value stream mapping can be used to make considerable improvements to the supply chain for one product group. These improvements can then be rolled out across other products, wherever appropriate.

8.3 REVOLUTIONARY CHANGE

Major, sustained change in a supply chain requires functional change in each link, strategic change in each company and strategic change in the composition of the chain.

Planning processes for the operations of entire supply chains require examination because business competition demands coherent strategies from them. Research into processes for strategic operations planning has defined the steps and procedures required. Some research has addressed planning processes for integrated supply chains. Section 8.4 specifies a process and investigates how a team of managers from the companies in a supply chain can be helped to formulate strategic plans for operating the whole chain, to benefit each company and to benefit the whole chain. Building on previous research,[6] we propose a framework to enable such a process. This chain-wide planning process was carried out in an Australian heavy metal fabrication supply chain, with encouraging results.

The process applies to all companies in an *integrated* supply chain because it attempts to involve all partner-companies, or intermediaries, in the supply chain planning process. The theoretical foundations of the process are:

1   The aim of the integrated supply chain is to achieve competitive criteria for end consumers at a profit.
2   Planning is a democratic, creative process in which natural process steps, which allow intuition, are used.[7,8] Such steps are preferred to a complex, logical series of planning decisions.[9]
3   The entity planned is the product family, which means a cohesive group of products going through a particular set of links or partners (a slice of the integrated supply chain) to the consumer. The entity includes the information that drives that process.
4   Planning aims to achieve leadership of the whole chain in one coordinated direction, involving the management of all partners in the chain.
5   A team representing all parts of the stream makes decisions on the policy, practices and resources required by the supply chain for a product family. These decisions aim to remove current weaknesses and, hence, to achieve the strategic vision for operations and logistics.

Developing these foundations further, three sets of parameters are defined which, together, provide the best context for supply chain planning to be undertaken. These parameters are shown around the outside of Table 8.3:

- Links, or partners, comprise all the intermediaries involved in the flow of materials and products from primary producers to manufacturers to retailers for a product group. The value-adding steps that are listed as links include both product development and manufacturing/distribution cycles. Information flow between links is included beside the links because of its importance to the planning process, since the flow of information between links controls the flow of products, although 'information flow' is not a link.
- Order-winning criteria are those needs of end consumers which are provided by operations and logistics, since those functions play a major part in satisfying requirements for many facets of the product, such as quality. The integrated supply chain aims to satisfy these needs by maximising the likelihood that the customers served by a product group will place orders with the chain through a retailer. The fact that order-winning criteria may change over time is emphasised by the criterion 'consumer change'. These criteria consist of 'order qualifiers', for which a certain level must be obtained before customers will consider placing orders, and 'order winners', criteria for which greater achievements will lead to a greater proportion of available orders being 'won' by the business.[10]
- Policies are structural and infrastructural decision areas that the management of supply chain enterprises configures to achieve the required flow of materials, products and information through the chain so that customer criteria are achieved at a profit. The policies required to achieve customer criteria comprise allocation of resources and development of capabilities to win business.

These three sets of parameters provide the context within which the process stages take place. The process stages are shown inside the parameters to indicate that the stages take place within the parameters' domain. The 'outputs' indicated on the right-hand side of Figure 8.2 are the set of action plans derived for each product group for each

Policies: / Links:	Facilities	Capacity	Link integration	Processes & technology	Transport	Product quality	Control policies & information	Supply logistics	Distribution	New product channel	
Farmer	Supply chain objectives & planning	Product channels									O U T P U T S
Dressing and chilling			Output competitive criteria								
Boning & manufacture				Link criteria	Link competencies						
Transport: inbound, bulk, delivery						Audit	Opportunities & threats	Formulate chain strategies	Formulate link strategies		
Distribution centre										Chain action plans	
Retailer										Link action plans	
Order-winning criteria:	Quality	Features	Safety	Price/cost/profit		Flexibility	Delivery	Shelf life	Reliability	Consumer change	

(Left margin vertical labels: INFORMATION FLOW / FLOW)

Figure 8.2 **Context for proposed process stages for supply chain planning**

link in the supply chain. The order-winning criteria record the customer requirements which the supply chain managers aim to satisfy by choosing combinations of policies that will be effective and economic. The links, or partners, comprise the specific intermediaries which should be designed to achieve this goal.

The supports to the process steps to form a supply chain strategy have many elements in common with socio-technical systems (STS). These elements include participative intervention processes involving relevant managers and employees from members of the supply chain[11] and structural change to organisations involving the creation of team-based parallel flows, which focus on particular products.

Recent work by Dutch STS researchers focuses on reorganising the task structure before redesigning the control structure to obtain 'whole tasks' or team-based flows centred on particular products.[12] Product flows can be segmented into a series of 'whole task' teams if required by the complexity of production. In this context, the operation of a supply chain is seen as a 'whole task', which cannot be planned effectively as a series of segments.

In addition to physical structure, supply chains are highly dependent upon the information which flows between logistics chain partners to plan and effect the flows of materials and products.[13] Researchers have found that *information distribution* is so important to supply chains that *it should have its own structure*, linking all producers, intermediaries and retailers, in order to optimise information flows serving these partners. Supply chain information can be typified as comprising transaction planning, order placement, operations scheduling and logistics organisation at each link (partner) in the chain. It must be very accurate. The purposes of such information are to provide better visibility of physical goods, to promote better communications between chain links, and to reduce the need for warehousing and distribution.

The underlying concept of the planning process is to find out the things that customers want that can be provided by the supply chain and then design the policies of chain operation to deliver those order winners.

8.4 STRATEGIC PLANNING FOR SUPPLY CHAINS

This section uses a simplified version of the Strategic Operations and Logistics Planning (SOLP) process to explain how to derive a strategic plan for an integrated supply chain for a group of products.[6] A case at the end of this chapter describes the application of the SOLP process in a supply chain.

Many companies work with their suppliers and customers to organise individual aspects of the supply chain, from both information and operations angles. However, it is believed to be quite rare for all the members of a supply chain to determine strategy for a whole chain together. This section explores how firms can improve the current business channel situation by carrying out strategic planning with supply chain partners.

Consider the situation where a company wants to craft new strategies for its whole supply chain. According to the SOLP process, it should bring together a planning team of seven to 12 managers to work together to form the new strategies needed. This team will work best if it has about seven meetings at weekly intervals and an external facilitator who is well versed in the process. In the student situation, we recommend groups of at least two students with access to a real supply chain and two months in which to carry out their assignment.

The SOLP process is a major modification of the manufacturing audit approach[14] for the operations and logistics functions of companies. It is implemented by a team of managers filling in a set of worksheets in a series of meetings. The progressive worksheets stimulate the managers to develop action plans for several families of products made by the company. The approach used is action research in which the facilitator engages closely with company personnel over a period of time.

The arrangement of stages to be followed by the planning team is given in Figure 8.3 with their inputs and outputs. The team, which represents all links in the chain, works together to plan the whole supply chain.

The preliminary step is to construct an outline diagram of the supply chain similar to that shown in Figure 8.4 but specific to the chain under study.

The gap

The first step is to decide the supply chain business objectives, such as delivery of acceptable products to particular customer-markets and return required on resources employed. This stage may include activities to motivate the planning team if required. An example of such an activity is measuring the gap of market requirements versus achieved performance.[14]

The second step partitions the range of products into a number of separate product or service groups. A product group can be distinguished because it serves a market segment or it requires a particular combination of processes to produce. A service group shares a common customer need and a similar service operation. By applying SOLP to one or two product groups, this reduces the complexity of the investigation. Frequently, the majority of strategies required by one group will apply across many other groups.

Order-winning criteria

In the third step, the team finds out the competitive criteria which, if attained, would cause customers to place orders. Hill[10] describes the following customer criteria for manufacturing strategy:

- price,
- quality,
- delivery speed and reliability,
- flexibility (demand increases),
- features (product range),
- design leadership, and
- technical support.

The specific criteria used will vary somewhat from one business to another. The method of deriving these order-winning criteria is described in section 6.2.

Table 8.3 gives an example of order-winning criteria for two product groups in a heavy fabrication business.

Audit

In the fourth step, team members audit the current capabilities of operations, information systems and logistics throughout the chain, for a product group, to determine how well they meet the capabilities required by the order-winning criteria. They consider performance measures that indicate the extent to which the desired capabilities have been achieved. Refer to section 6.5 for more detail on the audit process.

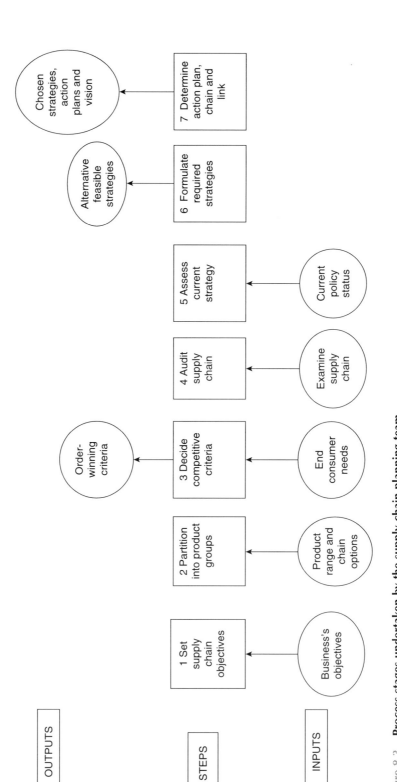

Figure 8.3 Process stages undertaken by the supply chain planning team

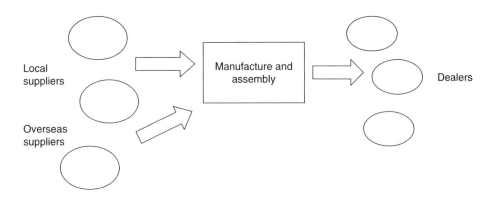

Figure 8.4   **Supply chain diagram for a heavy equipment manufacturer**

Table 8.3   **Example of order winners and qualifiers**

Competitive factors	Product group	
	Standard truck body	Custom truck body
Reliability of delivery	35 Q	30
Features (processing options)		
Quality (attainment of specification)	10 Q	25
Flexibility of design (specifications)		Q
Response to variation in volume	10	
Price/cost	15 Q	25
Delivery lead-time	30	20 Q
Total	100	100

Q = order qualifier

Current strategy

In the next step, we introduce the *policy areas* which enable the chain managers to provide processes and resources which will attain the required order winners. As with order winners, the policy areas chosen will vary according to the industry being planned. Suggested policy areas are:

- facilities,
- capacity,
- span of process,
- processes,
- human resources,

- quality,
- control policies,
- suppliers,
- distribution, and
- new product.

Team members consider the current strategy being pursued by the members of the supply chain. They assess whether the current strategy achieves the required order winners for each policy area, using Table 8.4. For each policy area (row) in the table, team members express the type of current practice achieved in a few words and then fill in each cell with a number in the range −2 to 0 to +2. If the current policy is perfect in supporting the customer's requirements, the cell is scored +2. If the policy is very poor in supporting that requirement, the cell is scored −2. A medium position would score a zero. It is not necessary to fill in all the cells in the rather daunting table. It is sufficient to make sure that all the negative scores are recorded and to concentrate on those columns which represent the highest order-winning criteria.

Strategy development

Now formulate the alternative strategies required in each policy area and the practices to be adopted by the whole supply chain, to modify its capabilities in order to attain the competitive criteria. A valuable technique to help this strategy formulation is to take the negative situation, uncovered in Table 8.4, and reverse it. What strength would remove the problem? It is then easier to think of ways to attain to required strength. For example, Table 8.5 shows a '−2' in the row 'Processes & technology' for the column 'Flexibility of design' due to a lack of tooling and fixtures to hold the components. The strength required is 'to reduce reliance on tooling' and the solution is to install robot welding.

Separate the chain-wide strategies, decided in this step, into feasible policies and practices to be followed by each partner in the chain for each product group.

Action plan

The final step is to use the strategies developed to drive an action plan which shows the specific actions required in each policy area against a timescale. Table C8.4 in the case at the end of the chapter gives an example action plan for truck bodies. Team members decide which actions are required to move from current to required policy settings and the sequence of those actions, in broad terms, across the whole supply chain. The emphasis is on concrete actions, such as 'install shot blast and paint facilities', rather than general comments, such as 'review processes required'. Hence this last step converts the chain-wide strategies into a number of time-phased actions required by each partner to achieve the overall strategies for each product supply chain.

Status of supply chain planning

In conclusion, how should *supply chain planning** be carried out so that information and operations will jointly provide integrated manufacture and delivery to end customers?

We believe that such planning must be done by small teams representing all significant parts of the supply chain for particular groups of products by particular channels. Members of this team must know the business plan of their constituent enterprises and have delegated authority to share information and build requisite strategies for approval by line directors for immediate implementation. Team members should be foremost business managers, not functional or discipline specialists. They need to have sufficient continuity and 'culture' to work in an open, trusting manner to enlarge the cake, before negotiating shares of the results. They must, among other elements, be comfortable with people matters, information systems and commercially appropriate actions.

Finally, the strategic planning process must be a separate, highly motivated, dedicated activity. It cannot be part of an annual budgeting process or a half-hearted affair.

Table 8.4   Assessing the current operations strategy (product group: custom truck bodies)

Policy area	Current practice	Order winners						
		Reliability of delivery	Features (options)	Quality – attain spec.	Flexibility of design	Response to volume changes	Price/cost	Delivery lead-time
Facilities (works)	2 factories	+1		+1	0		-1	-2
Capacity	120 hours 2 bodies per week	-1		0	0		-1	-1
Vertical integration	Assemble in-house	-1		-1	+1		-1	-1
Processes & technology	Fixtures	-1		-1	-2		0	-2
Human resources	Core team + contract	0		+1	-1		-1	+1
Quality	Self-inspection	0		+2	0		+1	0
Control policies	BPICS MRP II	0		+2	0		+1	-1
Producers	Cooperation	-2		+1	-1		0	-1
Distribution	Transport company	0		0	0		-2	0
New product	Formal process plan	0		+2	0		+1	-2

Given all these a priori conditions, supply chain teams can derive supply chain strategies for any manufacturing or service situation. They will follow the general method given in this section, modified for the particular circumstances in *their* industry serving *their* customers. Interruptions in the buying and selling of constituent firms must be expected. Elements of the supply chain may change on little notice. That is the risk of doing things properly towards a future goal. The supply chain strategy will be 'evergreen', losing some leaves continually, modifying itself to external conditions and new customer demands. A whole series of product group plans will result, with different firms being components of different product groups.

In this way modern enterprises can move into effective ways of working with their supply chain partners, when they are willing, to win business by delighting customers.

8.5 FUTURE CHALLENGES

Earlier sections in this chapter have suggested ways of measuring current performance, a method to improve a whole supply chain and a process to form logistics strategy for an integrated supply chain. Where does the future lie in supply chain integration? This section gives some concepts that determine the type of supply chain strategy required and define the aim point for supply chains. It also gives a word of warning about strategy implementation.

Researchers have recently derived a new framework for supply chain management.[15] Cigolini and colleagues consider that there are four main approaches to supply chain management:

1. The 'supply chain awareness' school, which emphasises material flow and involvement of all chain members but does not highlight information.
2. The 'modern logistics' school, which emphasises system-wide coordination of both physical and information flows.
3. The 'integrated process redesign' school, which studies how to redesign the whole supply chain to obtain more efficient and effective flows of materials and information.
4. The 'industrial organisation' school, which focuses on strategic alliances between partners of the supply chain to the exclusion of companies which are not strategic partners.

From their research across a wide range of manufacturing industries, Cigolini et al. propose three main factors that can play a major role in determining supply chain strategy:

- The dominant phase in the end product's life cycle from introduction to decline.
- The inherent structural complexity of the end product.
- The type of supply chain, whether it is aiming to be efficient, lean or quick in response.

This thinking leads to a demand–supply matrix (see Table 8.5), which predicates the supply chain management strategy preferred by various industries according to the chain's placing on two axes. The axes are supply chain type and demand type, according to product life-cycle phase.

A good model for achieving strategic change in a manufacturing supply chain is shown in Figure 8.5.[16] Soft systems, in the bottom right corner, refer to all the planning,

Table 8.5   **Supply chain management strategy according to the demand–supply matrix[15]**

Supply chain type	Demand type: dominant product life cycle phase			
	Introduction & decline	Growth	Complex products	Maturity Simple products
Efficient				A (grocery, pharmaceuticals basic apparel, classical books)
Lean		C (computers)	B (white goods, cars)	
Quick	D (fashion apparel; publishing best-selling books)			

organisation and information communication systems used in the supply chain. The figure means that the needs of the three corners of the triangle should be met in such a way that there are consistent policies throughout all parts of the supply chain.

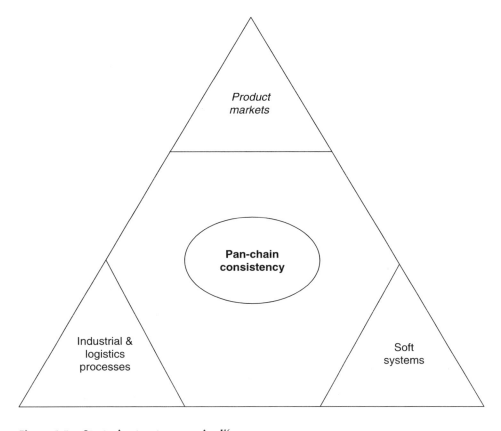

Figure 8.5   **Strategic structure required[16]**

In line with most of the literature, this book leaves supply chain strategy at the point at which a strategy has been derived. In practice, there is a major task to implement those strategies. Implementation is a systematic process of rigorously discussing *hows* and *whats*, questioning, tenaciously following through, and ensuring accountability. It includes making assumptions about the business environment, assessing the supply chain organisations' capabilities, linking strategy to operations (and the people who are going to implement that strategy), synchronising those people and their various disciplines, and linking rewards to outcomes.

Implementation also includes mechanisms for changing assumptions as the environment changes, and upgrading the supply chain's capabilities to meet the challenge of an ambitious strategy. Implementation is better known in the business world than in research circles. But, according to Bossidy and Charan,[17] it is essential to the success of companies and organisations.

Summary

Before change can be implemented in a supply chain, find out how well it is performing using measures that cover the whole chain. The challenge is to devise an individual solution for your supply chain and implement it with all the companies in the chain. This is harder than it sounds because the chain is really a network in which key links fade off into less significant players. Lean value stream mapping is an approach which frequently leads to considerable improvement. Owners of each link in the supply chain apply the five 'lean' principles. They progress from investigating every step in the current supply chain, for one product, to envisaging a 'future state' in which steps not required by customers have been removed. Working as a team assisted by external facilitators, the chain owners identify a series of actions which will take them towards the efficient future state over the next 12 months.

There is an enormous challenge to cope with change in a proactive way. With international sales, global competition and instant electronic information, the scene appears to move very rapidly. Many responses to change will be wrong, or wrongly timed. The challenge is to think through the correct actions to move your supply chain so that it can satisfy customers in the future.

Revolutionary change can be formulated by a strategic planning process called 'Strategic Operations and Logistics Planning'. This process assists a team of supply chain managers to determine the criteria that they must attain to satisfy customers and then design the policy settings throughout the chain to deliver those customer order-winning criteria. The output is a set of time-phased tasks in an action plan which must be implemented very carefully.

Finally, the chapter outlines the concepts that determine the type of supply chain strategy required and defines the point to which they should aim. The aim point is chain-wide consistency of logistics processes and soft systems in delivering the requirements of product markets. The challenges in managing supply chains will never stop coming!

Questions

1. What are the particular performance measures for a supply chain with which you are familiar?
2. Name the main stages in lean value stream mapping and explain the kinds of benefit that can result from its application.
3. Why should a company use the SOLP process with its supply chains?
4. What problems will firms face in strategically planning the whole supply chain?
5. How should the strategic logistics plan differ between a fashion clothing supply chain and one for supermarket groceries?

Case: Chain strategy for earthmovers

Alan, the Manufacturing Director of a branch manufacturer we shall call HFP (Heavy Fabricated Products), was not happy with the direction his assembly of large earthmovers was taking. He invited Ian and Richard, from Victoria University, to lead a planning process to develop plans across the whole supply chain.

The central company subsidiary in the supply chain, HFP, manufactures earthmovers and excavators in Melbourne, Australia, incorporating major components from its American parent company, a leading American heavy fabrication company with a global range. The manufacturing arm of HFP turns over about Aus$20 million per year and employs 300 people. HFP has been established in Melbourne for over 50 years. It has a conservative management, constrained by the slow reactions of its parent. The innate conservatism is demonstrated by their use of 15-year-old computer systems, although they are organised into teams.

Introduction

This case investigates the ability of a team from a manufacturer and its partners to formulate strategic plans of business functions for entire supply chains by using the Strategic Operations and Logistics Planning process. This assists team members to derive order-winning criteria and to design policy actions for several product groups. The process was carried out twice at HFP. The managers used the process to craft strategies while Ian and Richard studied the process. Strategic supply chain plans were formulated within given corporate plans. One application included representatives of supply chain partners while, in the other, the team was limited to manufacturer managers.

An action research approach is used to help a local fabricating and assembly facility and its partners create a strategic supply chain plan, within existing corporate aims, for selected product groups. Ian and Richard provide support so that supply chain members produce a coherent business strategy for the whole chain. This allows team members to concentrate on the plans rather than the process, while the use of group consensus allows all members to contribute and achieve results quickly.

The process used is the Strategic Operations and Logistics Planning (SOLP) process.[6] The steps required in this strategic operations planning process are, first, to find out the

(Continued)

(Continued)

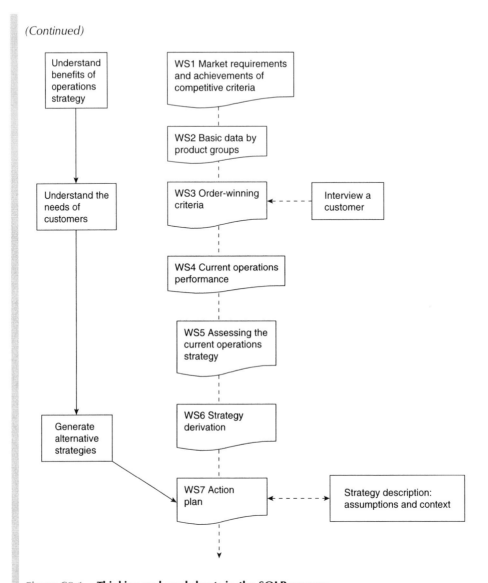

Figure C8.1   **Thinking and worksheets in the SOLP process**

business objectives; secondly, to determine a marketing strategy and analyse product markets; thirdly, to determine the order winners which operations need to provide for companies to win business in their chosen markets; and fourthly, to choose the operations processes and soft systems which will best achieve those winners.

SOLP requires a team of seven to 12 managers to form supply chain strategies over 18 hours in seven workshops. The 'managers' include employees who are directors, managers, supervisors or senior technical or marketing executives. Ian and Richard act as external facilitators. Seven worksheets, see Figure C8.1, are used to support strategy formulation so that each team member has his or her own input to the process. The process is carried out twice for the whole supply chain for several product groups at the manufacturer: once with supply chain partner representatives present, and once without external representatives.

(Continued)

Case method

Ian reflected on the work he and Richard did with HFP. They used a modified form of action research. Members of the supply chain had the task of deriving strategic plans, while the researchers acted as facilitators and used this position to observe the success and limitations of the process.[18] Action research-based case studies allow the researcher close access to the planning process to observe participants' reactions. Hence the researcher can observe at first-hand interaction between managers during meetings and can get to know them over an extended period. The chain partners were involved in a change to the system itself because the participative planning process adopted was different from that which the central organisation would normally use.

The method of research provided various supports through the steps of the Strategic Operations and Logistics Planning process, as follows:

- Steps and worksheets: the provision of help in carrying out each task, such as defining the task and providing worksheets, to guide its completion.
- Use of group consensus so that a group operates democratically to formulate strategy.
- Workshop organisation, breaking up the process into a number of manageable workshops.
- Tailoring to suit the individual company.
- External facilitation during formulation.
- Education in essential parameters of the management of supply chains.
- Embedding the process into the formal practices of companies.

The steps undertaken and the workshop organisation contain the following features (see Figure C8.1). Seven workshops are used rather than carrying out the whole process in one continuous seminar. Team members interview a major customer of the supply chain to develop a common understanding of the real needs of end consumers. A final worksheet lists actions in the various policy areas and their required time sequence. The need to embed the process into team members' normal practices by repetition to increase its effectiveness is recognised. Implementation assistance is not provided.

We believe that the operations planning process comprises a team thinking its way carefully to establish specific forward goals and the operations and logistics actions required to move towards those goals. Experience leads us[6] to argue that managers, once they are thinking strategically, tend to remain stationary unless a series of worksheets stimulates them to progress towards action plans. The two most important sheets are 'Order-winners and qualifiers' (sheet 3) and 'Action plan' (sheet 7). The other worksheets have only immediate value: the value comes from the strategic thinking process that they enable. Figure C8.1 shows the thinking process that team members go through, down the left-hand side:

- understanding benefits of operations strategy,
- understanding the needs of customers,
- generating alternative strategies, and
- deciding the strategic actions to pursue and their time order.

The worksheets assist members to think strategically about their goals for several product families and the actions needed to reach those goals.

(Continued)

(Continued)

The research application of the SOLP process was undertaken twice at HFP. The first process involved senior members from suppliers and the main Victorian dealer, whereas membership of the second process was limited to HFP managers, supplemented by telephone conversations with customers 1,500 kilometres away. In each case the researchers acted as facilitators and were able to observe the events in detail.

Team members were interviewed at the end of each SOLP process to get their views of the pros and cons of the process and the effectiveness of the outputs. After the second process, many members were interviewed to explore their perceptions of the process and the value of the results to HFP and its partners.

Process application

HFP management is dominated by engineers because of the high technical ability required from its earthmovers. Fabricated parts move slowly from one production area to another with much of the work done being welding. Most products are made to an individual specification. Imported parts, including complete motors and gearboxes, take four months to arrive from America after an order is placed. The need for imported parts to complement the products planned by SOLP slows down the tempo of production. The Manufacturing and Sales Departments of HFP have very different outlooks due to the Sales Managers being responsible for a wide range of earthmovers, many of which were imported directly from the USA. Hence they felt less directly responsible for the earthmovers manufactured in Australia. HFP managers were involved in an improvement process called 'Class A' which was mandated by the US Head Office for all subsidiaries. 'Class A' is a process driven by management consultants which nominates many key areas and trains some employees to organise improvement projects which will lower costs. HFP managers saw the outcomes of SOLP as making an important contribution to their improvement of the Australian business to 'Class A'.

Team members stated that getting new resources was a slow process in HFP because of the dominant, slow reaction by its American parent. Capital expenditure items needed to be included in the budget once a year. During the first SOLP process, operations were complicated because the Manufacturing Director became responsible to the Regional Vice President in Singapore instead of the Australian CEO of HFP.

Supply chain

Two suppliers were represented on the first SOLP process. The first was a large Australian steelmaker represented by its Victorian State Marketing Manager. The second was a smaller steel treatment company from New South Wales, represented by its Marketing and Sales Director. The third external company represented was the Victorian dealership, which sold most of HFP's earthmovers in that state, represented by its Regional Sales Manager, a very motivated and innovative individual. HFP sells only through its state dealers who are separate companies with a franchise agreement. These senior marketing and sales managers from the three supply chain partners knew the whole of their companies and their links to HFP. However, we consider that, except with the second supplier, general managers would have been more appropriate and would have contributed broader visions to the SOLP process. It is difficult, in practice, to get a general manager from the large Australian steelmaker to attend seven meetings interstate for a single medium customer.

(Continued)

Table C8.1   **Composition of teams in the two processes**

Affiliation	First process	Second process
HFP	Manufacturing Director	Manufacturing Manager
	Production Manager	Assistant Production Manager
	MRP Administrator	MRP Administrator
	Project Engineer	Project Engineer
	Materials Manager	Materials Manager
	Industrial Engineer	Master Production Scheduler
	Facilities Engineer	Engineering Designer
	Sales Representative	Sales Manager
	Internet Business Manager	Regional Sales Manager
Suppliers	State Marketing & Sales Manager	None
	Marketing & Sales Director	
Dealer	Regional Sales Manager	None

Before research started, several discussions were held with the Manufacturing Director to gain commitment to seven two-hour workshops by managers of the heavy fabrication business, its suppliers and a main dealer. In the first SOLP process, the team comprised nine members from HFP and three from other companies in the supply chain (see Table C8.1). All the HFP members, except the Sales Representative and the Internet Business Officer, were responsible to the Manufacturing Director in the Manufacturing Division of HFP. The number was high because the Director saw the process as a team-building exercise as well as a planning process. The Sales Representative had little interest in the products planned and he was passive in meetings.

First application

The first application of SOLP took place in seven workshops over six months. The 12 team members met in an HFP conference room to study strategies for two types of earthmover bucket. Each workshop was quite productive, and members were very positive, but workshops were at monthly intervals, due to the difficulty in getting people together. Consequently, time and momentum was lost until members regained the cognitive point which they had reached. The facilitator introduced the SOLP concept at the first workshop and then asked each member to fill in various worksheets. Completed sheets were summarised by the researchers, and fed back to the team. Members worked through one or two sheets per meeting. At the second meeting the order winners wanted by customers buying

(Continued)

(Continued)

Table C8.2   **Order winners and qualifiers**

| | Product group | |
Competitive factors	Wheel loader bucket	HEX bucket
Reliability of delivery	50	30
Features (processing options)	–	10
Quality (attainment of specification)	Q	Q
Flexibility of design (specifications)	Q 20	20
Response to variation in volume	–	20
Price/cost	30	20
Delivery lead-time	–	–
Total	100	100

buckets were derived (see Table C8.2). At the third, held at the dealer's premises, the team was addressed by a bucket customer. The direct customer input was an eye-opener for HFP managers, who had limited customer contact. For the last three worksheets, members were split into two groups, with each working on one product group to build a single set of strategic actions (Table C8.3). One researcher assisted each group. At the end, the team had constructed plans for two product groups. They were confident these plans could be implemented, provided the required capital expenditure was authorised by HFP's US parent. Table C8.3 shows the action plan derived for buckets and the assumptions made by that plan.

In the first process at HFP, two action plans were derived. Table C8.3 shows the plan for the wheel loader bucket product family. This plan shows that team members constructed a plan, for HFP policy areas, in considerable detail for the next 1.5 years and, for other supply chain partners, in limited detail restricted to immediate actions.

It is important to document these assumptions behind the action plan in case it is reviewed years later. The following dot points set down the assumptions for HFB's action plan in Table C8.3.

- Increase in wheel loader bucket sales is based on agreement for bucket manufacturing source change from divisions in the USA.
- Availability of wheel loader buckets was generally considered not to be a critical element of supply. A target of five weeks for small buckets and eight weeks for large was assumed.
- Inventory Stocking Project outcomes will be as expected (refer to Purchasing Manager).
- Scheduling system to give immediate availabilities by eight core measurements of Class A, and by the SOLP Process.
- The introduction of Pro-E in 2002 will play a vital role in the flexibility of design, as it will access to other HFP facility's designs.
- Bucket prices to dealers to be at competitive levels. This is to be compared with pricing from Atlas/Jaws/other Australian equipment manufacturers.
- Demonstrated labour capacities to be used as input for MRP to improve forecast accuracy.

Table C8 3   Worksheet 8: action plan for wheel loader buckets

Product group: Wheel Loader buckets

Policy area	Year 2001 Quarter 3	Year 2001 Quarter 4	Year 2002 Quarter 1/2	Year 2002 Quarter 3/4
For HFP				
Facilities	Review existing floor space	Layout design completed	Reallocate extra space acquired from CLS	Cell layout completed for additional production
Capacity	Examine feasibility of purchasing new press	Develop alternative suppliers	Placing orders for new equipment	Installation of equipment
Processes & technology		HFP	Review fixtures and robot weld	
Human resources	1 Hire of additional weld engineer 2 Review recruitment and training of welders	Recruit work tools engineer	1 Review business process 2 Complete training of new welders	
Quality		Review self-inspection	Train and Implement programme	
Control policies		Develop welding procedure		
Information systems	Use demonstrated capacity at all times by using BPCS	Achieve 95% plus eight core measurements for Class A	Use Internet-based tools to enhance communication	Continue supply chain communication processes
Suppliers	Investigate alternate suppliers	Find alternate material to avoid sub-contract heat treatment of edges		
Cost	Establish production costs			
Order processing	BPI project for process			
For Suppliers				
Capacity	Review alternate suppliers			
Human resources	Work with supplier B with regards to meeting specs			
Quality	Project already in place to improve delivery from steel suppliers			
For Dealers				
Delivery	Sales and operations planning process implementation as part of Class A initiative			

(Continued)

Second application

The second application of SOLP took place in seven workshops over six weeks, six months after the first. The team comprised nine members and was limited to HFP managers from engineering, operations, purchasing and marketing areas. Members included two managers from the national marketing and sales function (see Table C8.1). A newly appointed Manufacturing Manager, from outside HFP, replaced the Manufacturing Director as the most senior production manager on the team. Members developed strategies for three types of truck body for large ore trucks, in which the 'cab chassis' are imported from the USA for Australian mine sites.

This second application provides an interesting contrast to the first because of the lack of managers from other supply chain partners. It also had the new Manufacturing Manager on the team instead of the senior, long-experienced Manufacturing Director. We suggest that the Manufacturing Manager was less dogmatic than the Director and may have been motivated to build links to other team members, rather than promulgate a highly innovative strategic approach. Other work[6] indicates that team members become comfortable with a novel planning process as they repeat it. In this instance, only half the members of the second process were in the first.

A much faster timescale was achieved, since all the members worked for HFP in the same location. The two HFP Marketing Managers were interested in the process and provided much stimulation. Because the customers were located in northern Australia, 1,200 kilometres away, they were interviewed by conference telephone instead of attending a workshop. This conference was effective in giving team members a first-hand knowledge of customers' problems and views. A five-hour meeting was held at the last workshop. The team collapsed the product groups from three to one, compared to two in the first process. At the end, the team had constructed strategic plans for truck bodies along the whole supply chain (Table C8.4). They then reported the findings to the Manufacturing Director.

In the second process at HFP, only one action plan resulted because the three product families that were initially worked upon were collapsed into one plan. Table C8.4 gives the action plan (Worksheet 7) for that family, known as 'Truck bodies'. This sheet shows that a balanced plan was formed for HFP policies over the next two years and a patchy plan, limited to one policy area at each of the suppliers and dealers, was constructed. It is worth noting that, perhaps because of its authoritarian posture, members did not consider their American parent as one of the suppliers that should be planned. Rather, the attitude was that the parent division's actions were nearly immutable.

Discussion and conclusions

Some time after the end of work at HFP, Ian and Richard discussed what they had learned, using the interviews conducted three months after the second process.

The case shows that a team of supply chain managers are able to formulate a strategic operations plan for the whole chain. The use of a worksheet at each stage provided a task focus for operational managers who may not normally be comfortable with or capable of engaging in strategic thinking about a supply chain. The focus provided by the structure was viewed favourably by the team:'It had a very structured approach, a lot more structured approach to the way we would normally do things.'

From the above results and discussion, it is apparent that a team of supply chain managers can formulate a strategic operations plan for a complete supply chain in a heavy

Table C8.4 Worksheet 7: action plan for truck bodies

Product family: Truck bodies

Policy area	Year 1				Year 2	
	Quarter 1	Quarter 2	Quarter 3	Quarter 4	January–June	July–December
For HFP						
Facilities (works)	Freight costs equalised		Analysis of fully welded bodies v. kits. Allocate funds to 2003 budget	Develop plan for fully welding bodies in-house	Complete justifications for capital expenditure	Implement fully welded body plans
Capacity		Labour for two bodies per weet		Increase labour capacity by contractors		
Vertical integration	Validate Pro-Engineer software		Develop a plan for design and manufacture of tooling	Train CAD users in Pro-Engineer software. Better interface with suppliers	Implement Pro-Engineer review plan for fully welding bodies in-house	Purchase capital as required
Processes & technology			Shot blast and paint facilities for fully welding bodies in-house			
Human resources			Review support labour requirements & structure to support truck bodies		Implement labour and department structure recommendations	
Control policies			Update common goals for bodies, including stocking			
New product				Engineer to order and new product introduction (NPI) procedure developed		
Information services				Truck body forecasts in accordance with SOP		

(Continued)

Table C8.4 (Continued)

Product family: Truck bodies

Policy area	Year 1			Year 2	
	Quarter 1	Quarter 2	Quarter 3	Quarter 4	January–June	July–December
For Suppliers						
Capacity		Alternative suppliers established		Develop a link between C of A and suppliers to better establish capacity	Implement process for establishing supplier capacity	
Dealers						
Quality					Develop a truck body quality audit process for dealers based on supplier quality audit	Execute truck body implementation training programme for dealers

(Continued)

industry. The support provided by worksheets at each process stage provided a task-oriented focus for managers who do not often engage in strategic thinking. An important part of the research was the involvement of suppliers and customers in one process. They helped to challenge and expand the understanding of HFP managers of the supply chain, while giving suppliers and customers more insight into the inner workings and problems of HFP. Supported by results described in this case, we argue that SOLP is a robust process of supply chain strategy formulation which is likely to succeed in most manufacturing situations where managers have the capability to address wider strategic issues.

The relationship with suppliers seems to have improved as a result of the SOLP process. For instance, the purchasing manager said: '[major suppliers of steel] kept on referring back to their experience as a real positive. ... They talked about the alignment, customer needs and they articulated that as a real positive.' A practical outcome of this improved relationship was the supply of steel on consignment.

The processes show conflicting evidence on whether the supply chain strategy team should include members from all partners in the chain. There is a danger of 'not seeing wood for trees' in an organisation where a person has worked for many years. The SOLP process counteracted this, as attested by those involved, by comprising team members representing the complete supply chain. Being confronted by a major dealer and a typical customer shook members' complacency. Typical comments were:

I saw the value as actually hearing from the customers and getting an understanding of what their requirements actually were.

I can't think of anything we have done previously that brought the whole supply chain together like that.

This indicates an advantage of the SOLP approach over 'lean' approaches,[5] which analyse the existing scene in detail. This may not be productive if managers need to make major strategic change to the supply chain for future success.

The study suggests no simple answer to the question of whether the team should include members from all supply chain partners. The wider team membership opened the eyes of HFP managers to chain strategy but the process restricted to focal company members was very effective because more momentum was created. The Manufacturing Director, Alan, had wider aims than strategic plan formulation. In the follow-up interview he revealed he had two agendas in running the SOLP process: 'I saw the educational side as almost as important as improving the business processes we were looking at. I saw it as 50% business improvement and 50% education of the people. I said "It is part of your training for the year".' All the team members interviewed said they valued both the experience of having members of the whole supply chain present and the resultant action plans.

Richard asked Ian: 'Should our help be continued during the implementation phase?' Several team members saw a need for further meetings after the end of the process to track implementation of the action plans. Some of the partial application was due to the plans requiring expenditure for which no budget resources had been allocated. The company's budget cycle required new bids to be in by October for the following year, which conflicted with the timing of the first process.

The interview responses indicate both an understanding of the value of SOLP and a frustration with the lack of full implementation. Further, the inclusion of members of all echelons

(Continued)

(Continued)

in the supply chain increased the width and credibility of the strategic logistics plans derived. Almost all respondents believed that SOLP motivated managers to pull together and that results of the process were communicated to the management team. Together these answers support the finding that the process derived good logistics plans and members were encouraged to take part.

Repetition of the SOLP process provided insights into the learning curve for managers involved in the first process. One manager stated:

The first time we went through the process it was a journey of discovery so it took up a lot of energy. The second time around we knew the whole process and so we focused more on what we could get out of it. Obviously it is something you get better at the more you do of them.

Using SOLP for the first time in an organisation is more difficult than repeating the process because of the lack of comprehension of strategic supply chain thinking by those involved.[6] When a second SOLP process was carried out at HFP with different product families, the presence of new members prevented the gains of familiarity from being fully achieved.

Case questions

1. What are the strong and weak points about the SOLP process for strategic planning of a supply chain?
2. Should the supply chain strategy team include members from all partners in the chain? Why or why not?
3. Why should HFP use the SOLP process to form its future strategic actions in operations areas? How will the actions be implemented?
4. Is it sufficient to end external help when strategic action plans have been derived or is implementation assistance essential to put into practice the strategies derived?

REFERENCES

1   Ohmae K (1982) *The Mind of the Strategist*, Penguin, Harmondsworth. Page 24.
2   Harrison A and van Hoek R (2005) *Logistics Management and Strategy* (2nd edn), Prentice Hall, Harlow.
3   Supply Chain Council (2001) *Supply-Chain Operations Reference Model: Overview of Version 5.0. www.supply-chain.org,*
4   Jones D and Womack J (2002) *Seeing the Whole: Mapping the Extended Value Stream*, Lean Enterprise Institute, Brookline, MA.
5   Womack J and Jones D (1996) *Lean Thinking*, Simon and Schuster, New York.
6   Sadler I and Hines P (2002) 'Operations planning process for manufacturers with a supply chain focus: concepts and a meat processing application', *Supply Chain Management: An International Journal,* 7(4): 225–41.
7   Mintzberg H and Quinn JB (1991) *The Strategy Process: Concepts, Contexts and Cases,* Prentice-Hall, Englewood Cliffs, NJ.

8   Platts KW (1993) 'A process approach to researching manufacturing strategy', *International Journal of Operations and Production Management*, 13(8): 8.

9   Ansoff HI (1984) *Implanting Strategic Management*, Prentice-Hall, New York.

10 Hill T (2000) *Manufacturing Strategy: Text and Cases*, (2nd edn), Palgrave, Basingstoke.

11 Sharp JM, Hides MT and Bamber CJ (2000) 'Continuous organisational learning through the development of high performance teams', First International conference on Systems Thinking in Management, Geelong, Australia.

12 Van der Zwaan AH and De Vries J (2000) 'A critical assessment of the modern socio-technical approach within production and operations management', *International Journal of Production Research*, 38(10): 1755–67.

13 Lewis I and Talalayevska A (1997) 'Information structure for supply chains', *Journal of Business Logistics*, 18(1): 141–56.

14 Platts KW and Gregory MJ (1992) 'A manufacturing audit approach to strategy formulation', in CA Voss (ed.), *Manufacturing Strategy: Process and Content*, Chapman and Hall, London, pp. 29–55.

15 Cigolini R, Cozzi M and Perona M (2004) 'A new framework for supply chain management', *International Journal of Operations and Production Management*, 24(1): 7–41.

16 Jouffrey F and Tarondeau JC (1992) 'A methodological framework for the formulation of an industrial strategy', in CA Voss (ed.), *Manufacturing Strategy: Process and Content*, Chapman and Hall, London.

17 Bossidy L, Charan R and Burch C (2002) *Execution: The Discipline of Getting Things Done*, Random House, London.

18 Checkland P. (1991) 'From framework through experience to learning: the essential nature of Action Research', in Nissen HE, Klein HK, and Hirschhiem P (eds), *Information Systems Research: Contemporary Approaches and Emergent Traditions*, Elsevier, Amsterdam, pp. 1–7.

Glossary

ABC inventory control A method to manage the stock of large numbers of products or parts by dividing them into groups according to the size of turnover of each product. Different methods and frequencies are then devoted to each product group. Employs Pareto analysis.

Action plan A table of specific actions required to transform a supply chain from its present situation to a desired future state. In effect, these actions constitute the required strategic direction.

Active information The word 'active' is used to distinguish data and information, which are flowing within links or along supply chains to help their management, from other information, for example in ERP systems, which is not needed or not adding value.

Aggregate or capacity planning Calculating the resources of equipment, staff and inventory required to satisfy a forecast of product sales for the next year, say.

Agile A capability of the supply chain that aligns organisational structures, information systems, logistics processes and mindsets to satisfy demanding customers.

Backbone A central relational communication link between all of a company's computer systems. Enterprise resource planning systems provide a 'backbone' for all the data and information which a company possesses.

Barcode A machine-readable, permanent form of identification.

Channel A logistics channel is an alternative name for a supply chain.

Communications system It moves data and information up the supply chain, both within and between links, so that it is quickly available to operators, schedulers and managers.

Contract distribution An undertaking by a third-party logistics company to carry all the goods for a manufacturer, or distributor, for a year or more. It may include wider elements of distribution, such as storage and order-processing.

Corporate governance Conducting the policy and actions of a company.

Cross-docking Immediate sorting of incoming loads at a distribution centre to send the resorted loads directly out to customers.

Customer or end consumer The person or organisation which requires the goods or services to be provided by the supply chain.

Customer relationship management A software system which assists companies to improve their connection with customers.

Cycle time The time that it takes to make a product or the time that a customer must wait to obtain a product.

Decoupling point The position in the supply chain at which materials or products are designated to a particular customer. In international supply chains, decoupling points have a wider meaning, including major points of transfer, production and international distribution.

Delivery The act of supplying finished products to a customer or the whole sub-system of physical distribution of goods to end customers.

Demand Present and future requirement for the products or services being provided by the supply chain to end consumers.

Dependent demand inventory Requirement for parts, for example, which can be calculated from another measure. For example, the number of tyres required to make cars depends exactly on number of vehicles wanted.

Design Detailed consideration of the ways of achieving new or extensively modified supply chain (value stream, lean enterprise) objectives.

Distribution The outbound movement of finished products from production facility to end consumer.

Distribution centre A warehouse which receives finished goods from a production facility and holds them for despatch to customers.

Distribution requirements planning A computer system which tracks individual products through various distribution centres to the end customer for current and future time periods.

'Door to door' The logistics of one link (or partner company) from inbound receipts to despatch to the next link.

Double-Bell model A generic representation of a complete supply chain from sources of materials to end consumers of goods and services. The left-hand bell indicates many suppliers; the right-hand bell represents distribution to numerouscustomers.

Downstream A movement away from suppliers and towards customers. Conversely, 'upstream' is a movement towards suppliers.

Economic order quantity (EOQ) Is the amount ordered which will theoretically minimise the total cost of possessing inventory by balancing carrying cost against ordering cost.

Electronic communication Transferring data between two parties in digitised form by land line or radio transmission methods.

Electronic data interchange (EDI) A means of transferring data instantaneously between computers in different companies in the format required for each database.

Enterprise resource planning (ERP) A computer system which encompasses all the planning and control functions necessary to run a manufacturing plant and which records the current status of data in other functions throughout the divisions of a whole company.

Entrepreneur One who creatively matches customer needs to manufacturing or supply chain processes.

Essential information Comprises information elements which are considered to be absolutely necessary to manage the link facility: order-taking, purchasing, scheduling, inventory controlling and delivery recording.

Exclusive partnership *See* **Partnership, exclusive**.

Execution The production phase in which operating plans are carried out.

Factory or facility Building premises in which manufacturing, storage or sorting is carried out.

Flow The progressive achievement of tasks along the supply chain so that products are designed and physical movement from sources to customers is achieved without delays, waste or rework.

Flow-creating criteria Criteria which must be attained by various parts of the supply chain to satisfy the needs of customers and hence win business and ensure repeat orders. *See also* **Order winners**.

Focal company The organisation in the centre of the supply chain which is responsible for converting materials into finished products. In some cases, such as with imported goods, the importer or distributor may be considered the effective focal company. In service supply chains the focal company provides the service to customers.

Forecasting Prior estimates of the quantity of goods or services which will be required, based on historic quantities and a knowledge of current trends in customer needs.

Freight forwarder An independent company which arranges transport movements and documentation for a shipping company to any world-wide destination. The forwarder may or may not carry out the transport itself.

Freight transport A specialised form of transport to convey materials or finished goods to destinations along the supply chain. It can refer to any mode of transport.

Implementation A systematic process to ensure that activities required within a strategic plan are all effectively carried out.

Inbound logistics All the activities of supply and transport to bring materials into a manufacturing company.

Independent demand inventory A requirement for stock which cannot be calculated from a precedent situation because the demands are many, variable and unknown.

Information communication system (ICS) The gathering of electronic and other data and its movement to points of decision so that operators and managers have a greater understanding of current and planned conditions when they make decisions or allow automatic decisions. It is not information technology (IT) because the technology is not necessarily known to managers. *See also* **Logistics information system**.

Information flow Comprises the sharing of electronic and other information for use by any supply chain enterprise. Information flow has an overriding importance to the effective supply chain operation, although it is not a link in the chain.

Infrastructure The soft systems needed to run a company or a supply chain, comprising organisation, people and information systems.

Integrated supply chain Requires that the movement of material and product, and the provision of service, throughout the firms in the chain are planned and managed in a systematic way using electronic and person-to-person communications. Better design and implementation of provision and flow will dramatically improve the efficiency of the operation for customers and firms. Taking the system-wide perspective allows the firms to make appropriate trade-offs between costs such as purchasing, production, transport, inventory and distribution. Close coordination between these operations and the strategic environment produces high levels of service and performance for customers while reducing the total costs incurred. An integrated supply chain caters for one group of products within a supply network.

Intermediaries Organisations which are involved in the distribution of products with attendant services to end consumers. Intermediaries typically comprise wholesalers, retailers, importers, exporters and providers of storage and transport services.

Inventory Stocks of materials, components and products required for customers.

Kanban (Japanese for 'card') In a *kanban* system, cards are used to specify the number of containers of parts which are to be delivered to the next process or to a manufacturer.

Leader A leader promulgates visions of future forms of the company and the supply chain. He or she uses motivation, coordination and control to propel the company or chain towards that vision by strategic and operational actions.

Lean A method of removing wasted effort from processes while protecting and enhancing customer value.

Lean enterprise A conceptual name of supply chains optimally integrated from vendors to end customers to serve those customers with desired products at a profit.

Lean manufacture Achieving a waste-free production process by finding out what end customers want and reducing the manufacturing steps to the minimum required to achieve the customers' precise needs.

Lean thinking Using 'lean' principles and methods of thinking to remove waste from companies or supply chains so that they deliver value to customers and operating companies more effectively.

Lean value stream mapping (LVSM) A technique which allows a team to investigate a supply chain and use the 'lean' philosophy to remove wasted efforts while protecting steps required by customers.

Link A stage in a supply chain which performs tasks at one facility, contributing towards the eventual product. A link is often operated by a different company from other parts of the chain.

Logistics customer service The product and service delivery provided to end consumers by the supply chain, when and where they require it.

Logistics information system (LIS) The coordination and direction of people, equipment and procedures to gather, sort, analyse, evaluate and then distribute information to the appropriate decision-makers in a timely and accurate manner so that they can make quality supply channel decisions.

Make or buy decision A company decision to manufacture a component or carry out a service itself rather than buying it from another company.

Make-to-stock A method of production of goods in anticipation of orders.

Make-to-order Production of goods to satisfy orders received.

Manager A person who ensures that the aims of a company are met by regular oversight and decision-making. The term 'managers' or 'management' is used as shorthand for people in companies who make things happen for customers. The people concerned range from operators and supervisors to managers and directors.

Manufacturing Resources Planning (MRP II) An information system which contains all the data required by a company to carry out materials requirements planning and related functions, such as sales, accounting and human resources.

Mass services Mass services have high customer transactions with little contact time and low customisation. The offering is product-oriented and back office-dominated (e.g. retail whitegoods, petrol station).

Master production schedule A schedule of the number of products to be made in each forward time period. This schedule drives the production process.

Materials Inputs to the production process, such as primary products, components, sub-assemblies and modules.

Materials handling Movements between processes in the factory, by, for example conveyor or forklift truck.

Materials requirements planning (mrp) Using a computer system to convert a schedule of finished products into the detailed components and assemblies required for those products, by means of a product structure, for many future time periods. It also provides the number of materials to be purchased from suppliers.

Mode One means of transport to achieve the movement required between two stages in the supply chain (e.g. road or rail).

Module A large assembly within a product manufactured by a supplier from its own components and those of second-tier suppliers, reducing work by the manufacturer.

Network *See* **Supply network**

Offering Goods which are augmented by the addition of other products or services so that the customer obtains a more valuable product.

Operating decision Operating decisions are the huge number of decisions taken each day by each manager and operator to keep the company running properly in its current direction. Examples of operating decisions are: to purchase materials, to allocate fitters to maintain equipment, and to organise supervision of the entry of sales orders.

Order-processing All the business procedures from receipt of an order until the completed products or services are delivered to a customer.

Order winners The needs of end customers which, if fully met, will cause the customers to buy the product or service.

Outsourcing Using a contract with outside parties for services such as transport, warehousing and other distribution functions, often including concomitant information services.

Partners Separate companies which come together to provide one or more stages in the supply chain.

Partnership, exclusive The customer has sole rights over some supplier capabilities.

Partnership, strategic The customer wishes to improve some facet of the supplier's operations.

Partnership, transactional Business between two firms is conducted without commitment to a long-term relationship.

Performance measurement Using particular, relevant measures to show whether a supply chain, or a part thereof, is operating as effectively as desired.

Planning The preparatory phase in which future flows of material, products and information are mapped out and organised before execution commences. It is generally tactical, not to be confused with *strategic* planning.

Process A series of actions carried out as part of the provision or distribution of products or services. A process may operate on physical material or on information.

Product family A set of products which constitute a family because they have similar features in the eyes of the customers and/or the producers.

Production planning Deciding the amount of each product to be produced on major machines week by week for the medium-term future.

Professional services An intangible service operation with few transactions and a highly customised, process-oriented contact dominated by 'front office' work in which considerable judgement is applied (e.g. management consultancy).

Provision or manufacturing provision The four overall tasks, or processes, of purchase, produce, despatch and serve for customers. Put together, these tasks *provide* goods for customers.

Pull and push Pull is a supply principle in which providers manufacture and deliver only those products that the customers require. Push is the opposite principle in which goods are manufactured in the expectation that customers will require them.

Purchase orders Requests for suppliers to provide materials and services.

Relationship The way in which a supply chain organisation interacts with other organisations in the chain.

Reverse logistics The movement of products or materials *up* the supply chain in the opposite direction to the normal flow of products.

RFID (radio frequency identification) The identification or interrogation of goods at a distance by means of a microchip which is placed in the goods. The microchip contains information about a product or its shipment.

Safety stock Additional stock, beyond that known to be necessary, which provides higher levels of customer service or ensures uninterrupted operation of equipment.

Sales and operations planning (S&OP) A monthly procedure by which the disparate needs of sales, production, finance and other functions are resolved into one company plan for the forthcoming months.

Service businesses These carry out intangible acts which benefit, or meet the needs of, a person or a firm. Such businesses form a spectrum from mass service, in which there is little contact with the customer, through service shops, which provide a customised service with some contact, to professional service, which provides personal skills without any tangible product.

Service organisations These integrate value-adding activities in terms of outcome and experience by delivering a service product to customers by configuring resources and processes to create that service.

Servicescape The surrounds of the service operation, excluding the service product, which create an atmosphere in which the service is delivered.

Service shop A type of business which forms a class in the middle of the service spectrum. Such businesses have a medium number of transactions, medium customisation and medium front-office contact time. There are both process and product elements in the offering to customers (e.g. transport company).

Service supply chain The relationship and coordination of a number of organisations to create, develop and deliver a service product to a particular group of customers. The service chain creates value by the coordination of purchased goods and services with a suitable transformation operation and service delivery. Delivery may include passing goods or transformed objects to the end customer so that the customer perceives that the service is attractive and is likely to use it again.

Simulation An analytical technique for investigating the interaction of machines, operators and product movement by generating a probable picture of how events might unfold over time.

Sovereign companies Companies which are separately owned and managed although forming part of a wider supply chain.

Stage One level, or link, in the supply chain.

Stock-keeping unit (sku) An individual occurrence of a product variety, in which a separate stock may be kept.

Strategic business unit (SBU) A division of a larger company which operates under a distinct set of strategies.

Strategic decision A major decision which points the direction of the company and its supply chain for the future by committing considerable resources to achieve important outcomes (e.g a decision to purchase a new food packaging line which will replace numerous operators or a decision to attain quality accreditation).

Strategic Operations and Logistics Planning (SOLP) A process which assists managers from supply chain companies to formulate strategic direction and the actions required to satisfy the needs of the end consumers of the goods and services provided by the chain.

Strategic partnership *See* **Partnership, strategic.**

Strategic planning A process to determine the best future direction of an organisation or supply chain.

Stream A channel down which water and, by analogy, goods flow.

Supply chain (SC) A supply chain is the flow of one family of products within a supply network, which comprises all the significant product families in the network, with reference to one focal partner or firm. A supply chain runs from suppliers and their suppliers through manufacturers and distributors to satisfy end customers and obtain value for those companies. It is also known as value stream. *See also* **value stream**.

Supply chain management Requires that the movement of material and product, and the provision of service, throughout the firms in the chain is planned and managed in a systematic way using electronic and person-to-person communications. Hands-on control by managers can achieve better design and implementation of provision and flow, and hence improve the efficiency of the operation for customers and firms. *See also* **Integrated supply chain**.

Supply chain planning The process of deciding the direction in which all significant parts of the supply chain should head and the specific actions to enable the chain to reach that long-term goal.

Supply network The set of production and service companies which work with the *focal company* to assist it to produce a whole range of products. The facilities of companies in the network collectively source, produce and deliver products and services to customers. The supply network comprises a set of supply chains, each providing one group of products to industrial and individual customers.

Supply partnership An alliance between several service firms to work together to deliver a service to a group of customers.

System A collection of parts which work together to make a whole function. The prime emphasis is on the output of the whole system rather than the contribution made by any part.

Tactical decision A decision intended to change the company, like a strategic action, but through short duration tasks which fill out the overall strategy in some particular area. Examples of tactics are training employees in the methods of achieving quality assurance or involvement in an external body which overviews new guidelines for a particular industry.

Third-party logistics (3PL) A company which carries out logistics functions for shippers (the first party) or customers (the second party). The term '4PL' (fourth party logistics) is used in some quarters to mean the overall management of transport and other logistics services along the whole supply chain.

Tier Frequently, manufacturing companies receive parts from suppliers who in turn source components from their suppliers, and so on. Each stage in this supply process is known as a *tier*.

Total quality management (TQM) A management technique, prevalent in the 1990s, which tries to organise employees to optimise effectiveness by treating their internal customer as equally important as the eventual end customer. TQM uses statistical quality control and problem-solving methods.

Trade-off The choice to carry out a supply chain function at one point so as to save greater effort or cost at another point.

Transaction An individual process which forms part of the whole task of satisfying customer orders and frequently involves information transfer.

Transport The geographical movement of materials or goods between two partners, or to a customer. Transport is achieved by a particular mode and a carrier, such as a 3PL operator.

Transfer prices The price at which goods change hands between divisions of an organisation. Such prices may not represent the external value of the goods.

Transformation The physical and chemical changes made to input materials, such as steel or plastics, to convert them into finished products for consumers. In some industries transformation can comprise two separate links.

Transnational commodity supply chain A world-wide supply chain in which the manufacture of non-customised finished products is carried out in several countries. Suppliers of materials and components reside in many global locations and distribution is made to customers located in many parts of the world (e.g. the footwear supply chain).

Unitisation Building up the product into larger quantities for effective transport such as a pallet or container load.

Upstream A movement away from customers towards suppliers. Conversely, 'downstream' is a movement toward customers.

Value constellation The extra value created by a number of companies (i.e. stars) which work together to obtain synergy in the products and services that they are able to provide. Implicit in this definition is a move away from linear flow to a mixture of forward, backward and sideways flows.

Value stream The creation of a flow of a group of products or services from partner organisations to customers which provides more worth for the customer and the partners. Some authors use this term as a synonym for supply chain because it stresses the economic and need benefits which are provided.

Vendor-managed inventory (VMI) An arrangement between a supplier and a manufacturer or distributor whereby the supplier takes responsibility for replenishing stocks at the manufacturer's premises.

Waste An activity that consumes resources without creating any value. *Muda* can be physical or information waste. It originates from the Toyota Production System.

Warehouse management system (WMS) A computer system which records the status of stocks and movements of goods in a distribution centre.

Wholesalers Organisations that exist in the chain between manufacturers and retailers for some products to assist in the breaking down of bulk production and in contact. They occur as owners of distribution centres, distribution networks or headquarters of supermarket chains.

Index